THESE CRITICAL TIMES

THESE CRITICAL TIMES

Alloa At War 1939-1945

ANDREW HUNT

Reveille
PRESS

Reveille Press is an imprint of
Tommies Guides Military Booksellers & Publishers

Gemini House
136-140 Old Shoreham Road
Brighton BN3 7BD

First published in Great Britain by
Reveille Press 2023

For more information please visit
www.reveillepress.com

ISBN 978-1-9998900-2-5

Cover design by Reveille Press
Typeset by Vivian@Bookscribe

Printed in the UK

CONTENTS

ABOUT THE AUTHOR

Andrew Hunt was Principal Teacher of History at Alloa
Academy from 1978 to 2010. Over that time he taught
the topic of 'Life on the home front during the Second
World War' chiefly with S2 classes; but always held the
view that teaching through the use of local examples of the
impact of that war was the most effective way of capturing
and keeping an interest. Following his retirement from
teaching it was just a small step to get involved in the more
methodical and focused archival research which would
provide the material for a full book on the topic, to go with
his earlier book on *Alloa in the Great War*.

INTRODUCTION

In November 2018 when I published my book *In the Forefront: Alloa at War 1914-1919*, I was asked if there was another book in me and my response was, 'Alloa deserves to have another book written about its experiences going through the Second World War, but it won't be me writing it'. Well, by January 2019 I had changed my mind, heedful of the old saying, 'If not you then who, if not now, when?' Basically then, this book on the impact of the Second World War on Alloa, is my response to the kind comments of many people in Alloa, after writing the first book. They think that for the Second World War, just like the First, the people of Alloa, a town in Clackmannanshire of around 14,000 inhabitants in 1942, do deserve to have their story told and I'm prepared to step forward to do it.

Several research differences emerged. In the case of photographic evidence of what was going on in Alloa during the Second World War; there was slightly more of it by 1939-1945 and this history will be more pictorial than my book on Alloa in the Great War; although unfortunately, for Alloa, photos of local sporting events during the Second World War seem to be almost non-existent. There may also have been more information around. For instance, during the Great War, Alloa's newspapers were 4-sided broad sheets; by 1939 the size of the paper was often 6 and sometimes 8 sides. By 1942 though, it was back down to 4 sides. I'm not convinced that more was being reported; by 1943 it is surprising how much of the front page of the *Journal* was taken up by cinema adverts! Curiously, compared to my researches on Alloa in the Great War, there was not really that much more information available through the internet. The glaring exception here was on the story of Alloa's most decorated war hero, Squadron Leader Herbert H.K. Gunnis; there is so much available about him on the web that I could have compiled a small book just about him. On some topics I have been able to take advantage of secondary sources [which I have acknowledged] but for the most part this book still had to be researched 'first hand'; the materials that gave me my story were in the archives. Just as before, I felt that if some social group or club in Alloa had gone to the trouble of keeping a record at the time then I would make sure their thoughts were included, if they were about the impact of the war on their affairs.

Readers should keep firmly in mind that this book is an attempt to show the impact of war on a town; it isn't just out to say 'this was what life was like then'. It must be recognised that an awful lot of things about everyday life just went on as normal and had nothing to do with being in a state of war. This book is not out to show those normal everyday things. I imagine that some readers could well be interested in Headmaster, Mr Younie's constant state of dismay about the poor health [through scabies, impetigo, nits and head lice] of many of the children attending Park School in the early 1940s, but that ill health was not caused by being in a state of war, that was just the normal consequence for some, of the social conditions of the time, and will not be dealt with in this book. There are also some other things not in this book; there were some areas of wartime life in the town where it is almost impossible to find information. The outstanding areas of omission were to do with the impact of war on local railways, trade unions, the local accident hospital, and agriculture in general, including the Women's Land Army. These are the same areas where it was hard to pin down information during the Great War; the local press had passing references but the organisations or groups themselves did not keep any substantial records that showed the direct impact of either of the wars on their affairs. Any broad conclusions that I have been able to come to will appear in Chapter 6.

As before, wherever I have stated a historical fact or made a judgement based on evidence, I have end-noted it in that chapter so that any reader who may be concerned about the accuracy of my interpretation, can always go to the original sources themselves to see why I thought the way I did. Also as before; I consider this book a social and economic history, not a military history; it's about the changing lives of the people and businesses and institutions of Alloa during the war. It has got some military sections because the battles that Alloa men and women fought and died in, and the heroic military exploits of some of them, did affect the town in its view of how successfully it was undertaking its collective efforts to win the war. Where there were defeats the citizens had to rally to overcome their losses and disappointments; where there were successes, the town shared a reflected glory.

The main title of this book, *These Critical Times* was picked because it neatly implies that this is a history of the turbulent life of a town going through the strains of almost six years of war. The title is taken from a part of a minute of a meeting of the Kirk Session of St Andrew's Church in June 1940, particularly referring to the issue of whether, during these critical times, to conduct evening services through the summer months: but it did seem to lend itself to a wider interpretation.

As before, this book is a tribute to the people of Alloa and what they went through. Few are alive who fought in the war, but many are still with us who were children growing up through those critical times and have got firm memories of what it was like. I hope they feel I have done them all justice.

Andrew Hunt
April 2023

CHAPTER 1

ALLOA AND THE DECLARATION OF WAR ON 3rd SEPTEMBER 1939

If it could reasonably be claimed that the outbreak of the First World War in August 1914 caught people by surprise, that case certainly could not be made for the outbreak of the Second World War in September 1939. In the years through 1936 to 1938 the appeasers in the Government may have thought that war with Germany could be avoided by concessions, but by the time of the Munich Crisis which carved up Czechoslovakia in September 1938, though war was avoided at that time, even the appeasers conceded that preparations may now have to be made for how to defend ourselves in the event of a war. By March 1939, with the German occupation of the rest of Czechoslovakia in defiance of the deal that had been struck 6 months earlier at Munich, it was clear to everyone that war was somewhere on the fairly near horizon.

This recognition by the Government in 1938-39 that some war-like preparations might have to be made can also be seen in the case of the Burgh of Alloa. As early as April 1938 the Council was involved in Air Raid Precautions: it agreed to accept the rules and regulations of the ARP Act of 1937, and an ARP Joint Committee of Stirling and Clackmannanshire was set up in June 1938.[1] Then, on 5th September 1938 the Council nominated two local men, both council employees, to go on an ARP instructor's course for anti-gas measures and auxiliary fire-fighting.[2] The drama seemed to come closer to reality in September 1938 when the Council held a meeting during the actual Munich Crisis. The minute of that meeting refers to the 'International situation' and the instructions that were received from the Government

ARP Dept. about dealing with the safety of the civilian population; eg trench formation, distribution of gas masks etc. They really did think war was imminent. Provost Younger however, 'Commented on the fact that all steps which at present are being taken are merely precautionary and that there was still strong hope that war would be averted'.[3]

Captain James Paton Younger, Provost of Alloa 1932-1938 (*Alloa Academy Magazine*)

War was avoided in September 1938, but over 1939 the crisis gathered and by September 1939 it seemed that war could be avoided no longer. In terms of the response of the local newspapers; the *Journal* seemed to be superior to the *Advertiser* in the sharpness of its reporting of the sequence of events leading up to the actual outbreak of war on Sunday 3rd September 1939. It reported on

Alloa Advertiser

Telephone—Alloa 81.

SATURDAY, 2nd SEPTEMBER, 1939

War Emergency

After a week given over to rumours of war, but one, nevertheless, in which lingering hopes of a peaceful settlement of the Polish-German dispute were still being entertained by the peoples of the world, a day of grim drama was ushered in early yesterday when the shock intelligence was received of an aerial attack by Germany on Poland and the blockading of the Baltic by the former Power. British and Continental reactions to the situation which has arisen are being hourly reported in the National Press and provincial comment on the present state of flux would be at this stage both uninspired and untimely. Of more special relevance to this district is the Government evacuation scheme which had its inception in the county yesterday and which is continuing to-day. Between four or five thousand evacuees are being received in the county and reasonably complete arrangements have been made for their reception. We have no doubt that in this matter, as in others of a more calculable nature, the Wee County will not be behind other reception areas. It can be understood that the task of population re-adjustment will present many problems but with the goodwill and whole-hearted co-operation of the general public a smooth transfer should be effected. All who feel they can render any assistance should apply to their Town Clerk or to the County Clerk.

Editorial of *Alloa Advertiser*, Saturday 2nd September 1939

Saturday 2nd September of Germany's attack on Poland and 'the very grave news that reached the town yesterday forenoon, that Warsaw was bombed by the Germans at 9 o'clock in the morning...'[4] and that this would mean Britain would become involved in war.

The *Circular* however, had the edge on both its local rivals because it came out on a Wednesday; therefore being the first local paper to appear after the actual outbreak of the war. Its editorial on 6th September reflected its sense of disbelief that; 'After a weekend of grim drama and impending circumstance Britain finds herself – scarcely more than two decades after the Great War – once again a principal in a major European conflict'. An article in the paper itself noted that 'Somehow there has been an atmosphere of incredibility that such a situation could be possible and this has been emphasised by the perfect summer-like conditions of the beginning of this week'. It also observed that 'It is very noticeable however; an air of complete calmness prevails'.[5] This was picked up by the *Journal* on the following Saturday when it recorded that the reaction within Clackmannanshire County to the fateful event was 'calmness and determination'[6] and, without actually mentioning Chamberlain's famous radio broadcast, it observed that 'Sunday 3rd September will go down in history as one of the most momentous Sundays in the annals of this nation...'

It's worth pointing out that the Second World War was unique for British people on the home front in that it was the first major war Britain was involved in where people gained their news from the radio. The local press may not have mentioned Chamberlain's Sunday morning radio broadcast because by 1939, when there were 9 million holders of wireless licences in the UK tuning into the BBC Home Service, it was taken for granted that this was the way news would be spread. In fact, three weeks later the *Journal* while it commented on the rush to buy blackout material, also noted that 'the thirst for war news has sent sales of wireless sets booming'.[7]

There was another big difference in Alloa's reaction to the 'start' of the Second World War, compared to the First World War; this was in the length of time this 'reaction stage' took. In the Great War there was serious fighting and casualties within the first 6 months of the war, both on land and sea; so the period of the 'start' of the war was fairly short, and the brutal realities of being at war hit home quite quickly. In the case of the Second World War however, there was a prolonged period of relative military inactivity following the declaration of war, known as the Phoney War. This meant that the preparation/reaction stage for the people of Alloa was a much longer, more gradual and less dramatic process. For instance the story of the torpedoing of SS *Athenia* by a German U-boat on the very day war was declared, even with four named Clackmannanshire survivors to enliven the story, only got a week's coverage in the local press;[8] it didn't yet seem like a real war. It's likely that one of the first war-related deaths that Alloa suffered was Robert Fowell, a merchant seaman on SS *Abbotsford* which was lost with all hands 'to the perils of Nazi warfare at sea' in mid-March 1940. He was not born in Alloa but had lived in the town since he was a child when he went to St John's School. He had married a local girl, had three children and the family lived in Lambert Terrace. It's likely that his wife Barbara was Alloa's first wartime widow.[9] The reason it is difficult to accurately establish whether his was the first death is because the *Circular* reported that 'And so, with this tragic coincidence, it would appear that Alloa has lost yet another young citizen to the perils of Nazi warfare at sea'[10] which suggests that there had been an earlier one, but the paper had no details on who that might have been.

Then, it wasn't until May 1940 that Alloa got its first military casualty; the headline on an inside page of the *Advertiser* announced 'Alloa's First BEF Casualty – James Brophy's condition is improving'.[11] So that was 8 months of war before Alloa had an actual military casualty to talk about. It was only from about the middle of 1940 following the military evacuation from Dunkirk and the subsequent capture of most of the 51st Highland Division at St Valery could you argue that, for the people of Alloa, the 'start' of the Second World War was over. That's certainly what one interviewee in the *Alloa Docks Oral History Project* believed; 'It really started in 1940 at Dunkirk. That was when everybody got cracking then. Before that you thought there wasn't a war on. Oh they got cracking then'.[12]

In this 'starting' phase of the war, while it lasted, there were three obvious areas of war preparation that the Burgh Council would be deeply involved in; evacuation plans, blackout and air raid precautions/shelters.

EVACUATION

At first it seemed that the Burgh Council had its head buried in the sand; in November 1938 it deflected a request from the Provost of nearby Elie in Fife, to consider what action councils might to take to deal with evacuees. Alloa's councillors said it wasn't their business; they should wait for a ruling from the Convention of Burghs.[13] It was clear though that the Government was making some demands on councils and in February 1939 the Provost reported that under the government evacuation scheme, the Council had done a survey of housing in the Burgh. It was reckoned that there were 1,031 surplus rooms, and that Alloa had the capacity to provide 319 rooms for children, 147 for teachers and helpers and 48 for others. 454 rooms had already been reserved for private arrangements. This survey had largely been conducted by teachers of the schools.[14] In May 1939 the Council heard for the first time that it was to be a 'reception area' in the Government's evacuation scheme and now had to make more serious plans to receive evacuees.[15] On Saturday 2nd September, the day before the war started, the Advertiser's editorial was less concerned with the state of emergency than it was with the imminent arrival of evacuees; arguing that there was nothing much they could usefully say or do about the emergency, but there was plenty they could do for the evacuees![16] That editorial noted that between four and five thousand evacuees would arrive in Clackmannanshire. On that Saturday '772 are expected to arrive at Alloa station at 11.23 am, from where they will be escorted by receptionists to central quarters at Alloa Academy'. There were 70 billeting officers who would then escort the evacuees to their houses. That total included 581 children.[17] Tillicoultry had received its evacuees the day before. Rough totals for other reception centres in the County were:

Tillicoultry	received 549 of which 60% children
Alva	received 206 children
Sauchie	received 385 children
Tullibody and Cambus	received 303 children
Clackmannan	received 72 children

These figures from the Advertiser suggest that a few more evacuees arrived than the estimate from the Journal on 16th September 1939, which thought that 'the number of evacuated children in the County was somewhere around the 1,000 mark'.[18] It did not take long for issues to emerge but they were easily dealt with. There were concerns about the health standards of evacuees expressed at the meeting of the County's Public Health Committee, partly made worse by the fact that one child had contracted Scarlet Fever two days after arrival. However, Dr Finlator offered reassurance and said 'The County had been very lucky in that it had received a very good class of child'.[19]

The minutes show the Council had nothing to say about the process of evacuation in early September 1939, but it did set up an evacuation tribunal to deal with any complaints that arose from the billeting of evacuees.[20] October saw the arrival of 78 more evacuees, leading to concern about where they might be put. The *Journal* observed that 'Up to the moment, billeting has been voluntary, but if further accommodation is required and it is not forthcoming, compulsory powers may have to be exercised'.[21] In December 1939 the Council received a complimentary note from the Secretary of State for Scotland who 'made special mention of the work done in Alloa in connection with the Government Evacuation Scheme'.[22] The Council seemed astounded to then receive a note from the Government in February 1940, warning them to prepare for the arrival of 450 additional child evacuees.[23] The Council told the Government there were only 100 persons who had expressed a willingness to accept evacuees, and 'it appeared that compulsory powers would be required'.[24] The Council therefore put a notice in the local press saying they would enforce the compulsory billeting aspects of evacuation.[25] The problem now was that Alloa's Chief Evacuation Officer said 'he didn't mind trying to place children upon a voluntary basis, but that he desired to be excused if compulsion were to be employed'. The Council weighed up what to do if he did resign and suggested that 'a member of the teaching staff might be available' [apparently one local headmaster and one other person outside the teaching profession had expressed an interest in doing the job]. In fact the Council picked Charles Irvine, headmaster of Grange School as the new Chief Reception Officer, paying him an honorarium of £10 for fulfilling his duties.[26] The Council also decided that since it had the right to exercise its compulsory powers on this matter it would use them if necessary.[27] Mr Irvine had no such worries about the use of compulsion and another notice was placed in the *Advertiser* under his name stating that 'any house deemed capable of receiving an evacuee due to having room, will be given an evacuee'.[28] There was a right of appeal and many householders took this up. The *Advertiser* reported at the end of June that '208 pleas against taking in evacuees have been disallowed, 198 pleas had been allowed'.[29]

By July 1940 most evacuees had gone home[30], but the Council discussed an unsettling rumour that Alloa had been changed from being a 'receiving' area to being a 'neutral' area [ie an area which would not be receiving evacuees, and therefore by implication, an area slightly more likely to be bombed]. This was because the government had categorised reception areas into Plans A, B and C in terms of the order they received evacuees. The Council had been told that they were not on A but likely to be on B or C. That didn't mean that they were no longer a 'receiving' area, they had just been moved further down the receiving list; so that rumour was soon put to rest.[31]

BLACKOUT

Without having any real proof in 1938 that German bombing of Britain might be a night-time business, there was nevertheless a widespread belief that a blackout of Britain's towns at night would be a good idea. The Council agreed to hold a trial blackout, 'probably on 13th March 1939' [but in fact postponed to 27th] between the hours of 10 pm and midnight. All street lighting would be extinguished'.[32] It was also agreed, at the request of Alloa's Medical Officer of Health, Dr Finlator, to do some training for the blackout at the halls in the public baths.[33] Steps were taken in the town to prevent foreseeable difficulties; the *Journal* reported that, 'the lamp posts are having white bands painted on them to render them more distinguishable to pedestrians during darkness'[34]

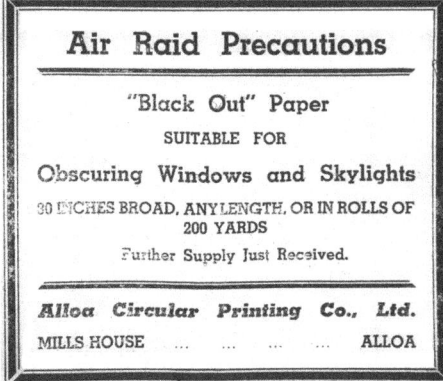

Blackout poster *Alloa Journal*
9th September 1939

Blackout material advert *Alloa Circular*
13th September 1939

and 'At Alloa station the platforms and bays have been edged with broad white lines... a sandbag shelter has also been erected. Down at the Shore, the edges of the docks were also being painted with a white line almost 6 inches broad'. The *Journal* noted that shops reported a rush on the purchase of black paper and other blackout material, stating that 'shops where such material has been on sale were besieged last weekend'.[35]

The local press reported on the government's determination to enforce a strict blackout. Only two days after the declaration of war the *Circular* had a column headed 'PUBLIC WARNED – Non-observance of Black-out Rules – Strict Enforcement and penalties'[36] and went on to list the penalties, including imprisonments of up to 3 months, fines of up to £100 and re-offenders getting 2 years! The Burgh magistrates were quite keen to enforce the blackout and within three weeks of the start of the war, five bicycle-lighting offenders had appeared in court for breaking blackout regulations. Two of them were fined 15/- or 5 days in prison![37] It was not until four months later that Alloa had its first blackout tragedy when a 76-year-old pensioner fell into the harbour and drowned.[38] The *Circular* for 3rd January 1940 reported on the 'Fatal mishap at Alloa harbour' where Angus MacMillan an OAP from Castle Street fell into the river from the harbour front. His friend, who also fell in but was rescued alive said 'they had mistaken their road in the darkness and stumbled into the river'.

The most notable local conviction for breaking the blackout rules occurred in November 1940 when Rev. William Gibbons, the minister of Moncrieff Church was fined £9. On 30th October it had been noted that he had two lighted windows in the upstairs of the manse in Alexandra Drive. When the police arrived he refused to give his name, became very obstructive and slammed the door in their faces. He had been warned on three previous occasions and was prosecuted. In court he said the manse had 43 windows and he was harassed. He didn't escape justice and was given a £9 fine or the option of 20 days imprisonment.[39] The Alloa magistrates did not let up on the severity of their approach; the *Advertiser* continually reported on the number of people who they fined for blackout infringements right through 1941 and 1942. Some of these offenders would not have seen the humour in the chirpy little poem in the *Circular* in January 1941:[40]

He rose and went to his window
And smiled, as the expert bid
But his smile lit the blackout of morning
And cost him a fine of a quid.

The blackout was a continual burden; in May 1942 the *Journal's* columnist depressingly noted 'we have now endured 1001 nights of the blackout'.[41] The regulations were still being strongly enforced even by late 1942 when the *Journal* noted that 'There is still considerable room for a tightening up of local black-out arrangements. A most reprehensible lack of attention to black-out details is being shown in some quarters, and lights showing prominently after nightfall have been the subject of much irate comment among the people living in the immediate neighbourhood, who rightly feel that their lives are being endangered by such flagrant carelessness on the part of others'.[42]

You can see why the *Journal* was so pleased in early September 1944 to announce that 'Blackout to be almost banished'[43] and also that there were to be big cuts in civil defence and fire guard duties.

The blackout regulations ended in the third week of September 1944; the *Advertiser* noted that '... after 5 years of blackout, street lights were switched on again at 8 pm on Sunday evening'.[44] For the last months of the war Blackout was replaced by Dimout; and the local press, for people's information, still listed the times for when partial lighting was allowed.[45]

LIGHTS GO ON AGAIN

End of a Five Year Ban

After five years of black-out, street lights were switched on in Alloa at 8 p.m. on Sunday evening. Councillor Young, Lighting Convener, officiating at Alloa Gas Works at a cheerfully informal little ceremony, which was also attended by Provost McKinlay, Mr Athol Brown (in his capacity as Lighting Superintendent) and Chief Constable D. Robertson (to whom in the first instance all local authorities in the County submitted their modified lighting schemes).

Following the switching on of the lights in the central part of the town the Councillors and officials made a tour of the streets to satisfy themselves that everything was in order

Alloa Circular 20th September 1944

AIR RAID PRECAUTIONS/SHELTERS

In March 1939 the Council considered whether to build some public air raid shelters on waste ground at the east end of Bowhouse Road.[46] On 4th September 1939, the day after war was declared, the Council agreed to let a set of trenches be dug in the West End Park for the protection of pupils from the Academy and Grange schools, as long as the Education Dept. paid for it out of its budget. Amazingly they also told the Education Committee that once dug, there would be no guarantee that these trenches would be for the exclusive use of school children.[47] This work was satisfactorily done; the *Journal* commented that 'there are now two large and well-constructed shelters in Alloa Public Park'.[48] In December 1939 the Council agreed to spend £4000 on air raid shelters for school children; Alloa Academy, Sunnyside and Park School would get 5 shelters, South School and St John's would get 2 and St Mungo's would get 3. Grange School would do some work in its basement to create 4 shelters.[49] The Council hoped that the government would pay for the cost of shelters but in December 1939 they received a note[50] that since Alloa was a safe area then no funding would be offered. In January 1940 when there was a petition from Alloa citizens demanding public shelters; the Council's view now echoed the logic of the Government's; that since Alloa was considered a safe place then it didn't need to provide them.

However, that had not stopped the councillors in September 1939 from setting up a mortuary to deal with 'civilian deaths through war operations'. The plan was to use part of premises belonging to Patons and Baldwins at Keilarsbrae; that company had apparently offered very attractive terms to the Council.[51] It was probably a surprise when in September 1940 the Council was told that the burial of enemy airmen was also their responsibility.[52] It was also informed, via Government Circular 203/1940, that it was the Council's job to salvage property and clear debris from air raids.[53] At the start of the war, when there was a widespread belief that the Germans would drop bombs containing poisonous gases, Dr Finlator reassured the Public Health Committee that Alloa was prepared and that the accident

Stirling and Clackmannan A.R.P. Joint Authority. Northern Division.

An issue of Children's Protective Helmets and Respirators will be made throughout the County on SUNDAY, 10th MARCH 1940, between the hours of 1 p.m. and 5 p.m. Parents must attend with their children under 4 years of age so that they may be fitted with the necessary equipment.

DISTRIBUTION CENTRES.

Menstrie	Public School.
Alva	Dalmore School.
Tillicoultry	Public School.
Coalsnaughton and Devonside	Public School.
Dollar	Public School.
Forestmill	Public School.
Clackmannan and Kennet	Clackmannan Public School.
Fishcross	Public School.
Sauchie	Public School.
Tullibody and Cambus	Tullibody Public School.
Alloa	Alloa Academy.
	Park School.
	St. Mungo's R.C. School.
	Sunnyside School.
	Grange School.

DAVID ROBERTSON,
Divisional Controller.

County Police Office,
Alloa, 5th March, 1940.

Alloa Circular, 6th March 1940

hospital had set aside '24 beds to the reception of gas cases'.[54] These were not to be needed.

In July 1940 the Council agreed to obtain more sand supplies so that householders could get more 'for the purpose of extinguishing incendiary bombs'.[55] Maybe some of that sand had a use elsewhere because in September 1940 it was pointed out to the councillors that many of the sandbags used to protect ARP buildings 'were now in a dilapidated condition' and the Burgh Surveyor was told to sort it out.[56] It also agreed to increase their supply of stirrup pumps for sale to the public [the Council meeting of 30th September 1940 noted that a good supply had been obtained and these were on sale for £1 each].

AUXILIARY FIRE-FIGHTERS IN ACTION

Alloa's auxiliary firemen showing their paces in a fire-fighting service demonstration at Shavelhaugh Bridge on the Alva-Alloa road last Sunday. Firemen in the group read (from left to right) R. Prentice, D. Hardie, W. Prentice, J. Irvine, W. Gray, and J. McMaster.

Alloa firefighters, *Alloa Circular*, 6th September 1939

A "CASUALTY" AT PATONS

Patons and Baldwins sports ground at Tullibody Road is one of many sites which have been taken over by the Government as a first-aid post in the event of emergency. The above picture was taken at a first-aid practice held there last Sunday afternoon when a local volunteer gives first-aid treatment to a "casualty." First-aid work of this description is run in conjunction with the Government scheme under civil defence.

Alloa first-aiders, *Alloa Circular*,
6th September 1939

Patons Mills Fireguard Squad 1939

By mid-1940 the government's attitude towards air-raid shelters in reception areas must have changed; in July the Alloa British Legion was still asking for shelters and the Minister of Home Security now agreed on 'the erection of domestic communal shelters in Alloa'. It was at roughly this time that Harlands [a large local engineering company] started camouflaging its roof, so someone was maybe expecting to get bombed![57] The Journal reported that the Council had received a letter from the ARP Joint Authority saying that Alloa was entitled to some communal air raid shelters which were big enough for 48 people. Alloa would get 27 shelters to be distributed throughout the council wards.[58] The number of shelters to be provided was '10% of the population for whom they were intended'.[59] The Council speedily got working on this and agreed to erect the shelters in accordance with approved designs from the Scottish Office. A draft site plan was submitted and approved with a few minor alterations.[60] The *Circular* reported in September that a contract to build 36 shelters had been placed with a Tillicoultry company at a cost of £2,645. 5/-. Each shelter was big enough for 48 people and all were to be built above ground 'of brick and cement specially destined (sic) to be bomb proof'.[61] The article went on to say that the Council would have built more shelters but there was a shortage of skilled labour and problems due to the rationing of cement.

In October the Government told councils that the full cost of air raid shelters would be borne by the government and would councils hurry up with the work.[62] This provision of shelters increased even more once the Blitz began; in June 1941 the Council was informed by the ARP Joint Authority that the Burgh could have communal domestic shelters for 1000 persons. They would start by providing some for the Dirleton Gardens Housing Scheme Area.[63] Things maybe did not always go totally to plan however, because by November 1941 the Council was discussing whether to scrap the Waggon-way air raid shelter. It was in poor condition, did not have seating, and it was now considered inadvisable to have a shelter big enough for 150 people. It would cost £130 to put in decent lighting, a satisfactory floor and toilets. The Council agreed to go ahead and do this.[64] It appears the Council may have been spending money to save its face here. An earlier article in the *Advertiser* pointed out that this had been an 'unofficial' shelter which the Council had authorised but the ARP Joint Authority hadn't. The *Advertiser* noted that the 'Burgh Surveyor informs us that an improvised shelter is being built on the Waggon-way by closing one end of the tunnel. The shelter is outwith the provisions of the official ARP scheme but will act as a reinforcement to the town's precautionary system'.[65] That 1941 reference to saving the Waggon-way air raid shelter was the last time shelters were mentioned in the Council minutes until July 1945 when there was 'Discussion about the removal of air raid shelters now the ARP Joint Authority had given its permission…'[66] This soon began; the *Circular* reporting that the Council had begun its demolition of air raid shelters… the one in Greenfield Street would be the first.[67] The Alloa squad of the ARP fulfilled its role right through the war and was finally dismissed from duty at its stand-down ceremony at the Gaumont on Sunday 10th June 1945.[68]

There were two other pre-war actions that showed Alloa's preparation for war. The first was the concern of the councillors in March 1939 that Harland Engineering would be getting war contracts and there would be a lack of local housing if Harlands got a big increase in its labour force because it was doing work of such national importance. It seems they expected to recruit aircraft workers, and these began to arrive in July 1939.[69]

Then the councillors also realised in June 1939 that under the terms of the Military Training Act passed in April, there were various employees of the Burgh who were now in the forces. As a result they now might be earning less, during training, than they were earning in their council employment. It was agreed that their pay should be made up to the level they were previously earning at.[70] This really was an absolute echo of what the Council decided to do in 1914 at the outbreak of the Great War. In respect of council buildings, it was noted in October 1940 that all the local authorities in the County had agreed on a scheme of mutual assistance in the event of war damage to property by air raids. A variety of building materials would be made available and there would be mutual assistance with work.[71] This was taken further in January 1941 when the Council agreed on war emergency arrangements for staff movement between different County Council and Burgh Council buildings, should one of them become 'the object of a successful attack by enemy aircraft'.[72]

ENDNOTES
_____

[1] Alloa Burgh Council minute book 25th April 1938. The Chairman of this Joint Committee was Captain James Paton Younger who had been Alloa's Provost for 6 years between 1932 and 1938

[2] Alloa Burgh Council minute book 5th September 1938

[3] Alloa Burgh Council minute book 26th September 1938

[4] *Alloa Journal* 2nd September 1939

[5] *Alloa Circular* 6th September 1939

[6] *Alloa Journal* 9th September 1939

[7] *Alloa Journal* 23rd September 1939

[8] *Alloa Advertiser* 9th September 1939. The *Alloa Circular* on 6th September 1939 noted that one of the survivors, steward William Fotheringham was from 13 Moir Street

[9] *Alloa Advertiser* 23rd March 1940 and *Alloa Journal* 30th March 1940

[10] *Alloa Circular* 27th March 1940

[11] *Alloa Journal* 26th July 1941 finally reported on his arrival home; that 'Private James Brophy of the Argylls, badly wounded at evacuation of Dunkirk has been welcomed home to East Castle Street'

[12] Alloa Docks Oral History Project 1987; Mr D born 1908

[13] Alloa Burgh Council minute book 4th November 1938

[14] Alloa Burgh Council minute book 13th February 1939

[15] Alloa Burgh Council minute book 8th May 1939, also called a 'recovery area' in some texts

[16] *Alloa Advertiser* 2nd September 1939

[17] *Alloa Advertiser* 2nd September 1939

[18] *Alloa Journal* 16th September 1939

[19] *Alloa Advertiser* 9th September 1939

[20] Alloa Burgh Council minute book 11th September 1939

[21] *Alloa Journal* 7th October 1939

[22] Alloa Burgh Council minute book 26th December 1939

[23] Alloa Burgh Council minute book 26th February 1940 and *Alloa Journal* 16th March 1940 reported a warning from Dept. of Health that Alloa should expect the imminent arrival of 450 more evacuees; the largest amount was 300 to Park School

[24] Alloa Burgh Council minute book 13th May 1940

[25] *Alloa Advertiser* 18th May 1940

[26] Alloa Burgh Council minute book 26th May 1941

[27] Mr Irvine was Chief Reception Officer until 28th May 1941 when the new Town Clerk, Mr Maltman was installed and took over the duties. He was also clearly willing to take the line of imposing compulsory billeting of evacuees if required. See Grange School log book 28th May 1941

[28] *Alloa Advertiser* 8th June 1940. Since this is the first reference to money it is worth reminding readers that Britain's currency in those days was pounds, shillings and pence: 12 pence to a shilling and 20 shillings to a pound

[29] *Alloa Advertiser* 22nd June 1940

[30] *Alloa Journal* 5th February 1944 reported that only 45 evacuees remained in Alloa at that date

[31] Alloa Burgh Council minute book 8th July 1940

[32] Alloa Burgh Council minute book 9th January 1939

[33] Alloa Burgh Council minute book 13th March 1939. Dr Finlator had been Alloa's MOH in the years before the Great War up until 1915 and had returned to his position after military service. He was still in post at the outbreak of the Second World War. He died in 1940

[34] *Alloa Journal* 2nd September 1939

[35] *Alloa Journal* 9th September 1939

[36] *Alloa Circular* 6th September 1939

[37] *Alloa Advertiser* 23rd September 1939

[38] *Alloa Advertiser* 6th January 1940

[39] *Alloa Circular* 20th November 1940

[40] *Alloa Circular* 8th January 1941

[41] *Alloa Journal* 30th May 1942

42 *Alloa Journal* 15th August 1942
43 *Alloa Journal* 9th September 1944
44 *Alloa Advertiser* 23rd September 1944
45 *Alloa Journal* 7th October 1944 contained a note of these times; plus a warning that if the air raid siren ever was heard then full blackout regulations came into immediate effect.
46 Alloa Burgh Council minute book 27th March 1939
47 Alloa Burgh Council minute book 4th September 1939
48 *Alloa Journal* 14th October 1939
49 *Alloa Advertiser* 15th December 1939
50 Alloa Burgh Council minute book 11th December 1939
51 Alloa Burgh Council minute book 25th September 1939 and 27th November 1939
52 Alloa Burgh Council minute book 8th September 1940
53 Alloa Burgh Council minute book 9th September 1940
54 *Alloa Advertiser* 9th September 1939
55 Alloa Burgh Council minute book 8th July 1940
56 Alloa Burgh Council minute book 30th September 1940
57 Alloa Docks Oral History Project 1987; George born 1899
58 *Alloa Journal* 3rd August 1940
59 Alloa Burgh Council minute book 29th July 1940
60 Alloa Burgh Council minute book 1st August 1940
61 *Alloa Circular* 18th September 1940. Was the use of the word 'destined' a typo? Did they mean 'designed' or was some higher fate supposed to be involved for those who took shelter there?
62 Alloa Burgh Council minute book 28th October 1940
63 Alloa Burgh Council minute book 30th June 1941
64 Alloa Burgh Council minute book 10th November 1941
65 *Alloa Advertiser* 28th September 1940
66 Alloa Burgh Council minute book 30th July 1945
67 *Alloa Circular* 5th September 1945
68 *Alloa Journal* 16th June 1945
69 Alloa Burgh Council minute book 21st March 1939
70 Alloa Burgh Council minute book 26th June 1939
71 Alloa Burgh Council minute book 14th October 1940
72 Alloa Burgh Council minute book 27th January 1941

CHAPTER 2

ALLOA'S INDUSTRIES

Alloa's industrial strength at the time of the Second World War was still largely based around the same 'big four' as during the Great War; coal-mining, the glassworks, Patons textile mills and the breweries. Just as in the Great War, Alloa's ship-building/repair industry grew up again; and there was the extra addition in the growth of The Harland Engineering Company as a major local employer and contributor of vital war materials. In the case of all these industries, the evidence about their growth and development during the years of the Second World War is very patchy; the companies' own records sometimes got destroyed during later mergers and takeovers, less evidence seems to have been placed in the National Archives, and the local newspapers did not report very much, probably under instruction from government censors. For instance, in their 'County Retrospects' in the *Advertiser* at the start of 1941 and 1942, the paper could find little more to say than the fairly obvious point that 'Trade throughout the County has been good during the year, but firms both large and small, face great difficulties as a result of the diminution of their staffs by the claims of national service'.[1] These problems were typified in the example, for instance, of the local metal manufacturer R.G. Abercrombie who took over Willison's Brass Founders in 1926; both companies manufactured products for the brewing and distilling industries but during the war, copper-smithing was not a reserved occupation and many of Abercrombie's staff were called up...[2] By January 1943 there was the more optimistic view in the *Journal* that 'Industry in the County has generally been brisk... the district has received a good quota of war work and this has meant increased employment' followed by the more pessimistic view that 'This has given rise to some problems, such as the billeting of war workers'.[3] More than 40 years after the war was over, Central Regional Council set up a group to interview many of Alloa's wartime workers and asked them about their experiences; this was the *Alloa Docks Oral History Project* of 1987.[4] It has useful, often quite detailed reminiscence evidence, particularly of working in the shipyards and at Harlands.

COAL

Ever since the time of the Great War, the Alloa Coal Company had extensive coal-bearing properties on both sides of the River Forth. However, in 1936 they sold off all their leases and holdings in Stirlingshire to the Carron Company and from then on, the ACC pits were all within the borders of Clackmannanshire. When an opportunity came up in 1938 to extend their holdings into New Cumnock Collieries in Ayrshire, the ACC Board voted against the purchase, although three Directors chose to go it alone and take over affairs there.[5] 1938 also saw a long-term lease being signed with Lord Balfour of Burleigh for his Brucefield and Kennet minerals, and an extension to a hundred years of the lease with the Earl of Mar and Kellie. Things therefore looked bright for the ACC in the last year before the Second World War started. The Managing Director was Sir Harold Mitchell, who had taken over from his father, who had run the ACC during the Great War.

The first major impact of the war on the ACC was that from almost the first days of the war, all main-line railway wagons owned by the Company were requisitioned and the Company had to fit in with government controls on how every aspect of their work should go. It is disappointing to note that many of the mistakes in government organisation of labour in the collieries that had been made in the Great War were simply repeated. For instance, the rapid expansion of the munitions industry meant that extra coal was now needed, which sounded like a good thing. Unfortunately these industries also attracted labour away from the pits at the very same time as the government was, as in 1914, encouraging young men to join the forces. There had been a schedule of reserved occupations drawn up before the war, including miners under 23; this was largely ignored and caused a big decline in output. To start with there had been a great effort to increase coal production and there was indeed a higher output. Maybe the pay rise for coal workers of 5 pence a shift from 1st January

1940 helped towards that.[6] *The Bulletin* on 2nd July 1940 reported that 'The Scottish miner's demand had been agreed to...' and the new basic rate was 10/- per shift; 90,000 Scottish miners would get this rate. The ACC had an increase of 56,447 tons in 1940 compared to the previous year.[7] But by 1940-41, production at the ACC dropped by 11,000 tons; the older men who were left working simply couldn't keep their production rates up when so many younger, fitter men had been called up. The coal industry made appeals to the Government to comb out miners from the Forces and send them back to the pits but they refused. However, in 1941 the Government did impose controls on the labour force in an attempt to retain the workers and get them to work harder; it applied the Essential Works Order to the coal industry. This meant no employee could now leave the industry without permission from a National Service officer, no manager could sack a miner without the same permission, and miners got a bonus of one shilling a shift as an inducement to reduce absenteeism [and therefore raise productivity]. The Government also set production targets for each coal-field; the target for the ACC in the Fife and Clackmannan coalfields was a 6.41% increase.

Controls of labour may have helped the supply side, but there were still problems with the demand side. Much of the early coal produced was exported to France to help their war industries but the collapse of France and the over-running of other neutral European countries in 1940 'brought the coal export trade to a standstill, and threw back on the home market an enormous tonnage of coal, for which new outlets had to be found...'[8] For a while there was too much supply and not enough demand. Curiously, this hadn't stopped the ACC developing a new mine. The *Advertiser* in June 1940 reported on the development of 'the ACC's new modern mine...' where 'despite delay due to wartime conditions, satisfactory progress is being made with the driving of a surface mine in the parish of Carnock'.[9]

The general issue of over-supply was partly solved later in the year when the Blitz started; since the Government now encouraged consumers to lay in extra supplies in case there should be transport difficulties as a result of the air bombardment.

During 1941-42 the ACC increased its output by more than 64,000 tons, although most of this increase came from the simple expedient of buying up other collieries [Tulligarth Colliery and Craigie Mine being two of them, providing 50,000 tons from that total]. The *Advertiser* neatly pointed out that 'the Company now control practically all the minerals in the County'.[10]

Alloa Coal Company's Meta Coal works around about the time of the Second World War

By the summer of 1942 the Government realised that its Essential Works Order was having little effect but they didn't do much to find a way out. By the autumn of 1943 the Government was facing a coal crisis due to lack of labour. The inspiration for the solution was Ernest Bevin, the Minister of Labour; he came up with the idea of using 1 in 10 of all the men who were conscripted for military service to be sent to the mines instead.[11] They became known as 'Bevin Boys' and by the end of the war the scheme had provided 48,000 workers as an additional labour force to the British mining industry. The first of Alloa's Bevin Boys was David B.H. MacGregor of 221 Ashley Terrace. He was posted to Bessie Glen colliery in Tillicoultry and started work there on 14th May 1944.[12] The *Journal* must have been expecting the arrival of extra manpower for the local mines because in February 1944 it reported on the announcement by Mr Telfer, the General Manager of the ACC, of the construction of 2 hostels for mine workers, one capable of taking 100 single men [Holton Square, Sauchie], the other capable of taking 100 married men [Fishcross].[13] The expression 'Bevin Boys' wasn't used but this must have been why most of them were coming; as indicated in the *Journal*'s October article referring to the fact that '33 young miners were already in residence in Holton Square'.[14]

Whilst it seems very difficult to get a clear idea of the ACC's wartime profits, it was the case that they continued investing in and initiating new developments in the coal industry right through the war. The local press reported enthusiastically on the opening of a new mine in December 1942, when Colonel Harold Mitchell cut the first sod at West Pitgober, near Dollar.[15]

It also seemed the case that labour relations were good and the trade unions responded to the opportunities that the ACC gave. At the opening of the Pitgober mine, 'Mr Andrew Rankine representing the Fife and Clackmannanshire Miner's Union said there had not been a ton of coal lost through any local dispute for 21 years'.[16] This may have been true then, but in March

Sir Harold Mitchell
(*Alloa Circular* 18th August 1945)

Alloa Coal Company's Devon Colliery pithead baths and canteen 1944 (J.L. Carvel)

Alloa Coal Company's Devon Colliery 1944 (J.L. Carvel)

1945 there were two 1-day strikes in two different ACC mines over objections to a dismissal [Devon Colliery] and firemen wanting more pay [Craigrie Colliery] so they must have lost a few tons of production there.[17] In February 1943, Sir Patrick Dollan, Chairman of the Scottish Fuel Efficiency Committee claimed

that Clackmannanshire miners were the 'Stalingrad heroes of British industry'...
their output was half a ton per man-shift greater than any other coal producing
area'.[18] Keeping going with its policy of innovation, on 18th March 1943 the
ACC opened a briquetting plant at their Meta Pit [near Sauchie Tower]. It was
officially opened by Major Gwilym Lloyd George, the Minister of Fuel and
Power [Minister from 1942-45, one of David Lloyd George's younger sons]. The
Journal commented that this plant 'will enable the small coal at this colliery to
be more economically used'.[19]

At the end of 1944 the *Journal* had a whole column under the heading 'Wee
County miners' wonderful record' which painted a glowing picture of the output
of Clackmannanshire coal workers
during the war years.[20] It reckoned their
man-shift output was nearly twice the
Scottish average [38.9 cwt compared
with 21.3 cwt]. After the war was over
however, Mr Telfer, the ACC General
Manager made a slightly more pessimistic
observation. He pointed out that for the
last pre-war mining year ending in March
1939, production was 342,538 tons, and
for the last wartime year ending in March

Alloa Coal Company's Meta pit
brickworks and briquetting plant 1944
(J.L. Carvel)

1945 it was 400,518 tons. That was all to the good, a 15% increase; but, over the
same period, absenteeism has risen from 4.1% to 10.6%.[21] This view was backed
up by a report in the *Circular* in January 1915 which expressed its concern that
higher wages in the pits due to the recent pay rise were causing less production.
This was because the miners were earning more than enough for doing the same
work, therefore they didn't bother turning up if it didn't suit them. There was a
rise in absenteeism and a recent court case showed this; a miner was fined £15
for not bothering to go into work.[22]

SHIPBUILDING

After a burst of success during the Great War, Alloa's shipyards had gone into
steep decline; only McLeod's yard still operated. In the first year of the Second
World War, Alloa's MP Arthur Woodburn was pushing within the government

for some sort of re-generation of Alloa's shipbuilding capacity to meet wartime needs, especially for repair and refurbishment. In a parliamentary question to the Minister of Shipping in December 1939 he 'Asked Sir John Gilmour whether he was prepared to use the shipyards and plant available at Alloa for the building and/or repairing of ships'. Gilmour replied that he was considering it for the repair of small ships.[23] The *Advertiser* believed he had a case, and in January 1940 it produced an article with the optimistic sub-heading of 'Busy Times expected ahead' even though it recognised the shortcomings of the present yards. It noted that in two yards, Forthbank and Kelliebank, 'the machinery in these yards has been entirely dismantled although the site could still be adapted for shipbuilding work'. But, it also claimed that 'At Kelliebank it is estimated that vessels of up to 13,000 tons could be constructed'.[24]

In April 1940 the *Circular* reported on the setback that Alloa had suffered in its 'Plea For Alloa Shipyard' when it noted that the Admiralty had commented 'The potentialities of this shipyard have been fully investigated. The yard… has not the facilities for repair work on a larger scale or for building ships, and I can find no evidence of there being the skilled labour available in the district as would be required to expand the yard's present activities'.[25] This pessimistic view didn't differ that much from the view, over a year later, of Sir Wilfred Ayre, who was sent to check out Alloa's chances of hosting a shipbuilding revival with a set of repair/refit or construction yards. In his view 'Facilities for the repair of naval auxiliary vessels on the east of Scotland, in July 1941, were found to be inadequate to meet the demands of wartime casualties. Sir James Lithgow requested me to make an assessment of the possibilities of utilising an old shipyard site in Alloa. I visited the place; it was a derelict prospect. There were no usable tools. A dry dock of ancient lineage was available for only small craft and was in a dilapidated state. Surplus skilled labour was scarce. Without this, repairs to auxiliary naval craft were not possible. During my inspection of Alloa I observed that two other derelict shipyards at Alloa might be pressed into some kind of activity. They appeared suitable for the assembly and launching of pre-fabricated tank landing craft. I discussed the matter with Lithgow who decided to accept my advice. The yards were equipped for the assembly of landing craft and were ultimately operated by two constructional steel companies using whatever class of labour they found available. Their efficiency was relatively poor'.[26]

The two companies which Sir Wilfred Ayre referred to were Sir William Arrol

Tank landing craft *LCT 4037* launched on 13th January 1945 by Commander Earl Beatty DSC
(© Imperial War Museum)

Commander Earl Beatty DSC with some of the workers who completed *LCT 4037*
which was later renamed HMS *Rampart* (© Imperial War Museum)

& Co which took over the Kelliebank yard, and Motherwell Bridge which took over the Forthbank yard. They and their workers set out to demonstrate that Sir Wilfred's damning views on their working abilities were totally without foundation, and the fact of the matter was that from late in 1941 until almost the end of the war, the rejuvenated shipyards in Alloa made a heroic contribution towards winning the war. The chief products of these two companies were tank landing craft, always known as LCTs.

About 3 months after D-Day the *Journal* contained a report of the success of Alloa-built tank landing craft at the D-Day landings.[27] It was reporting on an article in the Admiralty's official magazine *Spotlight*, which said 'Landing craft made at Alloa played a prominent part in the beach landings on the continent of Europe and one of them – LCT 608 – had earned the following mentions... There is something definitely Scottish about LCT 608, which was among the first craft to touch down on the beaches of France on Invasion Day. She was built by Scottish employees of the Motherwell Bridge and Engineering Company, her commanding officer Lieut. EC Mason... was a teacher in a Scottish preparatory school before the war and his First Lieutenant was... a former Glasgow office clerk. On the first trip '608' escaped without a scratch although shore batteries were raking the landing craft with shells and machine gun bullets in an almost unbelievable hail of fire. The second trip was more eventful. The craft was hit and a section of the bow was completely wrecked'. Elsewhere in that *Spotlight* magazine mention was made of other Alloa-built Landing Craft (T); '602', '604', '785', '789', '790' and '1041'. It further added that the first one built in Alloa was '601' which had already been the subject of a special comment at the landing in Sicily.

The Imperial War Museum has a fairly large collection of photographs of the construction and launching of landing craft in Alloa. They were mainly taken by Lt. F.G. Roper in April 1944 and Lt. J.E. Russell in January-February 1945, although the photo of Commander Beatty was taken by Lt. E.A. Zimmerman. The caption accompanying Roper's photo of the launch of *LCT 1169* was very complimentary; '60% of the shipyard workers were women and the yard was credited with building and launching landing craft faster than any other yard in Great Britain. Assembling pre-fabricated craft on four berths, one craft has been launched every seven days for the past two months'.

No story of Alloa's shipbuilding achievement would be complete without

Some of Kelliebank's female shipyard workers during the Second World War (*Alloa Advertiser*, with thanks to John McClelland)

Alloa Advertiser 17th March 1961

In 1942, H.M. Government commissioned Sir William Arrol and the Motherwell Bridge & Engineering Company, to build tank landing craft at the former Kelliebank and Forthbank shipyards in Alloa.

In the next three years the aforementioned companies handed over an amazing 122 of the large Mark 4 L.C.T.s, in preparation for the D-Day landings in June, 1944.

These were followed by 26 of the much larger ocean-going Mark 8 type, specially designed to meet operational requirements in the far east.
The Mark 8 prototype vessel was also built at Kelliebank.

68 Landing craft tank (Mark 4) (large) were built at Kelliebank.
24   "   "   "   (Mark 8) (large)   "   "   "   "

64 Landing craft tank (Mark 4) (large) were built at Forthbank.
2   "   "   " (Mark 8) (large)   "   "   "   "

Nos. 4085 and 4086 were the only Mark 8 craft handed over to the Royal Navy by Forthbank shipyard.
Number 4088 was dismantled on it's berth and the order for the remaining six Mark 8 craft was cancelled, due to the end of hostilities.

Mark 4 craft could carry 6 at 40 ton or 9 at 30 ton tanks.
Mark 8 craft could carry 8 at 30 ton tanks.

James P. Wright

a reference to the work of the late Jimmy Wright.[28] He wrote his own book *McLeod and Sons of Alloa* in 1996,[29] and had an epic set of photographs of many of the major refits that Alloa's third shipyard, McLeod's did during the war. Jimmy worked there himself as a welder during the war years and had a priceless knowledge of Alloa's shipbuilding and repair industry. The Clackmannanshire Archives has a note, hand-written by Jimmy, in which he itemises the contribution made by Alloa shipyards to the production of different types of landing craft.

McLeod's had been set up next to the Ferry Pier in 1925. William

T128 was a Dance class Anti-submarine warfare vessel, built at Leith in 1940 and was later renamed HMS *Saltarelo*. She arrived in McLeod's dry dock for a refit on 13th February 1942 and left a week later

J. McLeod ran the shipyard from 1935 and in his later years gave a talk to Alloa Rotary Club about its wartime activities.[30] He claimed that his yard was responsible for the conversion and re-fitting of about 300 vessels, including HM fleet minesweepers, minelayers, naval armament vessels, fleet rescue tugs, dance

LCT 468 in for repair at McLeod's yard
(Clackmannanshire Archives)

Mark 3 landing craft in for gun installation
at McLeod's dry dock in October 1944
(Clackmannanshire Archives)

Motor minelayer in for refit in March 1942. She
started life in 1939 as M34 and was renamed
HMS Miner II (Clackmannanshire Archives)

Cable vessel Z228 Dunavon in dry dock being
refitted in August 1942 (Clackmannanshire
Archives)

HMS Dornoch and HMS Fort York
(Clackmannanshire Archives)

HMS Brittany (Clackmannanshire Archives)

class escort vessels, boom defence vessels, netlayers, LC[T]s and LC[Q]s. There are many photos in the Clackmannanshire Archives of a wide range of naval vessels coming in for refurbishment and repair; a few of them are described and shown on the following pages. For the enthusiastic researcher there is a full list of all the vessels refitted at McLeod's during the war years, at the back of Jimmy Wright's book.

1943 saw the arrival of *HMS Dornoch*, the first of three Bangor class fleet minesweepers. She had only been built in 1942 in Troon but was in for a major refit. Then came *HMS Fort York* which had been built in Canada in 1941. After their refits both of these ships took part in the D-Day landings in June 1944.[31] Then in 1944 *HMS Romney* came in for a major refit which involved installation of radar and power-operated Oerlikon guns.

Netlayer *HMS Brittany* came in for refit in 1945. One interviewee in the *Alloa Docks Oral History Project* remembered that the *Brittany* was reputed to be the largest ship that was ever in the dock. It weighed 1,500 tons and had been a cross channel steamer before being commandeered during the war and converted to a submarine net layer.[32]

In his 1944 New Year's Address in the *Circular*, under a heading of 'Shipbuilding must be revived', Provost McKinlay expressed the hope that the end of the war would see the re-establishment of a thriving ship-repair industry in Alloa.[33] His hopes were not to be fulfilled. Within a month of VJ Day in August 1945, the *Journal* was reporting that '200 workers from Kelliebank Ship Yard received one week's notice that they would be laid off'.[34] There was some hope that Alloa's yards could pick up post-war work; a Pathe News film and commentary on the construction in Alloa of new dock gates for Le Havre and Dieppe in 1946 held out some promise; but it was not to be.[35]

GLASSWORKS

Times had been tough for the Alloa Glassworks in the early 1930s but had been generally improving since 1934, partly due to a Government Act of that year to encourage the provision of milk for children in schools. This led to a great demand for the production of a small 'third-pint' bottle. In meeting this demand, the turnover of the Glassworks for 1933-34 therefore increased by 32.5% over the previous twelve months.[36] In the later 1930s the Company experienced a period of prosperity and by '…midsummer 1939 the Company was in a stronger position than it had ever been before'.[37]

It did not take long for the impact of the war to make its presence felt. In September 1939 the Directors discussed the issue of insurance of stocks against air raids and whether to increase prices of bottles in view of the increasing costs of raw materials. There was an increase in demand for bottles due to a decrease in imports, but at the very same time there was the introduction of government controls and quotas. Raw materials became more difficult and expensive to source; for example, silver sand which had come from Belgium now came from Lochaline.

Just as in the Great War, the Company suffered severe labour shortages when the male employees joined the forces; the shortages of labour led to a rise in wages. Labour issues also affected the management; the Chairman, Colonel Harold Mitchell MP[38] was often called away on his military duties as liaison officer with the Polish Army and then Command Welfare Officer of Anti-Aircraft Command.[39] Another Director, Major Robert Moubray, was also given prolonged leave of absence to attend to his military duties. It seems that the remaining Directors did not shirk their duties in advancing the prosperity of the Company; they predicted a continuing and rising demand for glass and therefore put the Company's name down for the purchase of some advanced glass-making machinery once it should become available. On 12th August 1942, the *Journal* reported that 'Andrew Telfer, General Manager of Alloa Glass Company and ACC gave a well-received talk on national radio last Wednesday evening… on the importance of glassmaking as a wartime industry'.[40] Sales began to show an upward turn in 1943 but labour was scarce. By 1944 '…sales were up by a further £18,465 and the demand was the heaviest in the Company's history to date'.[41] It was during this time that Italian prisoners of war were employed to help keep up rates of production.[42]

Alec M. Mitchell, director of Alloa Glass Works in 1944 (J.L. Carvel)

By 1944, Colonel Harold Mitchell had become Vice-Chairman of the Conservative Party and was anxious to make a good showing of helping to run Party affairs during the first post-war general election, so he resigned as Chairman, leaving the running of the Company in the hands of his younger brother Alec.[43]

Alloa Glassworks in 1944 (J.L. Carvel)

Alloa Glassworks from the air, just after the Second World War

Things went well for the Company in the immediate post-war period; sales were up by more than 11% in 1945-46, and output for 1946-47 was up by 33% on the previous year. This would not have upset shareholders who, for a few years, had been receiving a dividend of 12.5%.[44]

PATONS MILLS

Shortly after the Great War this company underwent a merger and became a part of Patons and Baldwins. This merger made it much more difficult to work out what exactly was going on with the business in Alloa since it was now part of a much larger group based in Halifax. For instance, in October 1939 the *Journal* reported that Patons workers got a 10% pay rise but the firm has reduced the number of shifts... this meant most employees were earning the same money but working fewer hours.[45] During the Great War you would have known that such an increase applied just to Alloa workers, but now it just looks like it was part of a bigger decision taken elsewhere. During the Great War there was no local information about how many Patons workers had joined up; although the Patons war memorial told of the men they had lost. At least in the Second World War, the local press was able to report that Patons in Alloa had 150 workers on active service.[46]

In July 1940 the local press reported on how the company had done in the first year of wartime conditions. It recorded 'better results for Patons and Baldwins' with net profits of £487,000 compared to £305,000 for 1938-1939, but this total included their Halifax mills also. The company declared a dividend of 8½%.[47]

In March 1941 the government had a war-industry drive when it introduced a scheme to focus non-war production in a smaller number of factories, keeping them going at full blast, while the rest of the factories concentrated on war orders for whatever the government told them to do. It does seem that Patons welcomed this, obviously expecting more war orders for its yarns; a spokesman commented 'We have been engaged almost wholly on the production of hand-knitting yarns – the stuff of which soldiers' socks, gloves and pullovers are made... although our supplies have been rationed we have been able to keep on full time...'[48] However, it appears this optimism may have been premature; indeed the re-allocation of factory premises to suit the government's view of where to produce essential war materials may have been the reason why Patons came to be making a version of a bren-gun carrier at its Kilncraigs site by the middle of the war.

In terms of its economic success, things took a downturn and the 1941 annual report painted a depressing picture. In July 1941, Patons and Baldwins noted that they had reduced profits. Their surplus for the year to 3rd May 1941 was £292,000 compared with £487,000 for 1939-1940. They would pay a 5% dividend compared to last year's 8½%.[49]

In July 1942 the company announced that it would pay a dividend of 6¼%, which was an improvement on the previous year.[50] It had increased its profits by £95,000 to £387,000 but it did note that the company 'has suffered severely from the war'[51] and that 'these additions are fortuitous'. The Chairman explained that the previous years' profits had been hit by an allocation of £100,000 to meet an expected charge of Excess Profits Tax. This wasn't needed for 1942 and the present poor position was due to 'restricted output caused by the scheme of concentration in the worsted industry, shortage of labour, and rationing of home and export requirements on a more dramatic scale'. It was also the case that the company had to 'allocate £215,000 to a war emergencies reserve, particularly with reference to the substantial losses which may have to be met in connection with its mill in Shanghai' [which looked like it would be lost due to the Japanese invasion of China].

During the following two years things seem to have picked up; in July 1944 they announced their surplus for the year to 29th April was £430,000 and this included an estimated Excess Profits Tax refund of £80,000. There would be an interim dividend of 15% plus bonus of 2.5%, less income tax of 8/6 in the pound. The total dividend including a bonus amounted to 17.5%, which was less than last year'[52] but income tax was slightly less. As a result of all this financial success, the company gave a bonus to all employees of 'a fraction over 4%'.[53]

In 1945, after the war was over, Patons and Baldwins decided on a major reorganisation of its production facilities. It put a note in the *Journal* to re-assure the Alloa workforce that they would not suffer from this and that 'the 2,000 workers employed prior to the war' in their Alloa and Clackmannan mills would keep their jobs.[54] This is helpful in at least giving a clue to the size of the Alloa labour force at the start of the war!

HARLAND ENGINEERING

The British Electric Plant Company at Longcarse, Alloa was an engineering company from around the time of the Great War. It produced switch gear and dynamos for industrial and mining purposes. From 1919 onwards it was in a close association with The Harland Engineering Company which had been set up in 1910; the two companies shared a common directorate, chaired by

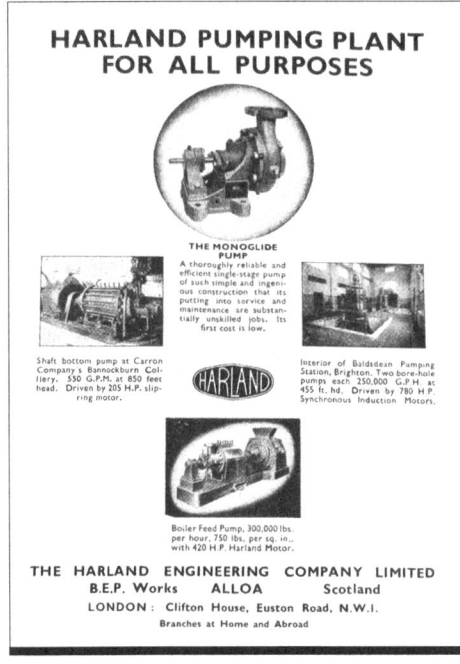

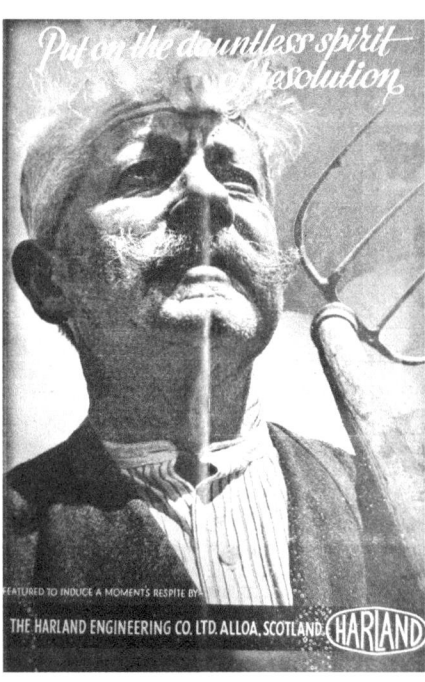

Advertisement for Harlands products
(*Alloa Academy Magazine* 1939)

A piece of morale building from
Harlands (*Alloa Academy Magazine* 1939)

one of the original founders of Harlands[55], Charles Atherton Atchley. In 1938 BEP voluntarily liquidated itself and all its assets were acquired by Harlands, whose main area of work was the manufacture of centrifugal pumps. At that time there were about 800-1000 workers at Harlands.[56]

By 1939 it was therefore a large and successful company, and indeed, was worth a royal visit in July 1943; but there is very little information available about what it actually did during the Second World War. A Burgh Council

Harlands test department round about the time of the Second World War (Thanks to Gordon Hamilton[57] whose father John was a manager in Harlands during the war)

minute of March 1939 showed they expected 'aircraft workers' but nothing more than that.[58] Indeed, in the local press there is not a single reference to what Harlands produced for the first four years of the war; it was only in November 1944 with the report of a visit by Sir Stafford Cripps, the Minister of Aircraft Production, to 'a war factory in the vicinity' do you get the first clue.[59] There's no proof that the article is even talking about Harlands but that has to be the assumption. Sir Stafford Cripps was accompanied by his wife who was given a 'tour of the air-frame section of the works' and met 'Miss Jessie Paterson, tail plane section, Miss Margaret Mack, pilot's coupe section, Mrs McEwan, wing tip section…' all of which provided the first factual detail in the local press about what Harlands did in the war. Maybe by late 1944 there was more relaxed censorship about what the local press could write.

Harlands ran a company magazine called the *Harland Magazine*, and it clearly took a keen interest in the international situation because in the April 1939 issue, the editorial, written by C.A. Atchley noted that 'Just as we go to press, Britishers and freedom-lovers all over the world have been heartened by the Prime Minister's declaration against aggression which was acclaimed by a united House of Commons, with hardly a dissentient voice. Things seem to be looking up. Imperially we have told the totalitarians that

bullying must cease or that we shall take sides against the bully, and that is a policy the Britisher can understand, and in the last resort if need be, fight for'.[60] In this same issue of the company magazine was a picture of Hugh Smiley with a Harland fire pump/trailer on his way to visit Hull and London fire brigades to convince them of the value of this piece of equipment in the event of a fire-bomb raid.

One interviewee in the *Alloa Docks Oral History Project* remembered how Harlands did quite well out of these fire pumps; 'we got orders for 500, then a 1,000 of these from the Government because we were told there would be a very heavy blitz when war broke out… In the end, Alexanders Buses of Falkirk made them'.[61] Another interviewee remembered that 'At the start of the war we made hundreds of auxiliary fire pumps for all the factories. They had to have a fire pump for incendiary bomb damage so we made hundreds of them'.[62]

One suspects however, that this was not the main way that Harlands expected to contribute to the war effort. Unfortunately for historians, there are no extant copies of the magazine from the war years in the archives to tell us what they actually did produce; and I suppose, in wartime reality, those magazines would not have admitted it anyway! Despite the loss of many men in its labour force to join the services, the *Journal* reported on its business success in June 1940 with the observation that 'Harlands reported that 88 of its employees were in the forces', that manufactured output last year was 30% greater in value than the previous year and it declared a dividend of 7%.[63] Maybe to make up for the lack of information in the local press about what Harlands actually did in the war, in October 1940 the *Circular*, under a headline of 'A Sun Tan at Harlands',[64] printed a rather facetious report about Harlands introducing an ultra-violet lamp into its factory. A week later the *Advertiser* echoed this story about the lamp giving 'beneficent rays' to the workers. It went on to say that 'The installation is fitted in Harlands elaborate underground ARP system'[65] which I suppose is revealing an interesting piece of information that no-one outside Harlands would have known about. However, one interviewee in the *Alloa Docks Oral History Project* did recall there were air-raid drills and 'they also had these sun lamps that you went to once a week, stripped to the waist, to try and keep you fit or give you some sunshine or something like that'.[66] Another remembered that 'you were working so much you werenae getting any sunshine so they designed a place in the factory where the men and women went at different times to get the sun ray lamps on them... I believe it was a gimmick... this was to boost you up for the war effort; a psychological effect'.[67] The *Circular* at least came to recognise its value and a week after its first article, under a heading of 'Harland Experiment – Sun Ray treatment explained', it included a much less frivolous piece stressing the health benefits and what a good idea the workers thought it was.[68]

Harlands may have done well as a war industry in 1939-40 but was penalised for it a year later. It was noted in the Annual Report in June 1941 that Harlands was reducing its dividend from 7% to 3%, in a year 'when record trading profits were earned'. It made the point that much more money seems to have had to be passed on to the government in EPT. This came about after Sir John Simon, the Chancellor of the Exchequer, had introduced his first war budget on 27th September 1939. Amongst his measures were a rise in income tax to 7/6 in the pound and the introduction of an Excess Profits Tax [in imitation of what had been done in the Great War]. This EPT was set at a 60% tax rate on all profits that were above the normal level of pre-war profits. This is what the Harlands annual report is complaining about,[69] but it does seem to suggest that Harlands was doing well financially out of the production of some sort of important war materials. This was shown at the end of the war, in June 1945, when Harlands announced a profit of £16,600 with a 7% ordinary dividend;[70] that was a return to the 1940 dividend level.

It was only when the war was over that the *Journal* first revealed what Harlands had been producing for the war effort. It printed an article in August 1945 discussing its 'Fine War Time Record'[71] which shows just what a great contribution this company and its Alloa labour force made towards winning the war. The *Journal* noted its 'War-Time Achievements', stating that 'During the war this factory has constructed large numbers of assemblies for Lancaster Bombers and Sunderland Flying Boats and it can be said that its achievement measured by the industry of the workers and their large output has played its part in the conclusion of war in Europe, the Battle of the Atlantic and the Far Eastern War. The main factory has been concentrating on large quantities of wartime machinery for all the Services, including certain still secret anti-submarine devices, and will soon be turning over to full peace-time production'. The *Circular* in October added a few more details 'of such interesting production statistics as the firm's output of 3,000 trailer pumps, 800 pairs of wing-tip floats for Sunderland aircraft, 550 Lancaster wing tips and 615 searchlight generators…. also a subsidiary factory in the town manufactured 500 tracked vehicles'.[72] It was only when the transcripts of the *Alloa Docks Oral History Project* came out in1987 that the information on the wartime activities at Harlands now came flooding out in the interviewees' reminiscences; the two chief areas being aircraft production and naval work, especially anti-U boat devices.

Firstly on aircraft production; one interviewee remembered he was told 'We're going to start building Sunderland flying boat's floats in Alloa' and he got taken on. 'They were about 16 feet long' and had 4 compartments with bulkheads. It was piecework… you were working two shifts… they built about 10 floats a week there. Maybe earned seven pound a week'.[73] The various bits of the Sunderland were sent to Shorts Belfast or Windermere or down to Kent for final assembly.[74] Another interviewee remembered 'the pilot's coupe [part of the cockpit] was partly made at Harlands then shipped down to Dumbarton for the final assembly on the main plane'.[75] Another recalls that 'they also built Bristol bombers. It was mostly the women who did all the riveting at that time'.[76] Later on in the war Harlands made 'great big metal lattices about 10 feet square to lay on the ground, for aircraft to land on… used in the Far East'.[77]

In regards to their naval work one interviewee recalled 'They built a terrific amount of stuff for the Admiralty'.[78] Another noted that 'We were making generators for the Navy… we were the firm that made the first two to combat the magnetic mines… we used to get orders for 5 or 6 hundred… in the machine shop we made the big eggs for the Asdic; there

"HEDGEHOG" SPIKED 32 U-BOATS

Alloa's Anti-Submarine Effort

"Hedgehog" is the pseudonym of the 24 projectible mortar, a device of pre-war origin first used by the Admiralty in 1942 and proved to be an invaluable anti-submarine weapon, so successful that from the date of its first kill—and note the date—Friday, 13th November, 1942 until the end of 1944, it accounted for the known sinking of 33 U-Boats, ignoring "possibles."

One of the secret weapons, some of which are still on the secret list, manufactured by the Harland Engineering Co. Lt., for anti-submarine warfare, the Hedgehog has six firing spindles on each of 4 pivoted interlocked beams, the spindles being set at various angles to give a definite pattern, to the points at which the depth charges hit the water, designed to obtain the utmost probability of at least one bomb actually striking the enemy submarine. The charges are fired ahead of the attacking ship and very precise automatic control gear keeps the Hedgehog aimed correctly despite the rolling of the vessel.

Article praising Harlands' war effort in *Alloa Circular* 26th December 1945 was one fitted on the side of the ship; we just made the shell, not the system'.[79] The generators which this interviewee referred to were used to power the boat's degaussing system which other interviewees also remembered. This 'actually turned the steel ships into wooden ships with the cable round the outside of the ship, it de-magnetised it because the mines were magnetic mines'.[80]

Another interviewee remembered the wider war work that Harlands was involved in, and echoed the earlier point about very good wages... 'They cleared out all the electrical dept. and they started building searchlight bases for wartime use... they also made huge pre-fabricated tanks and we found out these were for boom defence... they floated and below slung great big steel nets... the war took over and nobody could move jobs. You came under what you called the Essential Work Order. You were conscripted either for the services or the home front. Wages were static; money had good value during the war, anybody that had eight pound a week had a good job and they could save four pound a week off that'.[81]

Loyd carriers built at the Kilncraigs works, Alloa

Some interviewees still thought of Harlands as BEP, its old name. One of them remembered that BEP built bren-gun carriers and anti-aircraft guns... 'They built the bren-gun carriers up at Patons and Baldwins... I went up there to do the wiring on them... it was still called Patons and Baldwins but BEP had rented that building from them'.[82] People might have called them bren-gun carriers but they were in fact a lighter and less armoured version called a Loyd carrier whose main use was towing a 6-pounder gun or carrying up to 7 armed troops. In 1942 Harlands had problems in getting the trained staff and materials to produce the numbers that were required, shown by

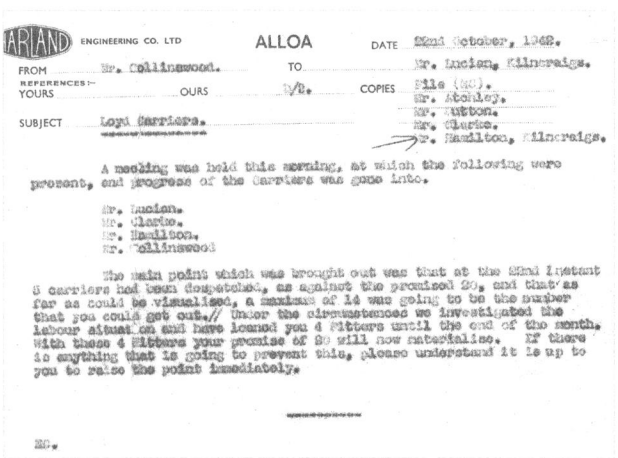

the memo which started off by stating that only 5 of the promised 20 had so far been built and basically threatening dire consequences if the loan of the extra fitters didn't produce the desired result of soon reaching the target of 20. In addition to working down in the town on the Loyd carriers, Harlands electricians were also involved in the wiring of the barges and tank landing craft at Forthbank and Kelliebank yards.[83]

BREWERIES

The obvious place to start a search for information on brewing in wartime Alloa is *Alloa Ale* written by Charles McMaster in 1984. However, despite dealing with the history of Alloa's seven main breweries in separate chapters, they contain very little information about what was going on in the breweries during the war; just snippets really. He argues that in the inter-war years Scotland was undergoing a consolidation in its brewing industry, and this continued. Ian Donnachie's history of Scottish brewing also claimed that what was going on in Alloa during the Second World War was no different from the wider picture in Scotland; 'The War of 1939-45 was not to have the dramatic consequences of World War I, with its great increase in government control at all levels, but it intensified many of the processes at work in the industry',[84] basically arguing that bigger breweries did well while smaller ones struggled or collapsed. When the war started it does seem that brewing, like many industries, suffered labour shortages, and this led to pay rises. The *Journal* in November 1939 reported a rise in pay of 3/- a week for all brewery workers over 21.[85] Maclay's accounts also show that they paid a war bonus increase in June 1940 which cost them £100. There is no suggestion in any of the evidence that the breweries considered employing women to make up for the shortages of labour.

What about the general state of Alloa's breweries during the war? In respect of Alloa's brewing companies; the original Bass Crest Brewery had been bought by Younger's and re-named Grange Brewery in 1919. It generally brewed 'black beers' which were non-intoxicating; this was to meet the threat from the temperance movement. 'The coming of the Second World War and the restrictions imposed by it, in particular sugar rationing, brought about the final closure of the Grange brewery. Brewing ceased in 1941, and subsequently the brewery was used for storing coal and grain, and for stabling horses and garaging dray wagons. From 1943 it was also used to house prisoners of war, who were employed in the Craigward and Ward Street maltings of George Younger's'.[86] Then the Mills Brewery owned by the Henderson family ran until the death of Robert Henderson in 1941 but by then it had become very decrepit and ramshackle, having been run as 'a virtual one-man operation'.[87] It was purchased by Calder's in June 1944 for £1,700, principally for its stocks of casks, since cask wood had been in short supply during the war.[88]

Apart from the local press and secondary texts, the best place to find information about the progress of Alloa's brewery companies in the Second World War is in the Scottish Brewing Archive in Glasgow. Maclay's has the largest amount of evidence about its wartime dealings but it is often fragmentary, without a 'full run' of information during the war years.[89] It does seem that they made good preparation for the war; their Stock Balance book on 30th June 1939 showed £4,782 worth of stock, audited and signed off by a director, but by 30th June 1940 they had got £10,012 worth of stock; which included a three-fold increase in the stock of hops and double the supply of barley and malt. By June 1942 the total stock was worth £14,583. Maclay's clearly intended to keep production rolling and indeed, in terms of sales income and production levels, Maclay's made good progress during the war. For instance, they owned/rented 16 licenced houses around the country [not including those in London] and these yielded a balance of £630 in March 1940, but almost £10,000 in December 1944. But not all of their business operations were successful. They had 21 outlets in London with bad debts amounting to £1,700, and in June 1941 they had to be written off.[90] Finances looked quite static in the early years of the war; the June 1940 Directors Report noted that £969 was to be carried forward; by August 1941 the figure was £868. However, that second Directors Report[91] had the following hand-written note on the front of it; 'The trading of the company showed a marked improvement throughout the year, but profits have been absorbed to cover losses due to enemy action'. This was a reference to their Old Kent Road brewing and storage premises in London being destroyed in a German air raid in October 1940.

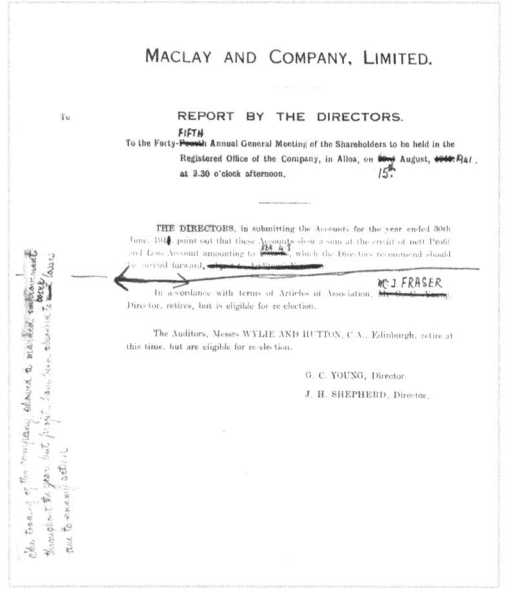

ABOVE: Maclay's Directors Report for 1941 with its marginal comment (Scottish Brewing Archive)

RIGHT: Maclay's Directors report of damage to brewery (Scottish Brewing Archive)

That wasn't the only bomb damage Maclay's had to deal with; in April 1941 their Angel and Crown pub in London was destroyed, and the Queenshead Inn in Cullercoats [near Newcastle] suffered damage in a German air raid.

Bottling at Brewery. Dozens.	½ Pints	Imperial	Nips	Barrels.	Total
Year-ending 30th June 1938.	1940	781	279		3000
" 1939	3,264	980	308		4,552
" 1940	8,483	1213	925		10,621
" 1941	14,232	1661	5152		21,045
" 1942	38,391	6813	1390		46,594
" 1943	39,768	7655	-		47,423
" 1944	64,670	10,450	-		75,120
" 1945	78,216	11,556	-		89,772
" 1946	73,921	10,717	-		84,638
" 1947	74,143	12,163	-		86,306
" 1948	77,267	15,924	-		93,191
" 1949	57,680	11,226	Dec.1948. 6634	1,762	75,540
" 1950	48,753	11,280	8431	1604	68,464
" 1951	41,498	10,497	7360	1404	59,355
" 1952	43,777	7380	7300	1316	58,457
" 1953	52,693	6849	8,851	1483	65,393
" 1954	55,628	6754	8048	1552	70,450
" 1955	56,308	6315	8102	1588	70,728
Record Heat Sep.1955. " 1956	63,645	8172	8826		80,644

Maclay's barrelage figures for the Second World War, showing the dramatic increase in production (Scottish Brewing Archive)

However, a look at their barrelage book shows that Maclay's increased production for <u>every</u> year of the war; in fact they bottled over 20 times more in 1945 than in 1939.

This had its effect on the Company's financial situation; in August 1942 the Directors Report noted that 'there had been a considerable increase in trade during the year'… and the balance in credit on 30th June 1942 was £23,000. By the date of the year ending 31st December 1942 they had sold £29,000 more beer than the previous year, but the government's excise duty on that beer, had risen to £24,000, so that year saw a net sales increase of £5,000, which was only 5.8%.

Its continuing success meant that in 1944 Maclay's hit the same problem that Harland Engineering had earlier experienced; the imposition of the Excess Profits Tax. In the year ending 30th June 1944 the records show that they had made a profit from their brewery and licenced houses of £29,000, yet had to set aside £22,000 to pay the government's EPT. They only declared a profit of about £6,500.

For Knox's Brewery, wartime restrictions on raw materials resulted in it being grouped along with Blair's Brewery and Maclay's for grain allocation, and also for draff sales.[92] These restrictions were in operation from 1941 until 1949. Despite these restrictions Blair's declared a net profit for year ending 30th December 1939 of £3,717 [against £3,791 the previous year] and a dividend of 4%.[93] Over 1940 it declared a net profit of £3,700 for the year to 30th September 1940 and a dividend of 6%.[94] Of all the local breweries, Blair's was the only one which regularly advertised in the local press; it had an advert at the top right hand corner of the front page of the *Advertiser* right through the war.

George Younger's found that the years of the Second World War had a marked effect on its export trade.[95] However, in March 1941 it announced

Barrel storage in Younger's Candleriggs Brewery, 1939

an 8% dividend from the previous year's business, with £37,000 being carried forward.[96] From then on, apart from 8% in March 1944, Younger's declared a dividend of 10% for every year, right up until 1949.[97] From these figures you can see that Younger's really was operating on a different scale than Alloa's other breweries. Like Maclay's, Younger's suffered some loss due to enemy action when one of its partner breweries, Fenwick's in Sunderland, was hit by German bombs.

It might seem unusual but some brewery workers were considered to be essential wartime workers. One interviewee in the *Alloa Docks Oral History Project* remembered that he worked at the Eglinton bottling stores and they dealt with the orders to fill up barrels [of beer] for troopships. He applied to join the Air Force but was turned down because 'he was counted as a necessity because the troops must get their beer'.[98]

ENDNOTES

[1] *Alloa Advertiser* 3rd January 1942

[2] Simon K. Marshall, *History of RG Abercrombie* (1998). The factory stayed open during the war but many of the coppersmiths began working at the local boatyards while the factory itself 'concentrated on foundry work, making castings, bushes and bearings'

[3] *Alloa Journal* 2nd January 1943

[4] There is a 50-year closure order on the actual recordings of those interviewed for this project, but transcripts of the interviews are available to view in the Clackmannanshire Archives.

[5] John L. Carvel, *One Hundred Years in Coal* (1944) p130

[6] *Alloa Journal* 4th February 1940

[7] J.L. Carvel p133

[8] J.L. Carvel p133

[9] *Alloa Advertiser* 8th June 1940

[10] *Alloa Advertiser* 3rd January 1942

[11] It was announced in Parliament on 12 October 1943 by Major Gwilym Lloyd George, the Minister of Fuel and Power

[12] *Alloa Advertiser* 20th May 1944

[13] *Alloa Journal* 5th February 1944

[14] *Alloa Journal* 14th October 1944. It was just typical of the local press that there was not a single wartime picture of Alloa's Bevin boys then in October 1946, when the war is well over, there was a lovely picture of 4 Bevin boys working for ACC who were 'stepping up output'. See *Alloa Journal* 5th October 1946

[15] *Alloa Advertiser* and *Alloa Journal* 2nd January 1943

[16] J.L. Carvel p137

[17] *Alloa Circular* 7th March 1945

[18] *Alloa Advertiser* 5th February 1943

[19] *Alloa Journal* 13th March 1943 and *Alloa Circular* 17th March 1943

[20] *Alloa Journal* 30th December 1944

[21] *Alloa Journal* 1st December 1945

[22] *Alloa Circular* 17th January 1945

[23] *Alloa Circular* 20th December 1939. The Sir John Gilmour who Arthur Woodburn wrote to, died in 1940. It was his son, who had inherited his father's baronetcy, who stood against Woodburn in the 1945 general election. The son was the nephew of Maud, who had married James, 2nd Viscount Younger of Leckie [died 1946]

[24] *Alloa Advertiser* 27th January 1940

[25] *Alloa Circular* 17th April 1940. The pessimistic purveyor of that news was Sir Victor Warrender who was Parliamentary and Financial Secretary to the Admiralty

[26] Sir Wilfred Ayre, *A Shipbuilder's Yesterdays* (1968) p57. The government was obviously making fairly slow progress on this because Woodburn had visited McLeod's Yard to inspect its facilities in March 1940 and was clearly pushing the case. See *Alloa Circular* for 27th March 1940

[27] *Alloa Journal* 9th September 1944

[28] He died in June 2019

[29] The book is published by Alloa Library Services

[30] This talk is reported at the start of James Wright, *McLeod and Sons Ltd* (1996)

[31] See *Our War: Clackmannanshire and Stirlingshire During the Second World War* (2006) p26

[32] Alloa Docks Oral History Project 1987; Mr M. born 1927

[33] *Alloa Circular* 3rd January 1944

[34] *Alloa Journal* 8th September 1945

[35] McLeod's Yard worked on, in worsening economic conditions; and finally closed in 1972

[36] John L. Carvel *The Alloa Glassworks* (1953) p68

[37] J.L. Carvel p73

[38] Harold was the son of Colonel Alexander Mitchell who had led the Company during the Great War but had died in 1934

[39] J.L. Carvel p74

[40] *Alloa Journal* 15th August 1942

[41] J.L. Carvel p76

[42] In 1943, Italy overthrew Mussolini and became a co-belligerent with the Allies. This did not bring much of a change in status for Italian POWs in UK however, since due to the labour shortages, they were retained as POWs. They could choose to become co-operators or non co-operators. Those who co-operated had some pay and more freedom of movement. This use of POW labour was 'of doubtful legality under the Geneva Convention'. The POWs used at the Glassworks probably came from the POW Camp at Fishcross but there is no official confirmation of there ever being a POW camp there. *Our War* (2006), quoting the reminiscence of Helen Hall, confirms that 'there was an Italian camp near Fishcross. They walked about the town. They weren't incarcerated or in prison. They wore brown jackets with yellow crosses on the back and that's how you knew they were prisoners of war' (p74). However, it could hardly have been that much of a secret because on 30 June 1943 the *Alloa Circular* printed a letter from an 'indignant householder' who was complaining about the 'decision of the County Roads Board to remove the bus stop outside the POW Camp near Fishcross to a point further on...' [that was to stop prisoners talking through the wire to people waiting at the bus stop]

[43] Colonel Harold Mitchell lost his Brentford and Chiswick parliamentary seat in the 1945 general election which was a 'Labour landslide', but he was created a baronet and returned to a position on the Board of the Glassworks as Sir Harold Mitchell. His fellow director, Brigadier GS Harvie Watt, also a director of ACC [since 1943] was also made a baronet; he was PPS to Churchill from 1942-45 and this award was for political and public services. See *Alloa Journal* 18th August 1945

[44] J.L. Carvel p78

[45] *Alloa Journal* 28th October 1939

[46] *Alloa Circular* 20th November 1940

[47] *Alloa Journal* and *Alloa Advertiser* 6th July 1940

[48] *Alloa Circular* 21st March 1941

[49] *Alloa Journal* 12th July 1941 and *Alloa Advertiser* 3rd January 1942

[50] *Alloa Journal* 18th July 1942

[51] *Alloa Circular* 26th August 1942

[52] *Alloa Journal* 8th July 1944

[53] *Alloa Journal* 5th August 1944

[54] *Alloa Journal* 6th October 1945

[55] Employees usually referred to it as 'working at The Harland' but the local press often referred to 'Harlands' which is what I have done to keep in line with Younger's, Patons and Maclay's etc

[56] Alloa Docks Oral History Project 1987; Harold born 1906

[57] Gordon Hamilton's father John was a manager in the section in Harlands which produced the Loyd carriers at Patons Kilncraigs site. His name is on the memo as one of those involved in the discussion on why production was not meeting targets

[58] Alloa Burgh Council minute book 21st March 1939

[59] *Alloa Journal* 4th November 1944

[60] *The Harland Magazine* Vol.3 No.2 April 1939. The editorial is presumably referring to Prime Minister Chamberlain's parliamentary response to news of the German occupation of the rest of Czechoslovakia in March 1939

[61] Alloa Docks Oral History Project 1987; James born 1913

[62] Alloa Docks Oral History Project 1987; Dick born 1914

[63] *Alloa Journal* 1st June 1940

[64] *Alloa Circular* 30th October 1940

[65] *Alloa Advertiser* 2nd November 1940

[66] Alloa Docks Oral History Project 1987; Mr D. born 1908

[67] Alloa Docks Oral History Project 1987; Dick born 1914

[68] *Alloa Circular* 6th November 1940

[69] *Alloa Journal* 5th July 1941

[70] *Alloa Journal* 23rd June 1945

[71] *Alloa Journal* 18th August 1945

[72] *Alloa Circular* 10th October 1945

[73] Alloa Docks Oral History Project 1987; David born 1905

[74] Alloa Docks Oral History Project 1987; Harriet born 1918

[75] Alloa Docks Oral History Project 1987; William born 1912

[76] Alloa Docks Oral History Project 1987; Jock born 1921

[77] Alloa Docks Oral History Project 1987; Jimmy born 1924

[78] Alloa Docks Oral History Project 1987; James born 1926

[79] Alloa Docks Oral History Project 1987; Mr D. born 1908 and James born 1926

[80] Alloa Docks Oral History Project 1987; Dick born 1914

[81] Alloa Docks Oral History Project 1987; Bert born 1920 and Dick born 1914

[82] Alloa Docks Oral History Project 1987; Bill born 1924 and Dick born 1914. Mr D born 1908 believes they were Bofors guns

[83] Alloa Docks Oral History Project 1987; Jock born 1921

[84] Ian Donnachie, *History of the Brewing Industry in Scotland* (1979) p237

[85] *Alloa Journal* 25th November 1939

[86] Charles McMaster, *A Short History of Robert Meiklejohn and Sons, the Bass Crest Brewery, Alloa* found in *Scottish Industrial History* volume 7.2 (1984)

[87] Charles McMaster, *Alloa Ale* (1984) p39

[88] Charles McMaster p40

[89] All the information about Maclay's comes from File GB248M held in the Scottish Brewing Archive

[90] The £1700 was just for London; Maclay's wrote off a total of £3,500 nationwide

[91] This is in the Director's Minutes. This Director's Report shows the name of J.H. Shepherd [but not that of P.J. Pettigrew, the Head Brewer]. The brewery salaries book shows that their monthly salaries in 1941 were around £40. They were both still there in 1962 when their monthly salaries had risen to around £130

[92] Draff is the spent grain in the mash tun, discarded at the end of the brewing process; it is sold as a protein-rich cattle feed.

[93] *Alloa Journal* 3rd February 1940

[94] *Alloa Journal* 28th December 1940

[95] Charles McMaster p62

[96] *Alloa Journal* 15th March 1941

[97] All the information about Younger's comes from File GB248GY held in the Scottish Brewing Archive

[98] Alloa Docks Oral History Project 1987; Richard born 1903

CHAPTER 3

SCHOOLS AND EDUCATION

Alloa had two schools providing secondary education during the years of the Second World War; Alloa Academy and Grange School. The latter was regarded as the more junior of the two, and was often referred to as the Technical and Commercial School. Pupils had to pass the Qualifying Exam to get into the Academy.

ALLOA ACADEMY

The Rector during the war years was Nathaniel Stewart. He tended to write up his log book on the Friday afternoon, covering the previous week's events. The roll of the school was round about 480 in 1942, having stabilised after the mass influx then exit of most of the evacuees [This figure includes those in the Primary Department; maybe just under 200 in that category].

Even when there were only war clouds on the horizon, there was still an impact on the school when the science teacher Mr Hovell was sent on an ARP course in April 1939 and had further training in June 1939. There is nothing in the log book at the outbreak of the war in September 1939 that refers to blackout, but the school did need to be blacked out; this was done 'by the woodwork pupils and some of the more recent former pupils'.[1]

The first actual impact of the war on the school was the arrival of evacuees, chiefly from Edinburgh in the first instance;[2] but a large number from around the British Isles in the weeks following. The log book noted that Alloa was 'a recovery area'. The fact that Alloa Academy kept such a good set of admission registers gives extra statistical insight into all sorts of aspects of this group of evacuees.[3] For example, there were more boys evacuated than girls [65 to 50], and as expected, the majority of the evacuees [100 out of 115] were in classes S1-S3. The Academy received a second mini-rush of evacuees in 1941 either in anticipation of or following the Blitz [12 from the Glasgow area and others from Hartlepool and Plymouth]. The evidence in the admission register suggests that at least a proportion of the evacuees from 'Other Districts' came to stay with relatives in Alloa. The game is given away here by recording the arrival from Bristol of Susan Erskine to stay at Alloa House, and the arrival of Robert Heeps from Glasgow to stay with the 'Heeps, Grange Road'.[4] How many more of the evacuees were in this family-connection category is difficult to say. For the Academy, all addresses of receiving families were noted; it is fair to say that the lower end of Claremont/Ochil St./North St. was the most generous area in taking in evacuees. It didn't take long before the evacuees started returning home and on 22nd September 1939 the log book referred to this as 'being the most unsatisfactory feature…' Out of all the 89 evacuees who arrived at the Academy in September 1939, only 2 stuck it out until 1942.

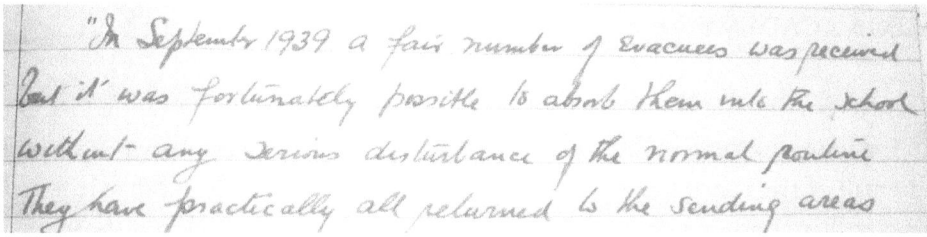

Alloa Academy log book note in 1942-43 Inspector's Report

The story of one evacuee is worth mentioning here. William Allan Meek stayed at 29 Ochil Street with the Dawson family;[5] he was admitted to the Academy on 11th September 1939 as an evacuee from Edinburgh [Admission No 3727E].

He was older than the average for Alloa's evacuees, more than 80% of whom were primary or lower secondary age; he was 16 years 7 months old.

William Allan Meek

He had been a pupil at George Heriot's School and he joined the Academy as a sixth former, wanting to complete his upper school education. He maybe would have gone on to university but he was called up and joined the Royal Navy. He served as a sub-lieutenant on *HMS Saxifrage*, a Flower class corvette used as an escort vessel on the Atlantic convoys from New York to Liverpool. He died on 5th October 1943 aged 20.[6] He was one of about 25 evacuees to the school who were born before 1926, who technically were going to reach an age to be called up, trained and then sent into action before the end of the war. As far as can be worked out by cross-checking the information in the school admission registers with the records of the Commonwealth War Graves Commission, it does appear that he was the only evacuee to Alloa Academy to be killed in the war.

Alloa Academy had a senior pupils/staff club called The Literary and Debating Society. It had been going since well before the Great War and it kept minutes of its meetings during the Second World War also. Some of the comments in its minute book give an echo of what was happening in the school and how the senior pupils saw things. For instance, they agreed at their meeting on 27th October 1939 that in future they should start it two hours earlier due to the difficulties of the black-out.[7] Then, on 24th January 1941, [the year following the school's first successful forestry labour camp at Langholm] there was a debate about the 'selfishness of individuals', where their minute book described how 'The after-speaking was quite brisk but soon degenerated into an argument on the motives of the senior boys for going to Langholm last summer...' On 26th September 1941 the club's topic for debate was 'That the ARP are as efficient as can be expected'. In the after-speaking to this debate '... arguments were in some cases very heated'. The debate on 21st November 1941 was 'That women should be conscripted' whilst that on 11th December 1941 was 'Should Conscientious objectors be tolerated?' By 18th February 1944 the issue for debate was 'That women should be allowed in the front line'. We can see that while there is no evidence in the school log books or these minute books that pupils' lives were blighted by the war, nevertheless many of them did have thoughtful and reasonable questions to ask about what was happening around them. Just as a reminder that pupils at this club did not spend their entire time asking deeply significant questions, the club occasionally had a 'brains trust' where a panel answered questions from the audience. On 18th September 1944 one of the questions was 'Where does the wool go when you get a hole in your sock?'

Since 1932 the Academy had also had a thriving Former Pupils Association.[8] This met regularly during the war years and was determined to do its bit to boost morale. It kept a log book of its activities but only up until October 1941. In October 1939 it agreed to raise money to send Christmas gifts to all FPs in HM Forces. To this end it held whist drives [the first one was held in November 1939[9]] and dances, encouraged donations of money and cigarettes, and was able to send out 41 parcels at that first wartime Christmas. It also agreed to set up a roll of honour of all serving FPs, although by October 1941 it was already a concern that 'More and more FPs are being called up and in many cases no intimation was sent to the FP Association. As a result, the roll was incomplete...' 118 Parcels were sent out at Christmas 1940, including donations of money sent to the Red Cross in respect of 6 FPs who were prisoners of war.[10] Fund-raising dances were held in 1941 to raise money for the gifts for Christmas 1941, when it was decided to just have a special card and a postal order on this occasion. By October 1941 the Association was already aware that 'a number of our members have given their lives for their country...' but didn't specify their names.[11] An FP Reunion was held in December 1944 and the FP Association collected £180 to send postal orders to FPs in the Services.

The Association produced the *Academy Magazine* throughout the war years. In its 1940 issue it expressed regret about the poor quality of the paper it was printed on, by the time of its 1942 issue it was apologising for the magazine's even smaller size and no photographs! Over the war years there were only a few articles related to wartime events; In 1941, a comment about the Battle of Britain, a description of life in air raid shelters and an article about fire-watching; in 1942, the Academy boys going to forestry camp and in 1943 a nice war-related frontispiece drawn by a former art teacher of the school.

Alloa Academy Magazine 1943

Then, in 1944 the *Magazine* showed an awareness that the Second Front had opened and in 1945 a recognition that the war was over. This last piece was a quite moving Editorial which recognised the war had been won but there was still a job to be done; 'Now that the long conflict in Europe is at last over, the mood reflected by this Editorial must certainly be one of profound and joyful thanksgiving, fittingly tempered by the knowledge that our task is yet far from complete...'

Apart from that, during the war years the magazine kept up morale by reporting on the distinguished military behaviour of FPs who had won gallantry medals. In 1942 it noted that Flight Sergeant John Kesson was awarded the DFM, and Flying Officer Herbert H.K. Gunnis was awarded the DFC.[12] In 1943 both of these airmen got their pictures in the magazine. The 1945 issue reported that Flying Officer Donald Beaton had been awarded the DFC. The 1946 issue noted that Squadron Leader Herbert H.K. Gunnis had been awarded a bar to his DFC, Horace Dempster had gained the DFC, Lieutenant John Hall in the Argylls was awarded the MC in 1945 for his actions at the Santerno Bridgehead in the Italian Campaign, and Lt Col William McKinlay got the OBE for his services in REME attached to the Canadian Army. See Chapter 10 for more details of all these men.

FUND-RAISING BY ACADEMY PUPILS

Pupils had been collecting for the Red Cross in a 'penny a week' fund [since October 1939] and this had raised over £100 in Session 1940-41. By Session 1942-43 it had risen to £260.[13] The Red Cross fund was closed on 30th June 1945 and the log book noted that, over the war period, pupils had given a total of £480. Pupils did get involved in the national War Savings campaigns. 'Wings for Victory' week in April 1943 led to the school raising £1,480.

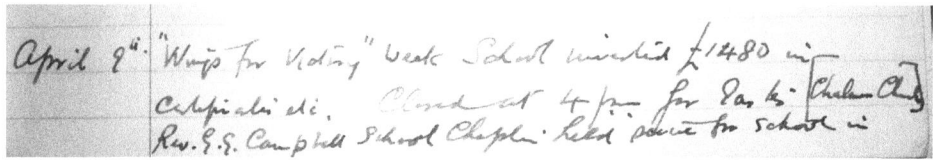

Alloa Academy log book 3rd April 1943

Apart from the issue of evacuation and the school being blacked out in 1939, there was precious little else in the log book which referred to the impact of the fear of bombing. There were only three references to it, with drills for air-raid shelters 3rd May 1940, and gas masks examined 7th November 1942 and 4th December 1942.

One war-related task that only the Academy pupils did was the writing of ration cards in 1941.[14] There were 60,000 needed for the County. This took almost three weeks to complete; the Rector wrote that it was 'a piece of necessary but very monotonous war work'.

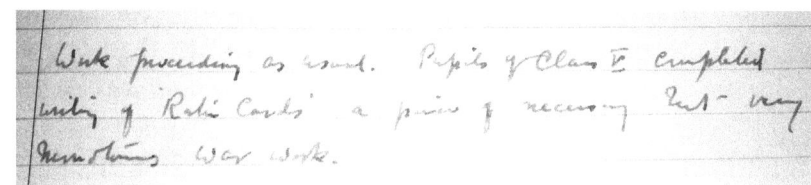

Alloa Academy log book 13th June 1941

This may have become a recurring annual duty [or maybe a sign of an additional area of the imposition of rationing], but the inspectors noted in 1943 that the pupils had written out another 30,000 ration cards.

Another war-related task which was unique to the pupils of the Academy was the establishment of work-parties of senior boys who went off on forestry camps during their summer holidays.[15] This started in July 1940 with a 'Labour Camp' at Langholm for 7 weeks. This received a very full write-up in the *Journal* including a reference to a photo of the pupils in that week's *The Bulletin*.[16]

DOWN IN THE FOREST!—Boys of Alloa Academy snapped during a break at their camp on the Duke of Buccleuch's estate in Dumfries-shire, where they are engaged in forestry work.

The Bulletin 21st August 1940 with thanks to ©CSG CIC Glasgow Museums and Libraries Collection: The Mitchell Library, Special Collections

There was also a report, possibly written by a pupil, about the work of the 20 boys on the Duke of Buccleuch's estate in Dumfriesshire who were billeted at Langholm lodge, a shooting lodge. Some boys did farm work, others tree felling etc. Another group of senior boys went out on 27th June 1941, again to Langholm because the Duke of Buccleuch had been so complimentary about the first lot that he had written to the school in January 1941 inviting them back. On 3rd July 1942, 27 boys went off to do forestry work near Elgin and on 30th June 1943, 23 boys plus 2 masters, 4 girls and 2 lady members of staff went off to do forestry work in Inverness-shire. This was for one month and the female contingent was sent largely to do the cooking![17] In terms of out-door work however; the Academy couldn't avoid the imposition that all other local schools suffered, the Burgh's decree on compulsory potato-lifting. The *Circular*'s headline reporting on this couldn't resist the military metaphor of 'Potato-lifting Campaign: 500 County Children Advance to the Attack'. The pupils worked at 49 different farms to lift 560 acres of potatoes. They were paid at the rate of 9 [old] pence an hour.[18] The autumn term of 1944 was the first time the log book noted the involvement of Academy pupils in this task, but they had done it the year before. The Rector wearily noted that it was 'another wartime activity' and that 'the progress of the classes involved will be badly affected'. 78 pupils from classes I to IV were sent off on 13th October 1944 for seven weeks work. The *Advertiser* had a short article on the County's contribution to the potato harvest which actually revealed the great extent of the labour that was being offered. Over 600 Clackmannanshire pupils would be dealing with over 550 acres of potatoes in farms across Clackmannanshire and Perthshire, with quite a lot of arrangements needing to be made for providing transport, feeding the pupils / staff and paying them the going rate.[19]

ALLOA ACADEMY STAFF SERVING IN THE ARMED FORCES

Unlike in the Great War, there was no suggestion anywhere that male teachers in a senior secondary school were somehow considered to be in a reserved occupation and therefore 'protected' from call up. The selection of the Academy's male staff for military service was really quite speedy. On 22nd September 1939 Mr Geddes, Principal Teacher of Maths was called up and left for his station in Ireland.[20] On 21st July 1940 Mr Farquaharson was called up for duty with the RAF, and on 27th September 1940 Mr McGregor reported for military duty.[21] The log book reported that on 11th October 1940 Mr Spence was absent on Thursday-Friday at an RAF depot for Examination, and that 'Being an Honours MA in History and holding the LLB degree he was naturally selected as an Air Mechanic'. Was there some sense of irony or sarcasm there?[22] On 29th November 1940 Mr Fraser joined the Army, and on 4th April 1941 Mr Gammie reported to a cadet training unit of the RAF. He knew he was going; the members of the Literary and Debating Society had said their goodbyes to him on 21st March 1941. Remembering the intentions of the idea of 'substitution' in the Great War, it is interesting to note that in every case of a male member of staff departing for service in the Second World War, he was replaced by a female. HM Inspectors offered something of faint praise for the efforts of these women. Their Report for 1944-45 noted that 'The absence [of the men teachers] had been keenly felt despite the devoted efforts of most of the teachers, mainly young women, who had temporarily replaced them'.

It went on to say that standards in Mathematics had not reached the normal standards of proficiency during the war due to the absence of men on service; but that the return of the Principal Teacher would soon restore the former high level of performance. The Inspectors had maybe raised their hopes too soon here! Mr Geddes did not have long to rectify the departmental shortcomings since he was appointed Rector of Brechin High School in early 1947. The log book in late 1945 and early 1946 reported the gradual return to teaching duties of 4 of the enlisted teachers. There is no suggestion that either of the other two were killed. The Rector did note in the school log book that the war had ended.

Alloa Academy log book 11th May 1945

To celebrate the end of the war, the school had its two days of holiday when VE Day was announced in May 1945. Then in June 1946 the pupils celebrated 'Victory Day' with a fun fair and each pupil received a new shilling. On 28th June 1946 the senior pupils held a 'Re-union Tea' to welcome home the teachers who had returned to the school after their military service.

GRANGE SCHOOL

The Headmaster during the Second World War was Charles Irvine and he was fairly conscientious in keeping his log book up-to-date concerning school activities.[23] He also wrote about an event on the very day it happened, he didn't keep his comments to a weekly overview written on Friday. In reading the earlier log book during the Great War, the chief ways that war left its mark on the daily lives of pupils at the school was either through their participation in various fund-raising efforts for war charities, or through the absence of female staff who took time off due to the loss of close relatives. The Second World War had a much deeper and more continuous effect on many aspects of school life.

War had been declared on Sunday 3rd September and almost straight away Grange School was affected. On Monday, 45 evacuated children, largely from Flora Stevenson School in Edinburgh,[24] reported to the school, along with several of their teachers. Classes were made up, the evacuees were enrolled, and the school was then closed for the rest of the week following the government order. Including the evacuees, the school roll in September 1939 was 437 pupils. It must be said that not many of these evacuees lasted very long.[25] On 12th January 1940 the log book recorded that 'Edinburgh evacuees are still drifting home' and by 3rd September 1940 there were only 10 left.[26] However, on 31st August 1944 the log book noted that there were still 6 evacuees on the school roll.

Following its week long holiday in accordance with the government order, school re-opened on 11th September 1939 with another 15 evacuees arriving; and in the light of the prevailing belief at that time that mass gas attacks from German bombers were imminent; the school had gas mask drills for all classes and the inspection of gas masks. Air-raid precaution drills were a regular feature of school life for the next 18 months. The log book refers to drills taking place on 30th October 1939 [including going down into the main cellars below the school and then to the ARP trench in the public park], 3rd November 1939, 9th January 1940 [including instruction in the playground on how to use a stirrup pump], 15th April 1940 [inspection of gas masks], 17th May 1940 [including a check on the air raid shelters], 23rd May 1940, 26th June 1940, 12th September 1940, 12th November 1940, 10th January 1941 [where the school was cleared into its shelters in 2 minutes], 4th February 1941 [including incendiary bomb practice and 'all male staff and senior boys passed into a smoke-filled room with a stirrup pump']. By early 1941 these drills had stopped, although carrying/wearing of gas masks was clearly still being done. On 25th May 1943 a consignment of 36 gas masks arrived for the pupils from the ARP authority in Stirling. That number did not make up for the return of 94 gas masks to the same authority; all defective for different reasons. Gas masks were still being examined on 21st December 1943, 13th January 1944 and 12th September 1944;

although by then you would surely have thought that the risk of a gas attack had now been totally discounted.[27]

I wonder if the air raid drills didn't stop because of the realisation that if there was going to be a day-time raid then there would be enough advance warning of it to get the pupils out of the school anyway. Also there was a clearer recognition that the main danger to the school would happen at night. The Luftwaffe took to night bombing attacks in late 1940 and Grange School's air raid precautions took a different turn from March 1941 with the Clydebank Blitz. The German aircraft attacking Clydebank were clearly seen and heard in Alloa as they flew across central Scotland, and there was perceived to be a direct risk to properties in Alloa. There was an air raid alert throughout the night of 13th March 1941 and the school was manned by three teachers and the janitor to guard against any possible fires. The following day the log book records that 'a rota of firewatchers was arranged and begun tonight. There will be two adults and two boys [on duty] during the hours of blackout including Saturday and Sunday nights'. This was voluntary labour to start with but from 22nd November 1941 fire-watchers [both teachers and pupils] were paid 3/- a night [backdated to 22nd September 1941]. This scheme lasted until May 1942 when pupils were barred from fire-watching duties since the government felt it could not insure under-16 year olds against war service risks. The rota was therefore taken up by 24 former pupils over the age of 16 and they were asked to do a duty every 16th night.[28]

FUND-RAISING BY GRANGE SCHOOL PUPILS

Just as in the Great War, there was a strong interest by the pupils in fund-raising activities to help the war effort. On 21st October 1939 3rd year pupils organised a sale of work and raised over £40 for the Red Cross, on 31 October 1939 there was a pupil collection for the British Sailors Society which raised over £35 and pupils started knitting socks. An example of the pupils' generosity which was not recorded in the log book was the gift of £3.15/- to the Finnish Relief Fund, out of the balance from their Christmas party.[29] Then a PE display on 25th June 1940 raised 27/- for War Funds and a children's concert organised by 3rd year girls on 28th September 1940 raised almost £4 for London's homeless in the Blitz. Right through the war there were tea parties, staff v pupils football matches, demonstrations of war-time cookery, concerts, scrap metal and salvage collections, whist drives and sales of toys; all to raise funds for various war charities. In February 1943 the school sent out the surplus from the money raised for the pupils' 1942 Christmas parties; £3 went to the Red Cross and £3 to aid for Russia.

A more systematic approach to helping the war effort was introduced in September 1942 with War Savings. There were savings targets for each class displayed in the hall, and the school's target for the 1942-43 session was £324. By November 1942 the school had reached £138, but by April 1943 they had already exceeded their target in reaching £466, and by July 1943, the end of that session, the total was £950. Further log book references show that £250 was raised over the Christmas term of 1943 and £200 raised in the spring term of 1944. The infrequency of references in the log book to the progress of this savings campaign suggests that Grange School did not take it anything like as seriously as some local schools.

A totally separate fund-raising idea which had not been seen in the Great War was the establishment by pupils, in December 1939, of a set of allotments, which were on the west side of Alexandra Drive.[30] There were 6 allotments, adding up to 1800 square yards, and six teams of ten boys were put up by the six classes. Each team would work once a week for up to two hours, with tools supplied by the Education Committee. In late December the *Journal* had a nice article about the boys getting stuck into their gardening work.[31] They couldn't always get down to work however; the log book for 8th January 1940 recorded that 'allotment ground was too frost-bound for work by the boys teams'. It was only on 20th February 1940 that 'the cultivation of the allotments begins again after the long and very severe frost'. The allotments accounts for the end of 1940 show the pupils raised almost £34 from the sale of their vegetables. At the end of 1941 it was almost the same; less than 10/- difference, although the size of the allotments had risen to 2100 square yards. In March 1943 the pupil allotment workers somehow managed to procure four boxes of American seeds. The allotment scheme was wound up on 12th November 1945 with a surplus of just over £51 transferred into school funds.

Another horticultural idea that was introduced to help the war effort was the voluntary 'conscription' of boys from the school for potato lifting. Now this may well have gone on anyway before the war, and the pupils risked breaking laws on truancy; but now it had government validation. On 20th October 1941 16 boys were 'temporarily exempted [from school work] for farm work with Mr Walker, Lornshill for two weeks. Three more are working for Kinross Hillend Farm for two weeks'. By 30th October 1941 the log book noted that '30 boys are at present engaged in potato lifting'. The pupils were getting into the swing of this and 16 boys were exempted in April and May 1942 for potato planting, then 12 boys were released for potato lifting in October 1942, capped in October 1943 when the school sent the Education Offices a list of 125 names of pupils for potato harvest! In fact 133 pupils were directed to report for potato lifting on 11th October 1943. Nine teachers were sent out to supervise them and the school was closed for 2 weeks. By October 1944 this was taken to its highest level when the log book proudly noted that there were 26 individuals out lifting potatoes at Lornshill, then 76 in West Perthshire,[32] 20 in Clackmannan, 17 in Tullibody and 2 in Fishcross. Given that the headmaster had noted that the school roll in August 1944 was 329 pupils; this suggests that over 40% of the school were out lifting potatoes for the first four weeks of October.

An event unique to Grange School were the 2 war-time visits of the merchant ship Captain James Struth. He was from Kincardine but had been corresponding with pupils in the school for three years. In July 1941 he was guest of honour at the prize-giving.[33] He gave a 'thrilling address' to the pupils in which he recounted how his last ship SS Benvenue had been torpedoed but he got the crew into the lifeboats in 11 minutes even though 2 lives were lost. In November 1943 Captain Struth, now in charge of SS Benares visited Grange School again, showing a collection of war relics.[34]

Grange School seemed fairly good at getting slightly more unusual people or groups to talk to them; in January 1943 the Journal reported that 'six cadet-officers from the Polish Brigade gave a team lecture on Poland to Grange School pupils last Wednesday.'[35] Then in November 1943 Flight Sergeant James Archibald of the New Zealand Airforce addressed the school on life in New Zealand.[36]

GRANGE SCHOOL STAFF SERVING IN THE ARMED FORCES

The departure of staff for military service was just as speedy as with the Academy. On 3rd September 1940 Mr Small from the Technical Dept. left the school to do essential war work in Dundee[37] then on 11th September 1940 Mr

Walker in the Art Dept. went off to join the forces.[38] On 7th February 1941 Mr McLeod [Commercial Subjects] went for his RAF Exams, was interviewed on 3rd March and on 24th April 1941 joined the RAF as a commissioned officer. In September 1941, Mr Inglis, Gym instructor left to go on military service. The log book for 3rd January 1946 noted that he had returned to duty since 'he has been demobilised following a spell of service in the RAF'.

On 21st February 1941 the log book noted that 'Peter White, an FP of recent years, drowned at sea while serving his country'. This death was not referred to in the local press at the time.[39]

In the log book for 17th April 1945, the Headmaster proudly noted that Pilot Officer James Hamilton, a former pupil and first boy school captain had been awarded the DFC. This was also reported in the *Advertiser*.[40]

In October 1942, just over half way through the war, the HMI Report for the school noted that 'Apart from a number of staff changes, mostly last session, the school has been relatively little upset by war conditions, evacuation causing neither stoppage nor half-time instruction'.

The log book noted that on 8th May 1945 with the word of the ceasefire in Europe, a holiday was given. The pupils also got a holiday on 9th May.

PRIMARY SCHOOLS

At the time of the Second World War Alloa had 5 primary schools; Park School [which was the newest and largest], Sunnyside [the second largest], St John's [which was associated with the Episcopalian Church], South School and St Mungo's School [which was associated with the Catholic Church].

PARK SCHOOL

Park School opened in September 1935,[41] it had 14 classes with a roll of round about 430 [by the middle of 1940 it was up to 522 but back down to 438 by 1944]. Its headmaster was James Younie.[42] He kept a very full and very, very neat log book. The impact of the war on Park School was very similar to that on all the other local primary schools.

The school week became disrupted as from 26th May 1939 when classes were adjusted to allow teachers to attend an ARP class for anti-gas instruction at Alloa Academy; these classes to be held on Mondays and Thursdays until

Park School just before the
outbreak of war

the summer holidays. Then, in the first school week following the start of the war, the evacuees arrived, '4 from Edinburgh and 10 from other districts'.[43]

The first note in the log book concerning air-raid drills was on 6th October 1939 but one suspects there must have been other drills before that date. The log book noted that 'Necessary practice in Air Raid precautions have been carried out... the teachers have also taken gas mask drill and have been fitting the pupils' gas masks'. In terms of air-raid drills/alarms, Park School log book was the only one to report that on 31st January 1941, 'an air raid alarm was sounded at around 2.45. Half of the pupils were sent home, the remainder were taken to the air raid shelters, where they remained for about half an hour until the all clear was sounded'. There must have been widespread fear in 1941, following the March bombing of Glasgow and Clydebank, about how things might now progress. The first response was, as with other local schools, that from 2nd May 1941, 'fire-watching, in conformity with Defence regulations, began in this school, and teams of 4 lady-teachers will be on duty each evening'.

On 9th May 1941 the log book noted that 'A considerable number of pupils were late on Tuesday morning as, during the night, a prolonged air raid had taken place'.[44] By October 1941 this led to the school making preparations to be 'used, under ARP control, as a first-line Rest Centre, and joiners are working to fit up a complete blackout'.

In 1940 had come the first news of the call up of male staff; on 4th October 1940, 'Mr Forrest absent, as he had leave to travel to Padgate, near Liverpool, to be examined for the Royal Air Force'. He was then given one month's deferred notice, and would receive 10 days' notice to join the colours. He joined the RAF on 6th December 1940. On 11th July 1941, Mr Fraser [primary V] 'received instructions to proceed to Huddersfield to join the Royal Corps of Signals'. In the case of the other local primary schools there was normally a mention of the return of male teachers who served. This was not the case with Park School since Mr Fraser was killed in action in August 1943, although this was not mentioned in the log book.[45] It did happen during the school holidays.

FORMER ALLOA TEACHER DIES OF WOUNDS

Mr Harry Fraser, Ashbank, Upper Mill Street, Tillicoultry, has received official intimation that his son, Harry Fraser, who was attached to the Royal Corps of Signals, died of wounds on 13th July. A graduate of St Andrews University, Mr Fraser, previous to joining the Army, was a member of the staff of Alloa Park School.

Alloa Circular 18th August 1943

For an unspecified reason it appears that Mr Forrest did not return either. There was one impact on staffing that was an un-anticipated consequence of Mr Forrest's departure for the RAF. In April 1943 he married Miss Dickson [the Infants teacher of class 2a]. This meant that whenever he was home on leave, she was entitled to time off to be with her husband, and her classes had to be looked after by other teachers. The log book noted that on 17th November 1944 'Mrs Forrest absent with permission for three days this week since her husband was home on leave from RAF'. Also on 23rd February 1945 she was off for a week for her husband's leave, and 1st June 1945 and 28th September 1945.

War savings played a part in all the pupils' school lives, but only get a couple of mentions in Park School's log book. 28th March 1941 was the first school-day of 'War Weapons' week and a total of £37 was subscribed... 'By Friday, the close of the special effort, a total of £112.18/- had been collected'. In April 1943 it was 'Wings for Victory' week. The target set for the school was £100; this was easily exceeded, and by Friday, a total of £221 had been subscribed.

There was only cursory reference to Park School's contribution to the potato lifting, which was such a big feature during several autumns of the pupil life in other local schools. Only on 13th October 1944 did the log book note that '29 pupils from this school were out gathering potatoes'.

When war came to an end, Mr Younie had his own quite verbose style of recording that fact; he noted on 11th May 1945, that 'In the afternoon [of Tuesday] a broadcast announcement was made that the German High

Command had accepted terms of unconditional surrender, and consequently the European war was concluded. In consequence the school was closed on 8th and 9th May to celebrate Victory in Europe'.

SUNNYSIDE SCHOOL

J.A. Atkinson had been Acting Headmaster of Alloa Academy Primary Department for all but three weeks of the years of the Great War, and had been appointed to the full position in May 1919 when the former headmaster Mr P.T. Moodie, returning from war service, declined the Council's offer to resume his position. Mr Atkinson was subsequently put in charge of the South School when it opened in 1928 then later [in 1936] transferred as headmaster to Sunnyside School where he was in charge up until the end of 1941. He was succeeded as headmaster for the remainder of the years of the Second World War, by another old hand, Mr Sidney Perry, who had been headmaster of St John's Primary School for the entire time of the Great War.[46] Both of these men were conscientious in writing up the log book but, from our point of view, it is disappointing how few references there were to the direct impact of the war. Nothing seems to have been recorded about air-raid drills, gas masks practices / inspections or air raid shelters, even though Sunnyside School had its own air-raid shelters dug below the school playground;[47] nor male staff leaving to join the forces…. yet those were some of the key things that, for instance, Grange School log book commented on. Luckily, for Sunnyside School, reminiscence evidence is able to fill in some of the missing details. Graeme Cairns remembered that 'Blackout curtains were hung on every window, the windows and glass partitions between classrooms were pasted with black mesh and all the lights were lowered and heavily shaded…. Air raid drills became a regular feature of school life. We all carried gas masks, in cardboard boxes…. Once there was a 'daylight raid' [on Clydebank] during the week at two o'clock in the afternoon. The school was immediately evacuated. Miss Keith panicked and kept shouting 'Down the stairs children' and Miss Hunter cried'.[48]

As with Grange School and Alloa Academy, the first impact of the war was the arrival of the evacuees, chiefly from Edinburgh. Even after only a week, the log book reported that 'A number of evacuees have gone and new ones have appeared'. By 11th September 1939 there were '45 evacuees from Edinburgh and 13 from other areas who had come to stay with friends'. As with other local schools most of them soon went home. The log book noted on 6th September 1940 that there were only 11 evacuees on the roll... but some must have stayed because when school opened on 31st August 1944 for what would have been the final war-time session, there were '12 evacuees from London and the South'. It looks like the Edinburgh evacuees had gone home but those from the South, who had maybe been sent up to Alloa to stay with friends or relatives, had stayed the course.

The introduction of the blackout right from the start of the war soon had its effect on the school; on 24th November 1939 it changed its hours of opening so that it could close at 3 pm to allow the pupils to go home in daylight.

A key aspect of school life which was a consequence of being at war was the incredible enthusiasm shown by the 400 [approx.] Sunnyside pupils [and their parents presumably] for War Savings. On 14th June 1940 the log book noted that 'this week is War Savings Week ... and the amount collected in school amounts to £136.10/-'.[49] What we now see is that after this terrific start to War Savings, this almost becomes Sunnyside's 'thing' and the log book spares no detail on the continuing glorious tradition of War Savings that the School then embarked upon.

On 24th March 1941 the log book noted that this was 'War Weapons' week; £551 was invested throughout the school of which £380 represented certificates sold.[50]

On 15th February 1943 the Chairman of the Education Committee and the Director of Education visited the school to

Alloa Journal 15th April 1941. Posters like this one would have encouraged school children to buy War Savings certificates

address pupils and congratulate them on reaching their 100% membership of the National Savings Association. The School had a roll of 419 and was the second largest school to achieve this result. There was a long article in the *Circular* talking about 'Sunnyside School's Splendid Record' and the way in which they had hoped to double their savings but in fact had trebled it.[51]

On 10th April 1943 it was 'Wings for Victory' week; the amount invested in the school during the week was £1,170.16/-. Then 7-8th April 1944 was the

The 7-8 year olds in Miss Dudgeon's Class Infants 3 at Sunnyside School in 1943

start of 'Salute the Soldier' week and Sunnyside pupils responded true to form. The total amount invested during the week was £1,245.14/- in National Savings Certificates and £200 in Defence bonds. The school had its own savings 'thermometer' in the school hall, recording the rate of savings; just like the one for Alloa in front of the town hall.[52] On 18th September 1944 the log book noted that 'A.C. Marshall, Director of Education, visited the school this morning to congratulate teachers and pupils on having their success in the National Savings campaign announced on the radio'. The pupils even managed to save £242 during the summer holiday. Sunnyside's reputation for War Savings had been good in the Great War, but they surpassed themselves [and almost every other local school apart from the Academy on occasion] in the Second World War. That was a tremendous achievement.

And the pupils still had time to save and give to the Red Cross. They gave £76 on 23rd July 1943, £75 on 29th June 1944 and £50 on 25th June 1945 but that was only part of it. The log book proudly noted on that last date, that pupil donations to the Red Cross took place 'over two and a half years and they have given no less than £526 which averages £1 for every school day during the whole period'. And there was even more; Sunnyside gave £236 for parcels for POWs right through 1944 to pay for 2 parcels for POWs on every school day. They did that and still had 72 extra parcels.[53] VE Day meant that the school was closed for 2 days on 8-9th May 1945.

ST JOHN'S SCHOOL

Sidney Perry was headmaster for the first two years of the war. J.W. Ross, a teacher from Sunnyside School was promoted to headmaster at St John's as from January 1942. The school roll was round about 150 in 7 classes but this had declined to 5 classes by 1944.

As early as 26th May 1939 the school prepared for war by reorganising its school day on Wednesdays and Fridays to fit in ARP classes for the teaching staff. Once war started there was the usual round of air-raid drills, gas mask practices[54] and alterations to the timing of the school day in order to mitigate the worst effects of the blackout.[55]

There were only a few evacuees placed at St John's; 15 from Edinburgh and one private evacuee from London.

The pupils of St John's were quicker than the other Alloa primary schools to get an idea of some of the realities of war, because in March 1940, Leading Torpedo Operator Roy G. Fullerton, a former pupil who had actually been in action on *HMS Exeter* in the Battle of the River Plate, visited the school for its Easter prize-giving and gave a short speech about his experiences.[56]

With thanks to Bert Fullerton, also in *Alloa Journal* 23rd March 1940

He even presented the school with a memento; a 2 pound lump of shrapnel which had hit the ship, part of one of the *Graf Spee*'s shells.[57] The *Journal*'s report of his visit noted that the 'Exeter hero' had visited St John's school with a 'grim souvenir'.[58]

One aspect of the pupils' involvement with war business was their focus on knitting 'comforts' for those in the services. By December 1941 they had provided 44 pairs of socks, 9 pairs of bed socks, 22 scarves, 16 cap comforters, 9 cap and scarf comforters, 24 pairs of mitts, 10 helmets, 10 pullovers, 6 knee rugs, 12 blankets and 84 cretonne utility bags [containing toiletries].

There is only one reference to potato lifting in October 1943 when it was noted that the school would be closed for two weeks.

There must have been fund-raising efforts by the St John's pupils, but they did not get anything like the prominence of entries in Sunnyside's log book. One bit of fund raising which was reported in the *Circular* was that in December 1941 'Pupils of St John's School have sent £3.5/- to the Admiralty to assist in the purchase of a depth charge to destroy a U-boat in the Atlantic'.[59] On 5th March 1943 a Whist drive was held in the school which raised £25 for 'Wings for Victory' week and on 6th April 1944 a special effort was made by the pupils towards 'Salute the Soldier' week. The sum realised was £192. That was it as far as references to fund-raising.

The last war-related entry was on 8th May 1945 when the log book noted that the school would be closed for two days holiday following VE Day.

SOUTH SCHOOL

This school opened in March 1928. Pupils were taken from the Academy Primary Department and Grange School. The starting headmaster was Mr J.A. Atkinson who was promoted on to Sunnyside as headmaster in July 1936. W.H. Andrew was appointed headmaster starting in September 1937 and he was in charge throughout the war years, retiring in July 1945.[60] In January 1942 the roll of South School was 188, but it fell to 166 by January 1944.

On Monday 4th September 1939, the day after war was declared the school opened and received its share of evacuees; the log book recorded 'School assembled with children evacuated from schools in Edinburgh and, unofficially, Glasgow, Dundee, Clydebank and Rosyth [total 46]'. As with the other local schools, they didn't all stay very long; by January 1940 at the start of the new term, it was 'Evacuees now Edinburgh 10, others 6'.[61] In 1942 there were still 8 evacuees on the roll.[62]

Over 1940-41 the school had its usual programme of air raid drills; in May 1940 was the 'First Air Raid test evacuating to shelters [two] now complete', followed in July by a test evacuation of classes in view of possible air raid warning.[63] In October 1941 the school tried to help out the Council, who were short of hall space due to the military requisitioning, by blacking out the gymnasium and corridors so they could be let out at nights.[64] The first German bombing of Scotland was in March 1941, but South School seemed to be organised for fire watching at an earlier date than the other local schools; on 25th February 1941 its log book records that it was 'grouped with Library, Bank Street, Mill St. to Cross. 4 ladies, 1 man once a fortnight at First Aid Post, Gas Showrooms'.

There were only two log book references to wartime fund-raising in South School. In March 1941 the pupils committed their savings to 'War Weapons' week and raised £153.[65] South School's log book was the only one to record that as a promotional encouragement for this, a 'Messerschmitt was on exhibition in playground'. This was widely reported in the local press. In April 1943 the school also raised £293 in 'Wings for Victory' week.[66]

There were two other war-related events that only South School's log book recorded [although surely the other local primary schools would have been involved in both cases?]. The first was the provision of Mid-day meals from the end of April 1942 'from County Cooking Depot, Keilarsbrae, under auspices of Ministry of Food. First Week - 94 meals [4d per meal, 1/8 per week, prepaid]'.[67] The *Advertiser* had plenty to say about this; crowing about what a bargain it was. Its article[68] claimed that communal feeding for Alloa school children was going to start on 27th April at 4d per head for a 2 course meal. The County would be paying 17% of the true cost with the government picking up the rest of the bill. A very fine new kitchen, paid for by the Ministry of Food, was being set up in Keilarsbrae.

The *Journal* chipped in with extra details… '1,600 children had indicated a desire to have meals but [the Education dept.] had made provision for 3000. It would cost £2,000 a year but the Government grant of 83% would reduce that to £340.'[69]

Secondly, only South School's log book picked up on the watching of wartime propaganda films provided by the Ministry of Information.[70] The films watched were '100,000 Women' [Russia], 'The Building of a Tank' and 'The Siege of Tobruk'.

In 1943 and 1944, a small number of pupils joined in the potato lifting. In both of these years, the school only had 5 pupils over the age of 12 who were eligible to be exempted from school attendance.[71] This didn't mean that there was a lack of interest in horticultural affairs in South School; in May 1944 the Council agreed to pay the expenses of a 'Dig For Victory' exhibition that had recently been held there.[72] 8th February 1945 must have been a special day for some reason, because the log book reported that 'School bell (turret) rung for first time since outbreak of War'.

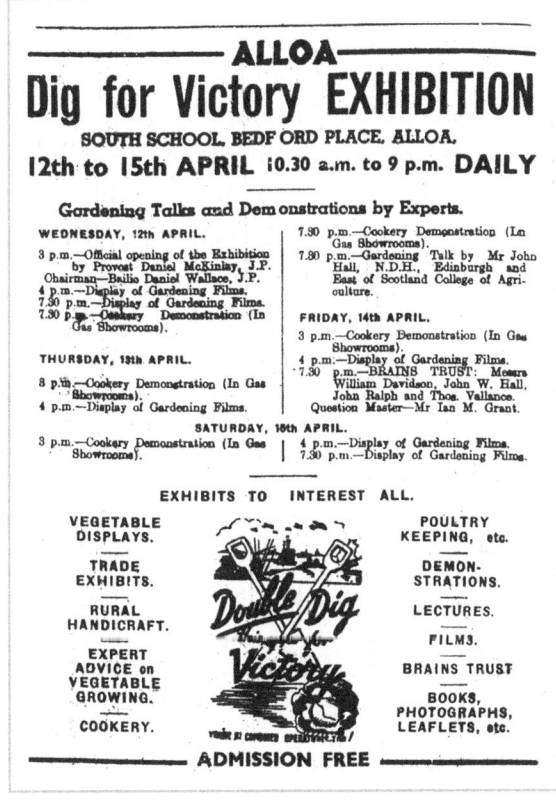

Alloa Advertiser 1st April 1944

The ending of the war was announced in the log book by '8-9th May 1945 VE Days – public holidays following unconditional surrender of Germans in Western Europe'.

ST MUNGO'S SCHOOL

The Headmaster during the war years was Hugh Campbell, who began in September 1937. By 1942 it had 2 infant classes, 5 primary classes and a secondary division [of 41]; and its total roll was 321. Of all the primary schools in Alloa, this one's log book is most conspicuous for saying almost nothing. Again and again, all that is written is 'Routine Work throughout week'.

However, here and there in the records are some notable war-related activities and indeed, some war-related events unique to this school.

As with the other primary schools, war preparations began well before the war started. The log book noted on 24th May 1939 that every Wednesday and Friday timetable is to be adjusted to allow teachers off during the afternoon to attend ARP classes in First Aid and Anti-Gas measures. On Friday

1st September 1939, 2 days before the declaration of war, the headmaster and janitor, under orders, opened up school buildings in readiness for use under the Evacuation scheme. These evacuees began arriving but the log book on 11th September 1939 recorded that 'Only 11 evacuees reported to this school'. That wasn't the end of the evacuation story however; the log book on 16th May 1941 noted that 'During the past few weeks an increasing number of evacuated children have reported. The number of evacuated children on the roll is now 44. Nearly all of these come from Glasgow and are distributed among the various classes'. None of the other local primary schools reported this significant boost to evacuee numbers which occurred almost two months after the Glasgow/Clydebank Blitz but only a week after the bombing of Greenock.

St Mungo's took its air raid drills seriously and there were many references in the log book through September 1939 to its plans for the pupils to speedily reach the air raid shelters.[73] From Friday 2nd May 1941 onwards, when there seemed a more realistic prospect of bombing, fire watching duties by teachers began.

In 1940, the log book reported two military impacts on school life; in July and November the Army took over the school yard then the school gym for drilling, then as from 1st November 1940, 'Mr MacLellan left today to begin his service in RAF'.

Pupils did get involved in fund raising and from their own perspective it was very successful... but the inspectors had commented on several occasions that this was a school with an intake which often came from families in very deprived circumstances. On 24th June 1941 the log book noted that 'Children's savings amounted to £24 during 'War Weapons' week – nearly 8 times the normal weekly average'. Two years later, in April 1943, during 'Wings for Victory' week, the children contributed £123.

In the later years of the war, as with all the local schools, there was serious pupil involvement in potato lifting. On 8th October 1943 the school was closed for two weeks to allow children to collect the potato harvest. This closure had to be extended into November due to bad weather. The headmaster sadly noted on 25th October 1943 that 'Because the potato harvest is not yet finished children are being allowed to be absent from school to assist the farmers. The result is that the secondary classes are practically empty'. Then in 1944 it was the same; on 9th October 1944 'Children over 12 were exempted for potato lifting'. 35 Children were allowed out to farms along with one teacher. There was a spell of bad weather which led to it being suspended, but this went on until 10th November.

As with all the local schools, the ending of the war in Europe on VE Day in May 1945 was the start of a two day holiday. The schools expressed this with slightly different degrees of emphasis. St Mungo's log book said 'VE Day - German Capitulation' which seemed to sum up a certain satisfaction. The last war-related reference in the log book was on 8th October 1945 when it was noted that 'Mr Ronald MacLellan returns to duty today after service with the RAF'.

ENDNOTES

1 *Alloa Academy Magazine* 1940
2 Alloa Academy Rector's log book 22nd September 1939 refers to the number of evacuees being around 100. In fact, the admissions register [pages 43-46] records 67 Edinburgh evacuees and 48 from 'Other Districts'
3 All of the Alloa Academy admission registers, covering most of the 20th century and even some of the 19th century were kept in the school until 2020, and were then passed on to the care of Clackmannanshire Archives and Local History Service
4 This boy at least stayed at the school for a while; the Rector's log book for 24th January 1940 noted that 'R. Heeps (pupil evacuated from Glasgow) won the Flynn Cup – Heeps' father is a native of Alloa and an FP of the school'
5 The Dawsons were among the most generous of Alloa families in offering a home to evacuees; they took in three unrelated boys, all from Heriot's School. Two of them had perfect attendance at the Academy until they both left on 10th November 1939. Curiously, the Dawsons did not take in W. Allan Meek's brother Ian who went to stay at the East Lodge of Inglewood House. He continued his studies at the Academy until July 1942
6 His death was not caused by his ship sinking since the ship survived the war. In fact it was sold to the Norwegian Navy in 1947 and became a weather ship and is still around [in 2020] although it had now been retired from active duty. *HMS Saxifrage* was heavily involved in defending Convoy SC122 from 11-23rd March 1943. There were 65 merchant ships in this convoy of which 9 were sunk by German U-boats. Maybe in this attack he was killed, and either lost or buried at sea. His name is on Plymouth Naval Memorial [panel 84 col 2]
7 Almost a year later, on 18th October 1940 they agreed to reverse this decision
8 Alloa Academy FPs Association log book for October 1940 says its membership was 490
9 Alloa Academy Rector's log book 17th November 1939
10 The FPs running the magazine kept in as good touch as possible with FPs who were prisoners of war. They were glad to offer congratulations in the 1945 issue of their magazine to 'Warrant Officer Geo Mitchell, POW Stalag Luft 3, for having passed the December 1943 Intermediate Examination of the Association of Certified and Incorporated Accountants. (Special congratulations these!)' This information was also reported in the *Alloa Journal* for 22nd July 1944
11 By 1942 the Alloa Academy FPs Association was more aware of which FPs had been killed, and started to include lists of names in its magazine. In 1942 there were 5 named FPs
12 See Chapter 11 for the full story

[13] This is referred to as 'very creditable' in the HM Inspectors Report on the school in 1943

[14] Alloa Academy Rector's log book 13th June 1941

[15] This was to chop down trees, chiefly to be used for pit props in the mining industry.

[16] *Alloa Journal* 24th August 1940. *The Bulletin* which was referred to was for Wednesday 21st August 1940

[17] I know this because about 30 years ago I spoke on the phone to James Doyle, a former pupil. He was on this particular work party and remembers that Miss Arkieson was in charge of the girls and the cooking. The HM Inspectors were particularly impressed with this aspect of wartime life in the school. The HM Report for 1945-46, oblivious of any sexism, said that 'A noteworthy feature has been the forestry camps attended each summer since 1940 by parties of more than 20 senior boys, at which catering has been entrusted to senior domestic science pupils.'

[18] *Alloa Circular* 20th October 1943

[19] *Alloa Journal* 14th October 1944 and *Alloa Circular* 18th October 1944

[20] Mr Geddes joined up as a lieutenant in the Gordon Highlanders [*Alloa Academy Magazine* 1940, p38] but then became a captain attached to the Irish Fusiliers [*Alloa Academy Magazine* 1941, p34]

[21] Mr McGregor joined the Scots Guards [*Alloa Academy Magazine* 1941]

[22] Maybe the Rector was right to have a high opinion of Mr Spence's abilities; he was appointed Director of Education for Shetland in 1947

[23] Mr Irvine was obviously ambitious to progress up the educational ladder but he did lead Grange School for the duration of the war. In December 1944 he was leeted for but failed to get a position as Assistant Director of Education for Ayrshire [See *Alloa Journal* 2nd December 1944], but in July 1945 he moved to be headmaster of Darroch Secondary School in Edinburgh; a much larger school than Grange School [See *Alloa Advertiser* 7th July 1945]

[24] A note in Grange School log book margin suggests that additional pupils came from Bellevue and Tynecastle Schools in Edinburgh

[25] Grange School roll for September 1940 was 375 pupils, in September 1941 it was 332 pupils

[26] Pupils didn't just come in to Grange School; some maybe left. On 27th June 1940 the log book noted that '7 boys and 5 girls are registered for evacuation overseas'. Whether this was a further evacuation of Edinburgh children or an evacuation of Alloa children was not specified

[27] September 1944 was 3 months after D-Day. By then any sort of German air control had totally disappeared, meaning there was no effective way of getting poisonous gas to the British Isles.

[28] Alloa Burgh Council minute book 11th September 1944 shows that the Government gave permission for Fire guard duties to be relaxed as from 12th September 1944

[29] *Alloa Journal* 3rd February 1940

[30] The log book entry for 4th May 1945 refers to 12 half-plots in Alexandra Drive. Earlier mentions of the allotments did not say where they were but in fact, these were the ones in Alexandra Drive because the Burgh Council minutes for 23rd October 1939 reveal a discussion on how to increase the number of allotments and a site was suggested on the west of Alexandra Drive. In the Council minutes for 15th November 1939, the Burgh Surveyor said that pupils at Grange School would take over part of this new plot

[31] *Alloa Journal* 23rd December 1939

[32] Grange School log book for 26th October 1944 noted the names of the 10 farms in Perthshire and said how the pupils lifted 63 acres

[33] *Alloa Advertiser* 12th July 1941. Grange School log book for 10th July 1941 says his talk was called 'Being Bombed'

[34] *Alloa Advertiser* 11th November 1943

[35] *Alloa Journal* 13th January 1943

[36] Grange School log book 9th November 1943

[37] Grange School log book entries for 4th and 5th September 1945, referring to Mr Small's return after

5 years absence, noted that he was 'on essential shipyard work'. John McClelland remembers Mr Small telling the class that he was engaged in making RDF rooms on board ships safe for operators while under attack; apparently they tended to be housed in wooden shacks as steel was causing interference with the equipment

[38] Grange School log book for 1st November 1940 noted that 'Miss Michie [Gym Mistress] and Mr Walker [Art Master] are to be married tomorrow. Mr Walker is due to go to the Air Force at 10 days' notice'. On 24th December 1940 the log book noted that he had been ill and his call up had been postponed

[39] *Alloa Journal* 31st January 1942 contained an In Memoriam notice from his mother, noting that the death had occurred on 31st January 1941. He was aged 19, serving on *HMS Huntly*, a Hunt class minesweeper, when it was sunk by German aircraft off the coast of Egypt, His name is on Portsmouth Naval Memorial [Panel 51 Column 2]

[40] *Alloa Advertiser* 14th April 1945. *Alloa Circular* 18th April 1945 also had a report

[41] Park School inherited pupils from other local primary schools. South School log book reported on 6th September 1935 that 234 of its pupils were transferred to the new Park School

[42] James Younie had been a teacher at Sunnyside School before the Great War, and then served in the Royal Garrison Artillery in Mesopotamia during that war before returning to his teaching duties in Alloa in November 1919, and later being promoted to headmaster of Park School upon its opening in 1935

[43] See Park School log book for 8th September 1939. The entry for 15th September 1939 noted that the figure of 14 evacuees remained constant, but by 6th September 1940 there were only 5. However, others must have kept coming in because the log book for 25th April 1941 noted that 'the school roll stands at 538 of whom 35 are evacuees'; and the entry for 2nd May 1941 stated that '6 evacuees from the West of Scotland have entered school this week', whilst the entry for 4th September 1942 noted that '2 evacuees from West Hartlepool have been enrolled'

[44] This was not an actual air raid on Alloa, it was the noise of the westward passage of German bombers along the route of the Forth valley on their way to bomb Greenock, and then eastwards back to their bases in France or Norway. There was no reference to this in the local press

[45] *Alloa Circular* 13th August 1943. CWGC records that Harry Fraser [No. 2372624], aged 34, died on 20th July 1943. He was buried at Syracuse War Cemetery, Sicily; grave ref. II.A.12

[46] Sidney Perry was born in 1880 and became headmaster of St John's Primary School in 1907. On the face of it, his transfer to Sunnyside in 1941 looks like he was being sent as a war-time stand-in; yet from looking at the Council discussion of the appointment, they clearly regarded it as a well-deserved, if late, promotion to a larger school. Mr Perry retired, aged 65, on 11th July 1945

[47] In *Our War* (2006) Graeme Cairns writes about his memories of the air raid shelters at Sunnyside School on p93

[48] *Alloa Advertiser* 25th February 1994. Graeme Cairns was a former pupil of Sunnyside School

[49] Compare this to Grange School log book entry for 25th June 1940, where it noted that the total collected was 27 shillings!

[50] Grange School's total for this date was £51, their total for 'Wings for Victory' Week April 1943 was £216, and their return for 'Salute the Soldier' Week in April 1944 was £376

[51] *Alloa Circular* 17th February 1943

[52] Reminiscence evidence from George Hutchison

[53] *Alloa Circular* 27th December 1944

[54] These were logged on 26th September 1939 and 7th May 1940

[55] These were logged on 20th November 1939, 18th November 1940 and 6th and 10th December 1940

[56] His words as a survivor of that battle may have had additional impact since it had been reported in the *Alloa Advertiser* on 6th January 1940 that another local seaman serving on the same ship, a man from Tillicoultry, had been killed

[57] *Alloa Advertiser* 23rd March 1940. This visit was not mentioned in the log book

[58] *Alloa Journal* 23rd March 1940

[59] *Alloa Circular* 3rd December 1941

[60] W.H. Andrew had been a long-serving member of staff of Alloa Academy; he was in the staff photo for 1909-10, but was not fit enough for war service in the Great War, despite the government's attempts to re-classify him. He died in 1948

[61] South School log book 4th January 1940

[62] South School log book 1st September 1942

[63] South School log book 4th July 1940

[64] South School log book 25th October 1940

[65] South School log book 28th March 1941

[66] South School log book 10th April 1943

[67] South School log book 27th April 1942

[68] *Alloa Advertiser* 14th March 1942

[69] *Alloa Journal* 14th March 1942

[70] South School log book 9th June 1942. The *Alloa Journal* on 23rd April 1942 had reported on the good attendance at a viewing of a large selection of Ministry of Information films at Alloa Academy; although the ones that were watched seemed slightly less 'military' than those watched at South School

[71] South School log book 11th-22nd October 1943 at Muckhart, 19th October 1944 at Sheardale and Blairingone, at a payment of 9d an hour

[72] Alloa Burgh Council minute book 29th May 1944

[73] St Mungo's School log book noted on 15th September 1939 that 'the whole school gained the shelters in 5 and a half minutes'

CHAPTER 4

SPORT AND THE WAR

The effects of the Second World War on Alloa's sporting life were almost the same as in the Great War, although it seems that more of an effort was made to keep some sporting fixtures going to help morale rather than just as fund-raisers. So, the big team sports like football and cricket both declined (cricket less so) simply because, in the days of conscription, it was difficult to guarantee that a team of sufficient quality could be assembled on a regular basis, that is, every Saturday. So football disappeared altogether and cricket became a game just of 'friendlies'.

Sports which were played as individuals or small teams were easier to keep going; golf and bowls especially carried on throughout the war. Their problem was not the lack of players as much as the lack of greenkeepers to keep the venues in tip-top shape.

The sports so far mentioned all had well established clubs in Alloa before the war and they kept records which give some reasonable evidence of how the wartime conditions treated them; other small scale sports like billiards at the Liberal Club, curling, homing pigeons and tennis all existed and received occasional reports in the local press, but never enough to build up a general picture of their response to the rigours of war.

FOOTBALL

Alloa Athletic had a great season in 1938-39. They were managed by Jimmy McStay [before he was poached by Celtic to be their new manager in February 1940[1]] and he led them to a decent run in the cup, and promotion into the First Division following the last match of the season, at home against Brechin.

Their 1939-40 season-opener in the top division was a victory at the Recreation Ground [known as The Recs] against St Johnstone, where 7,600 spectators watched Alloa win 3-0.[2] However, by the time of their fifth match of the season against Partick Thistle, that just about coincided with the start of the Second World War. There were only 5 games played in this

Alloa Athletic FC, players and officials at Montrose on the last away match of the season (with thanks to John Glencross), also in *Alloa Advertiser* 26th February 1960

curtailed season and the *Advertiser* did carry reports on them. The Scottish Football Association took the decision to suspend all players' contracts from 3rd September 1939... effectively ending professional football since, with conscription already in place, no team could guarantee that its players would not be called up for military service.

The *Circular* dramatically called this 'The Football Blackout' and noted that 'Managers are quite in the dark as to what might be expected of them in the future' since 'The war breaks all contracts, and managers as well as players are affected'.[3] At that time, Alloa Athletic were sixth from bottom of the division and hadn't yet won an away match. However, professional football of a

ALLOA FOOTBALL & ATHLETIC CLUB, LTD.

RECREATION GROUNDS

REGISTERED OFFICE, 41 MILL STREET.

Directors.
THOS. MURRAY, Chairman.
WM. STANTON, Vice Chairman.
WM. L. CRAWFORD.

Colours.
ORANGE & BLACK HOOPS.

Manager.
Mr JAMES McSTAY.
Telephone No.: Larkhall 227.

Secretary.
Mr GEO. R. MATHEWSON.

Telephones.
GROUND, ALLOA 64.
OFFICE, ALLOA 100.

41 Mill Street,

Alloa. 8th.September 1939.

Dear Sir,   The War and Football.

The following decisions were made at a Special Meeting of the Scottish Football Association held on 6th.inst.
1. In conformity with the Government order,all football in Scotland shall be suspended until further notice.
2. The registrations of the players with the Association shall remain effective meantime. (Players are debarred from playing for any Club other than that for whom they are so registered)
3. All contracts or agreements between clubs and players shall be suspended as from 3rd.September -the date of the Government's decree.

The Directors very much regret in the circumstances having to suspend your contract until further notice and sincerely trust it will not be long before you will be recalled to commence playing again.

Expenses due are enclosed for which kindly acknowledge receipt.

Yours faithfully,

Secretary.

P.S. In order that same may be stored away at the Ground kindly return boots and spikes recently purchased.Postage will be refunded.

Alloa Athletic's letter to Alex Izatt informing him of the suspension of his contract (With thanks to John Glencross, Alloa Athletic FC)

kind did carry on for the whole of the 1939-40 season following the declaration of war. The *Circular* announced that football was to resume with 2 sectional tournaments and that 'details had been sent to all senior teams this week'.[4] Scotland was divided into two divisions, and Alloa Athletic was placed in the North Eastern Section. This meant that they would not play divisional matches against Celtic or Rangers. There was however, a full programme of matches right until the end of April 1940 where Alloa played Aberdeen, Dundee, Stirling King's Park, and Edinburgh teams like St Bernard's. For example, the *Journal* reported on 11th November 1939 that Alloa played Hearts 'under War League auspices' and lost 3-2.[5] At the start of 1940, half way through this league's season, Alloa were fourth in the table. There was also play in the Scottish Cup (War Emergency Competition) where Alloa were knocked out by Rangers over two legs, losing 6-3 on aggregate in February 1940.[6] The club's annual report showed they made profit of £221 over the 1939-40 season with a reduction in gate takings but an increase in season tickets.[7] However, the board of directors did not think that was good enough and at the club's AGM in July the decision was taken to have 'no more football till war ends'. Without the players realising it at the time then, the last wartime professional fixture for Alloa Athletic was on 4th May 1940; a 0-2 defeat in its home match against St Bernard's.[8]

The *Circular* reported of the decision at the AGM to suspend club activities, that 'The Board, after consideration, decided not to take part in any war-time football, owing mainly to the fact that the majority of the playing staff were liable for military service or engaged in work of national importance, and it was going to be very difficult to field a team in these circumstances'.[9] The secretary also claimed that 'the Eastern League would never pay, and to go into such a league would be to lose any money they had' and further argued that Mr McStay's departure was a 'blessing in disguise' since they would have had to pay his salary at least until the end of the season.[10] The club still felt it could take an optimistic view of their future, believing of their earlier performances in the First Division, that 'in a restricted season they had taken 4 points out of 5 games... which, if not suggesting championship honours, at least gave hope of First League status being retained',[11] that is, whenever football resumed after the war.

Although professional football by contracted players was now over for the duration of the war, clubs were allowed to 'retain' players on their books 'should hostilities end'. For the 1940-41 season Alloa Athletic retained 15 players, but as the war progressed and some of these men either enlisted, moved to reserved occupations elsewhere, were retained by other clubs or simply became unavailable, then the club cancelled that player's retained status. By 1942-43 the number had dropped to 6 players and these same 6 men were retained right through the war until the 1945-46 season provided an opportunity to play again.[12]

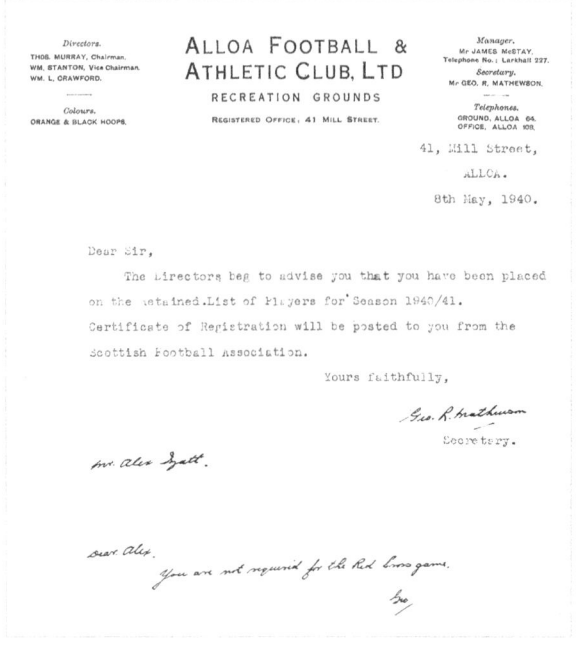

Alloa Athletic's letter to Alex Izatt informing him of being retained by the club in 1940 (With thanks to John Glencross, Alloa Athletic FC)

From July 1940 onwards, as the *Advertiser* acknowledged itself in November 1940, 'senior football was very much a dead letter for Alloa for the duration'[13] and rather poetically reported that 'Untrodden by all but youthful vandals the Recs brooded silently throughout the autumn and early winter months'; a reference to an earlier crime by youths who had broken into and vandalised a refreshment hut.

But some further matches still took place. The most unusual of these occurred on the last Saturday of 1940 when what was billed as 'A Wartime International' took place at the Recs. This was between teams representing the Polish Army and the British Army and was in aid of the Welfare of Troops Fund. The Polish President-in-exile Raczkiewicz arrived shortly before half-time and the teams were presented to him at the interval. The British Army team won 7-5.[14]

The *Advertiser* did its best to keep going with the memories of Alloa Athletic's football successes. In March 1941, a long article under the headline of 'Wasps still stinging', reported on the subsequent [mostly] military careers of all the players who were in the last Alloa Athletic side that was disbanded as they all got called up.[15] One of these past players who did **not** pursue a military career was John Fitzsimmons who had gone on to Clyde FC, but by September 1941 was now a qualified doctor, working in Glasgow and treating survivors of the Blitz.[16]

There were other occasional exhibition matches at the Recs; for instance, in February 1943 a McLeod's Shipyard select played a Polish Army select. The *Journal* noted that 'This is a try-out for the Poles because they play a British Army select in Edinburgh next Saturday'.[17] Then in March 1943 a team from the Polish Brigade played a Black Watch team, with a 2-2 score. On 28th August 1943 there was a match between a Polish Army XI and a British Army XI to raise funds for the Clackmannan County Hospital.[18] The *Circular* reported on this match, which the British Army lost 6-0. Its report included a disgusted comment from a watching policeman who said that 'Even if the British Army could carry on playing until the end of the war, but they still wouldn't score'.[19] In April 1944, as a fund-raiser for 'Salute the Soldier' week, the Recs saw a match between a 'County Select team of Junior footballers' against a Polish Army XI, then on the following Wednesday a team from the Royal Navy took on the Poles.[20]

By January 1945 when it seriously began to appear that the war would soon be over, there was a burst of local enthusiasm for getting Alloa Athletic Football Club set up again, ready for a start in August. The *Advertiser* reported on this local interest, and that 'Optimistic officials' hope 'it will be in the first division of the Scottish League, claiming they were in the first division when the war started'.[21] At a well-attended meeting in March at the Townhead Institute, the club Chairman reported that they needed a manager but he had received calls of interest from 3 internationals, and that the ground was in good order but the stand needed repairing.[22] He very optimistically reported that they should be in the first division because 'with a good crowd we can average 10,000 at our home games'.[23] The club Chairman at least had some local industrial support for the revival of the club; Younger's Brewery had purchased 100 shares in Alloa Athletic FC at £1 each.[24]

At the beginning of June 1945 the Scottish Football Association announced the new leagues. The generally over-optimistic views that had been held in Alloa were not to be rewarded; when football started again in August, Alloa Athletic would be placed in Division B.[25] That however, was better news than that which faced the newly reconstituted Stirling King's Park [now to be called Stirling Albion] who found their bid for a league placing rejected on the grounds that they could not yet guarantee proper playing facilities.[26]

It was only at the end of June that Alloa Athletic appointed a new manager. They had drawn up a leet of 5 and picked Mr James Crapnell, the former Scottish international.[27] He had a whirlwind couple of months trying to buy players, and assembled enough of them to have a trial match between his A and B teams on 4th August, watched by several thousand spectators.[28] Everyone must have thought they were onto a winner here, when their new centre forward, McKay, an ex-Celtic player, scored 7 goals![29] However, Alloa's opening league match of the first post-war season was away to Albion Rovers on 11th August, and they lost 6-2.[30]

Jimmy Crapnell didn't have the success he hoped for; Alloa Athletic only won one of their first 4 matches and their form fluctuated during the season. He didn't last that long; in May 1946 he was sacked [as from 7th June 1946].[31] He went on to manage St Johnstone.

There is evidence from the war years [presumably 1942 and later] that there were local women's football teams in action, some as in the picture below, from the local industries which employed large numbers of young women. They were maybe playing matches as part of fund-raisers for war savings campaigns or in a local league. The local press had nothing to report on this at the time, or where they actually played, and the later report alongside the photo in the *Advertiser* did not have a date.

These Kelliebank Ladies had the footwork

In the intervals of giving their attention to the biggest game of all—the beating of Hitler—these young ladies of Kelliebank, surely a trim and workmanlike combine, proved themselves a difficult proposition for any other football feminity combine in this part of Central Scotland (And we're sure they could give a few tips to the men, too!) Their goalkeeper is now Mrs Isabelle Mitchell, 102 East Castle Street, Alloa.

Alloa Advertiser 26th May 1961

CRICKET

The war started just as Clackmannan County Cricket Club's 1939 season was coming to an end; the last match played was a non-league match against Stenhousemuir. This match ended in a draw, where J.M. Hardie for Stenhousemuir top-scored for his own side, and then took all seven Clackmannan County wickets to fall.

The issue now was what the club could do in subsequent seasons. The club's AGM was held in March 1940 and the club President spoke in epic terms of the task facing the club; 'Gentlemen, we are faced with many difficulties - travelling restrictions, depleted ranks, an empty purse and falling revenue – but, do not let us forget how petty these troubles are alongside the paralysing tragedy being enacted on the world stage'. It was agreed that no championship matches would be played that season, just a series of friendlies; and the Second XI fixtures would be dropped.[32] That was indeed what happened in 1940; the club played 20 friendly matches; mostly against their old county rivals but also a few against Army XIs or regimental teams for charity purposes. The most interesting was the match at Clackmannan CC's home ground, the Arns; against an Army XI in May when the match ended in an exact tie... both sides scoring 113.[33] In August there was a return match between the Army and Clackmannan County; this time the County got the better score.[34]

The Arns was not just used for cricket matches; there were several ladies hockey matches played by the County team, and also a gala sports day in September 1940 hosted by the Polish army. This really was a special event; admission was by ticket only and there were 1,500 guests. Those who couldn't get in watched from the slopes of the Pleasure Grounds which were 'thickly populated'. The guests of honour were President Raczkiewicz of Poland and General Sikorski who was Prime minister, Minister of National Defence and C-in-C of Polish forces.[35]

The 1940 cricket season was considered a successful one; only 2 matches were cancelled due to the inability to get a team. At the AGM in April 1941, J.T. McLaren in his Secretary's Report showed the club's spirit in a time of adversity and a determination to overcome any obstacles; noting that 'Conditions are becoming, and will become, increasingly difficult, but as long as we can get together 11 men, a scorer and an umpire, we shall endeavour to carry on'.[36] It was further noted that good wartime economies were being made in that 'A club which normally had an expenditure of around £540 had carried on successfully with one of not much more than £150'.[37]

Over the 1941 season Clackmannan County played 17 matches and won 8 and there was even Sunday cricket at the Arns on 13th July 1941 where the Scottish Counties XI beat the KOSB XI.[38] The season was regarded as a success, ending with a financial surplus for the year of almost £65.[39] The *Journal* reported on the same 1942 AGM but put an even more positive spin on it; maybe charmed by Mr J.T. McLaren's eloquence in his Secretary's Report. This time he noted that '1941 bristled with difficulties... fixtures were difficult to arrange, players were few, petrol was scarce and transport was difficult...'[40] but basically all this was overcome.

Mr McLaren continued his eloquence a year later at the 1943 AGM, reporting on 1942's season... 'In an atmosphere of world-wide tragedy and glory, we are happy to be able to say, that despite difficulties that seemed almost insuperable, we were able to carry on another season's cricket'.[41] No doubt he would have been heartened to read in the *Journal* in July 1943 that one of the club's pre-war players, Lieutenant F. Gilmour now a POW, had written from Oflag VII.B to say he was still running cricket matches there. [42]

The Annual Report in April 1944, looking back over the 1943 season noted that the club had continued with fixtures of 'a happy-go-lucky nature', and despite the 'many difficulties and heavy going' they hoped to continue with at least the same amount of restricted activities for the coming season.[43] In fact, the 1944 season was the most successful wartime season they had; they were still unbeaten at the end of July, but faded a little bit after that. On 19th August they were well-beaten by Stenhousemuir in their last home match,[44] but won their last match of the season away to Stirling by 47 runs.[45]

By the time of the AGM on 14th April 1945 the war in Europe was all but over so, although the Club Secretary agreed that the 1944 season 'was one of the most successful they had had' (Played 15 won 11) he had much more important news. He had arranged for there to be a Victory Match at the Arns which would hopefully take place on 25th June 1945, where the famous pre-war West Indian cricketer Learie Constantine would assemble an 'International Eleven' who would compete against an equally famous 'Services Eleven'.

When this match took place it must have exceeded all expectations.

There was an attendance of over 3,000 and 'the weather was ideal, brilliant sunshine tempered by cooling breezes'.[46] Both of the prospective candidates in the forthcoming general election were among the spectators, plus the Earl of Mar. Learie Constantine's team batted first and declared at 164 for 6 after a fine innings of 67 by the Cheshire opener H. Brown who was at the crease for over 2 hours. The 'Services Eleven' reached a total of 85 for 8 so the match was drawn. It was certainly seen as a 'victory' for Learie Constantine's team, especially since he had 'the fine analysis of 6 wickets for 12 runs' in his team's response.[47]

GOLF

During the Great War, Alloa Golf Club had been based at Braehead, but by the time of the Second World War it had moved to Schawpark in Sauchie where, in 1935 James Braid had designed a brand new course; and the majority of the members moved to it. The President of Alloa Golf Club for all the war years was T. Craig Lennox. The main concerns of the club in facing up to the impact of the war; were on greenkeeping and other staff issues, treatment of military/members, club facilities being turned over to government or military use and a small amount of war-related fund-raising.

Even before the war had started greenkeeping became an issue when 'the captain reported that one member of the staff was shortly to leave for military service...'[48] By April 1940 things were at crisis point when the club realised the pressures that the head greenkeeper McPhee was under. The club minutes noted that '...in view of the younger men having been taken for military service, it would be necessary to find other assistants for McPhee'. The club committee wondered what to pay them and the head greenkeeper, and agreed to ask other local clubs whether 'the wage of their greenkeepers had been increased since the outbreak of the War'.[49] They apparently had because in June 'it was decided that [the head greenkeeper] should receive a war bonus of 10/- per week in addition to his present wage'.[50] Things didn't improve for McPhee's working conditions; in December 1940 'It was reported that McPhee was alone on the course and had been unable to procure assistants'.[51] He soldiered on but 1941 saw a slight misunderstanding when the club minutes reported that McPhee wanted to resign his post. It was agreed to advertise for a replacement in the local and national press.[52] However, the club then realised that he hadn't as much 'resigned' as been 'instructed to report for duty' with the Auxiliary Fire Service on 8th September. This meant that 'it was quite clear that the latter did not resign his appointment and the club would accordingly require to consider his re-instatement at the end of the war'. The second assistant, Mr Aitchison was made up to head greenkeeper at £3 a week with a war bonus of 10/- a week.[53]

The club also had a club mistress who looked after catering and cleaning. In April 1941 it was noted that the club mistress, Miss Mitchell, was finding it difficult to make any profit from the 'sale of commodities in the club house'. 'It was agreed that her wages be increased from 12/- to £1'. It was further agreed that this should be regarded as purely a wartime increase.[54] The club risked losing her altogether in late 1942 following the conscription of women. The club minutes noted that Miss Mitchell 'was now to be regarded as liable to be called up for work of national importance...'[55]

As far as the treatment of military members went; there was very much a repetition of what had gone on in the Great War. In February 1940 it was agreed that 'the invitation which had been recently extended to the officers of the Gordon Highlanders billeted in the town should be extended to the personnel of the Black Watch, who were now billeted here'. It was also agreed that 'members of the club on active service should not be asked to pay an annual subscription but should have the courtesy of the course during their period of service'.[56] It was agreed that members of the club on active service could enter all club competitions if they were able to.[57] At the AGM on 23rd February 1942 it was noted that 'there were 40 members on active service who had not been asked to pay the annual subscription'. The AGM reported that, over 1941 they had a drop in income of £70 but had managed to retain a surplus of £54.[58]

The club found its life quite disrupted by the demands of the military and the government. From October 1939 the club house was taken over by ARP authorities as a First Aid Depot. It was unclear, even after discussion with Dr Reid [Director of Medical Services] as to whether 'the clubhouse was to be regarded as wholly taken over by the authorities or only partially so'.[59] This obviously caused local concern because in January 1940 the club put a big notice in the *Advertiser* saying 'Schawpark Golf Course – Not to be taken over by the military'. The club has been told that 'the military authorities have no intention of taking over Schawpark golf course as a military training ground'.[60]

They must have been re-assured in February 1940 when they were informed by Dr Reid that 'the clubhouse had still to be regarded as under the control of the club, and would only be used for the purpose of a First Aid Depot during ARP exercises on a Sunday afternoon'. The club agreed to delay consideration of what rent to charge until the roof had been repaired.[61] The ARP's Sunday use was obviously not trouble free; in October 1941 the club submitted a claim of £15.15/- for damage done to the clubhouse by the ARP 'through the building of sand bags and damage to the roof'.[62]

As far as interference from the military was concerned; in December 1940 the minutes noted that '... two weeks ago [at the end of November] the clubhouse had been requisitioned by the military authorities for the use of some 15 soldiers who had taken over the common room and cloakroom accommodation as a temporary billet'. This billeting would last for about a month.[63] The minute continued that at least the club would be able to claim compensation for the accommodation of the military unit which had occupied part of the club premises, although there were a lot of forms to be filled in.[64] Then again, in February 1942 the *Journal* reported that 'The military authorities have requisitioned the main club room and Gentleman's cloak room for a period of approximately three weeks and for the accommodation of 36 soldiers'.[65] By now the club was beginning to learn the lessons from previous such 'occupations' and the first thing the committee did was agree 'that tables and chairs would be removed to the kitchen, and notice of the proposed occupation should be given to the insurance company'.[66] They were taking no chances this time, neither did they in 1944 when the Secretary 'reported fully on the position of the claim made upon the Home Guard authorities for compensation for damage, following the manoeuvres at Schawpark...'[67]

Besides its clashes with the military, the club also suffered as a consequence of other decisions by the government. The club had a practice ground in two fields adjoining the course which were leased from a local farmer, but in January 1941 the government issued a formal order that these two fields must be ploughed up... 'the club's arguments against this proposed cultivation had not been accepted as sufficient in the circumstances'.[68] Things got worse in October. There was clearly pressure from the government's Agricultural Committee and in 1941 the club agreed that 'some part of the course should be voluntarily offered for ploughing purposes'. They also agreed there should be more extensive grazing, even of dairy cattle, on the course. The President and the club Captain proposed that roughly 16 acres, embracing the 9th and 10th holes should be conceded to the Agricultural Committee. The course effectively became a 15-hole course.[69] This didn't go down well with all the members; at the AGM on 23rd February 1942, questions were asked about '... the rotation of holes in competition play, in view of the recent taking over of part of the course for cultivation...' One advantage which came to the club from this was that they decided to approach the Alloa Coal Company [the club's landlords] for 'some reduction of the present rent for the duration of the war, in respect that a large portion of the course was now ploughed up...'[70] and in February 1943 it was reported to the Club Committee that the ACC had agreed to 'allow the club full remission of rent for the duration of the war and for six months thereafter'.[71] At the 1945 AGM it was noted that 58 club members had been in the forces and 52 were still serving; 6 had made the supreme sacrifice. The accounts showed a surplus of £144.[72]

There was also some small but steady war-related fund-raising in the club; chiefly by the Ladies section. It was noted at the AGM on 27th February 1940 that ladies from the club had knitted a quantity of woollen garments for the local war charity schemes and had also collected 13/3 as a contribution to the Warmth For Warriors Scheme. A further £2.2/- was collected at the AGM towards this scheme. At the next AGM on 25th February 1941 it was noted that lady members were still knitting [292] garments for the Warmth For Warriors Scheme and at the following AGM on 22nd February 1943 a collection for Warmth For Warriors was taken, amounting to £2.10/-. It was a small contribution but consistent in its giving. The Men's section did little more than agree to organise a competition to raise money for the County's 'Warship Week' in 1942.[73]

One last point to make about the impact of the war on Alloa Golf Club is that, despite the total lack of reference to it in any official minutes of the club, it may well be that the most war-related thing to happen to the club was that a German bomb fell on the golf course during the war! This is referred to on page 19 of the 1990 Club Centenary book where it says that 'Despite the loss of those holes [to the Government's Agricultural Committee] the course continued to be played over 15 holes. This must have upset the Germans because they actually bombed the course. To their credit they hit the centre of the fairway of the 8th hole. No mean feat as the members will testify. The bomb caused a large crater – it is unfortunately not on record as to whether play continued or not – probably the crater was deemed 'ground under repair' and players allowed a free lift and drop! What is on record is the club's request for damages from the War Damage Commission'.[74] This rather facetious telling of the story gave no date for when the bombing happened, but tried to position it as though it occurred <u>after</u> the loss of the holes to meet the government's agricultural plans in late 1941. In reality the evidence suggests this bombing happened at 3.15 in the morning of Thursday 24th October 1940. That is what is referred to in the evasive [obviously censored] article in the *Advertiser* on 26th October about bombs dropping on a golf course NE of an unnamed industrial town in Central Scotland, and the comment at the end of the above quote from the Centenary book about the club claiming damages. This is surely is a reference to the club minute in December 1940 about the sudden unexplained arrival of 15 soldiers – and the club being able to claim compensation even with a lot of forms to fill in. The *Journal* in early December had a partially accurate story which gives further support to the timing being in October 1940. It noted that a local golfer got a hole in one on the 7th hole but went on to say 'This is the same hole, by the way, which was presented with a ready-made 'bunker' a few weeks ago by an 'anonymous donor' who made the presentation in the small hours of the morning'.[75] This story, with its unsubtle reference to the bomb dropping, just had it happening at the wrong hole since the bomb dropped on the 8th which is a par 4 and the golfer could never have got a hole in one.

Braehead Golf Club

After the move of Alloa Golf Club to its Schawpark location, Braehead Golf Club was set up to continue using the old site. It was therefore the newer and more junior of the two clubs in Alloa. It struggled during the war but managed to keep going. It lost members quite quickly; the *Advertiser* in February 1940 reported that 'it had lost 45 members, mostly juniors'.[76] The *Journal*'s report on the club's 1940 AGM and annual report was more optimistic: claiming that Braehead Golf Club had 'A good year' with 205 members, 1,207 visitors and a profit over the year of £18.[77]

At the club's AGM in February 1941 it reported that it was still losing members and had a balance of £9 over the year.[78] Like the Alloa Golf Club and the Alloa Bowling Club, they realised that greenkeepers were in short supply during the war; but in April 1941 they advertised in the *Journal* for one; offering 50/- a week plus a free house and shop.[79]

Then in late 1941 the club was struck by the same agricultural blow as Alloa Golf Club at Schawpark; they were asked by the government to cultivate seven and a half acres at the east end of its course. That would leave just 9 playable holes.[80] This could have been disastrous because the club had already got a 'depleted membership' but a plebiscite within the club led to a good majority for carrying on and hoping for the return of its members who were serving in the military. The club hung on and in March 1942 it was able to report that financially the club was £30 in credit.[81]

The club held its AGM in January 1943 and noted there was an increase in club finances of £55. This led the club to reduce subscriptions to 25/- for men. The club President noted that 'It is hoped old members will rally round and play as often as possible to back up their enthusiastic Committee since that is all that is now wanted to keep the flag flying till victory allows our serving members to return to find Braehead as bright a place as ever...'[82] The *Advertiser* observed that the club had reduced its fees, partly due to the smaller number of holes that could now be played.[83] At the 1944 AGM it was noted that the club's financial balance was up by £10 and 'this was most satisfactory considering the reduction in annual subscriptions'.[84] By the time of the 1945 AGM in January 1945 that surplus had risen to '£74 in hand'.[85] Once the war was over it obviously took a while to get the course back into shape, and it was not until the AGM in March 1946 that the club was able to report that 'the 6 holes in the western section of the course would soon be put in order'.[86] Curiously, since it didn't ever seem that the club itself was actually defunct during the war; at this AGM 'it was formally agreed to re-start the club'.

BOWLS

Alloa had several bowling clubs, including the Alloa East End Bowling Club, the Alloa Bowling Club, Patons Bowling Club and the Co-op Bowling Club. They all played regularly during the war years but not all kept records. The Alloa Bowling Club in Coningsby Place has some records in the archives which give a flavour of the impact of the war on this area of social recreation.

The war started just as the 1939 bowling season was coming to an end. This had an instant impact on the Alloa Bowling Club since it usually had a special celebration for the prize winners held in some fancier location. This time though, it was agreed that 'The prizes for the various competitions to be presented there [ie in the clubhouse] this year, owing to the present crisis'.[87] The Committee had considered proposals for the re-levelling of the green, but at the November 1939 Committee meeting it was agreed that 'owing to the present crisis we had decided to let the matter drop in the meantime'.[88]

In March 1940, several resolutions were unanimously agreed; the first was that evacuees would be allowed to play on the green for the payment of the annual subscription during their stay in the district, and that they would be exempt of the entrance fee. The second was that members of His Majesty's Forces who are bowlers and stationed temporarily in this district will be welcomed on the green for a game when convenient. It was also agreed that teas should not be offered after the matches in the County of Clackmannanshire owing to the present crisis.[89] A further recognition of the demands of war came in March 1941 when 'It was proposed that owing to the War, we should grow vegetables in the plots surrounding the Green, instead of flowers'.[90] The club's AGM was held in March 1941 and showed that they ran at a profit in 1940, carrying forward a surplus of £5.[91] In May 1941 the Scottish Bowling Association had raised money from clubs all over Scotland to contribute to its war relief fund, and had raised nearly £11,000. Some members of Alloa Bowling Club thought that it could make a better contribution towards this... and agreed to have a special Rink Competition where the entrance fees would raise money. Two committee members offered to put up the prizes.[92] At the 1943 AGM it was reported that the bowling club now showed a credit balance of £124.[93]

In March 1944 at the AGM, Mr John Gordon became the new President, after two years of Mr D.M. Robertson. At that time the club's account showed a credit balance of £190.[94] The new President 'expressed the fervent hope that Victory and Peace would come about during his tenure of office';[95] his wish was two months short of being granted!

Although the club was financially viable it could hardly be said that the club prospered during the war. It never had a proper greenkeeper and relied on the part-time services of the greenkeeper from Alloa East End Bowling Club plus the support of a couple of members. The green was in fairly bad condition, with a lot of repair work done to it which didn't always work. However, it did manage to run competitions and club championships throughout the war. The minutes in 1945 made no reference to the end of the war. Maybe, given that 1945 was the centenary year of the club, the Committee and the 125 members had more important things to think about; especially long-standing members like T.S. Knox who had joined back in 1887.

SWIMMING

Alloa had two ladies swimming clubs in existence for at least the early years of the war, but it is difficult to get accurate information about what exactly happened to them. The *Journal* noted in October 1939 that 'Alloa Ladies Swimming Club and Alloa Norwood Ladies Swimming Club have suspended their activities, at least until February next year'.[96] The minutes of the Norwood Ladies Swimming Club in April 1940 support this view;[97] they state that 'At the outbreak of War on 3rd September 1939, it was decided to close the Club for the winter months. This was made inevitable owing to black-out regulations, and at that time the Baths were not suitably darkened to permit the use of the Pond after daylight. It was intended the Club re-open in the spring'. At that time Margaret McKinlay was the Club Vice-President. However, it appears that when they wanted to re-start in the spring of 1940, things did not go their way. Although they had appointed Bessie Dewar as their new coach in late April,[98] the *Advertiser* reported that the club was told by a meeting of the Council's Baths Committee that 'they wanted the Baths to be a better paying proposition' and a reservation fee of 2/- would now be charged for the use of the Pond for one hour. The Club's reaction was that 'The financial position of the Club is very difficult under present conditions and if the new proposals were enforced it would make it impossible to carry on the Club'.[99] The club minutes claim that they were going to attend a council meeting on 24th May to make their objections known. There were no more minutes after this one and it looks like the club packed up. There were no references in either the local press or the Burgh Council minutes to how these problems were resolved.

Yet, almost a year later there was supposed to be a big swimming gala held at Alloa Baths where the military would perform.[100] However, they pulled out at the last moment but they were replaced by local swimmers, the *Journal* reporting that there was 'a demonstration by Alloa Ladies Amateur Swimming Club', so it still must have been in existence. Indeed there was yet another swimming gala in March 1942 when the *Circular* reported that 'Alloa amateur ladies took part'.[101] This club did show staying power; they complained again to the Council in August 1943 about not getting enough pool time even though they had 107 members. The Council, noting their 50 years of existence, agreed to give them a dedicated evening slot on a Wednesday.[102]

However, the *Journal* did report in July 1943 on the demise of one of Alloa's two ladies swimming clubs; 'Following the disbanding of the Alloa Ladies Norwood Swimming Club, the Hon Treasurer has handed the entire funds of £45 to the Red Cross Week'.[103] The other ladies club kept going; shown by the *Journal*'s report in October 1944 that 'Alloa Ladies Swimming Club held their Halloween swimming gala last Wednesday'.[104]

ENDNOTES

[1] During his time as Celtic manager, until mid-1945, there were no competitive games played by Celtic; his wartime record was P220, W112, D38, L70, WP50.9%. See the website 'fitbaStats'. I assume this means they were all friendlies, exhibition matches etc., not in proper recognised football leagues

[2] *Alloa Journal* 12th August 1939

[3] *Alloa Circular* 6th September 1939

[4] *Alloa Circular* 6th September 1939

[5] *Alloa Journal* 11th November 1939

[6] *Alloa Journal* 24th February 1940

[7] *Alloa Journal* 6th July 1940

[8] *Alloa Advertiser* 4th May 1940

[9] *Alloa Circular* 2nd July 1941

[10] *Alloa Journal* 13th July 1940

[11] *Alloa Advertiser* 13th July 1940

[12] See Stuart Latham and John Glencross, *The History of Alloa Athletic FC* (2022) for further statistical information about Alloa Athletic's players and matches during the war years

[13] *Alloa Advertiser* 30th November 1940

[14] *Alloa Advertiser* 4th January 1941. This was not the first time these two teams had played against each other. On 2nd September 1940, 10,000 spectators watched the British Army beat the Polish Army 4-0 at Firhill

[15] *Alloa Advertiser* 22nd March 1941. Alloa Athletic's nickname was 'The Wasps' due to the black and gold hoops of their jerseys.

[16] *Alloa Circular* 17th September 1941. He also played for Falkirk and Hamilton Academicals. In 1953 he was appointed as Celtic's Club Doctor and held that post until 1987

[17] *Alloa Journal* 27th February 1943

[18] *Alloa Journal* 28th August 1943

[19] *Alloa Circular* 1st September 1942

[20] *Alloa Journal* 1st April 1944

[21] *Alloa Advertiser* 13th January 1945

[22] *Alloa Advertiser* 10th March 1945

[23] *Alloa Circular* 10th January 1945

[24] Minutes of Board of Directors of George Younger's Brewery for 22nd February 1946

[25] Daniel Gray, *Stramash: Tackling Scotland's Town and Teams* (2010) p42-45

[26] *Alloa Journal* 16th June 1945. Also see D. Gray, Chapter 6 for a reference to the bombing of Stirling's football ground in July 1940. This was the old ground down near the John Player's factory. The newly reconstituted club would have a new ground, at Annfield, much nearer the centre of town, but it couldn't yet guarantee its fitness for matches

[27] *Alloa Journal* 23rd June 1945

[28] *Alloa Journal* 11th August 1945

[29] *Alloa Circular* 8th August 1945

[30] *Alloa Journal* 18th August 1945

[31] *Alloa Journal* 4th May 1946

[32] *Alloa Advertiser* 30th March 1940

[33] *Alloa Advertiser* 18th May 1940

[34] *Alloa Advertiser* 17th August 1940

[35] *Alloa Journal* 7th September 1940

[36] *Alloa Advertiser* 5th April 1941

[37] *Alloa Journal* 5th April 1941

[38] The King's Own Scottish Borderers were stationed fairly locally

[39] *Alloa Advertiser* 4th April 1942

[40] *Alloa Journal* 4th April 1942

[41] *Alloa Journal* 11th April 1943

[42] *Alloa Journal* 10th July 1943

[43] *Alloa Journal* 5th April 1944

[44] *Alloa Journal* 26th August 1944

[45] *Alloa Journal* 9th September 1944

[46] *Alloa Journal* 19th June 1945

[47] There was in fact a Clackmannan County player who turned out in this match; L/Sergeant J.P. McGhee played for the 'Services Eleven' and scored 3 runs

[48] Alloa Golf Club Council minutes 17th July 1939

[49] Alloa Golf Club Council minutes 1st April 1940

[50] Alloa Golf Club Council minutes 17th June 1940

[51] Alloa Golf Club Council minutes 5th December 1940

[52] Alloa Golf Club Council minutes 2nd July 1941

[53] Alloa Golf Club Council minutes 10th September 1941

[54] Alloa Golf Club Council minutes 2nd April 1941

[55] Alloa Golf Club Council minutes 13th November 1942

[56] Alloa Golf Club Council minutes 2nd February 1940

[57] Alloa Golf Club Council minutes 27th February 1940

[58] *Alloa Journal* 28th February 1942

[59] Alloa Golf Club Council minutes 26th October 1939

[60] *Alloa Journal* 30th December 1939 and *Alloa Advertiser* 13th January 1940

[61] Alloa Golf Club Council minutes 2nd February 1940

[62] Alloa Golf Club Council minutes 22nd October 1941

[63] Alloa Golf Club Council minutes 5th December 1940

[64] Alloa Golf Club Council minutes 30th January 1941

[65] *Alloa Journal* 21st February 1942

[66] Alloa Golf Club Council minutes 9th February 1942

[67] Alloa Golf Club Council minutes 7th February 1944

[68] Alloa Golf Club Council minutes 30th January 1941

[69] Alloa Golf Club Council minutes 22nd October 1941

[70] Alloa Golf Club Council minutes 13th November 1942

[71] Alloa Golf Club Council minutes 6th February 1943

[72] *Alloa Journal* 3rd March 1945

[73] Alloa Golf Club Council minutes 2nd April 1942 and *Alloa Advertiser* 28th March 1942

[74] Alec Moffat and Don Laurence, *Alloa Golf Club: A Centenary History* (1991). Back sometime in the 1980s, playing a round of golf with Alec, he showed me exactly where the bomb dropped; there's not a sign of it now!

[75] *Alloa Journal* 7th December 1940

[76] *Alloa Advertiser* 10th February 1940

[77] *Alloa Journal* 10th February 1940

[78] *Alloa Advertiser* 15th February 1941

[79] *Alloa Journal* 12th April 1941

[80] *Alloa Advertiser* 15th November 1941

[81] *Alloa Advertiser* 7th March 1942

[82] *Alloa Journal* 13th January 1943

[83] *Alloa Advertiser* 13th February 1943

[84] *Alloa Journal* 18th March 1944

[85] *Alloa Journal* 3rd February 1945

[86] *Alloa Journal* 2nd March 1946

[87] Alloa Bowling Club Committee minutes 20th September 1939

[88] Alloa Bowling Club Committee minutes 7th November 1939

[89] Alloa Bowling Club Committee minutes 7th March 1940

[90] Alloa Bowling Club Committee minutes 24th March 1941

[91] *Alloa Journal* 29th March 1941

[92] Alloa Bowling Club Committee minutes 10th May 1941

[93] *Alloa Journal* 27th March 1943

[94] *Alloa Journal* 25th March 1944

[95] Alloa Bowling Club Committee minutes 22nd March 1944

[96] *Alloa Journal* 28th October 1939

[97] Alloa Norwood Ladies Swimming Club Committee minutes 20th April 1940

[98] *Alloa Advertiser* 27th April 1940

[99] *Alloa Advertiser* 13th May 1940

[100] *Alloa Journal* 8th March 1941

[101] *Alloa Circular* 4th March 1942

[102] Alloa Burgh Council minute book 2nd August 1943

[103] *Alloa Journal* 24th July 1943

[104] *Alloa Journal* 28th October 1944

CHAPTER 5

WOMEN AT WAR

During the Great War Alloa had been lucky to have a couple of women in very prominent positions within the community; Lady Violet Erskine, Countess of Mar and Dr Ethel Cassie, both of whom, in many different ways, had led from the front. However, by the time of the Second World War, Lady Violet Mar had died, aged 70 in 1938, and of course, Dr Cassie had already left the Burgh Council's employment in 1918.[1] They were not replaced by any similar outstanding individual female leaders. Maybe though, by 1939 that need was less; during the Great War, the mobilisation of women into war work and/or taking a lead in the community, seemed almost to be a revolutionary thing; but by the time of the Second World War, it was just about taken for granted that women of any rank would have a major part to play in fitting into the demands of the country in whatever role the government decided.

What maybe is surprising is the length of time that the government took in actually bringing about the mobilisation of this vital labour force to meet the needs of the military or the wartime economy. It did seem that they had a reluctance to break with conventional attitudes towards what a woman's role was, especially if they were married and had families. To start with therefore, after 18 months of war, the government targeted unmarried young women to be more intensively involved in war duties. In April 1941 the government introduced registration of women at labour exchanges, just like men had to. The *Advertiser* carried a notice about 'Girls born in 1920 registering for war work'.[2] Then it just went like the men; every month a different year group registered. In June 1941 the *Advertiser* reported for Alloa that 'women born in 1918 registered at employment exchanges. 217 compared to 261 for the 1919 class and 391 for the 1920 class'.[3] In September 1941 the *Journal* reported that 'Women born in 1915, many with babies in their arms, registered at labour exchanges' and 'At Alloa, there were 200 registrations'.[4] None of this was compulsory yet in the sense that these young women were **not** being forced to join up, they were simply registering so that the government knew how many of them there were; but everyone could see where it was heading. By August 1941 it can be seen from the tone of the short article in the *Advertiser* that there was serious support / expectation for the idea of some sort of enlistment for women.[5]

RECRUITMENT OF WOMEN.—Efforts to encourage the recruitment of women war workers are being steadily intensified. Disappointment at the comparative slowness of response so far is admitted frankly by Ministerial authorities. The possibility of the use of compulsory powers cannot be altogether dismissed, but a strong feeling exists against the application to women of such rigorous methods as real conscription would entail. Views on this subject are conflicting, and the advocates of compulsion are frequently women themselves.

Alloa Circular 21st August 1941

JOBS FOR WOMEN.—No responsible person questions the fact that the women of the country are making a worthy contribution to the nation's war effort. In the Services, in industry, in welfare activities and other directions they are playing a notable part, but it has become increasingly clear that the business of mobilising women for war work now demands greater attention than ever with the available surplus man-power now to vanishing point. In the Services alone, it is estimated that 100,000 recruits are still wanted, the A.T.S. being in more need than the other two branches at the moment. The Parliamentary Secretary to the Ministry of Labour has made it clear that although there is no conscription of women for the Forces in the normally accepted use of that word, there is certainly compulsion for war work, and compulsion is to be applied in cases where it is necessary.

Alloa Advertiser 30th August 1941

By November 1941 the *Advertiser's* editorial column was echoing this; recognising the value of the Minister of Labour Mr Bevin's latest actions in '... extending to women between 20 and 30 years of age the provisions of the Restriction of Engagement Order under which no woman can obtain a post or change her occupation except through the Employment Exchange'.[6] The *Advertiser* admitted that women at that moment of time could not be forced to enter the auxiliary services but it must have been little surprise when, in December 1941, the government introduced the National Service Act (no 2) which effectively was conscription of women aged 20-30. They had to choose whether to enter the armed forces or go into farming or industry. In the same month, speaking for the government, Arthur Woodburn MP gave a speech in Alloa where he rounded out the details of this new policy; 'Referring to the calling up of girls and women, Mr Woodburn said that those who had no domestic ties would be sent where required. A girl who had domestic responsibilities would be sent later and would get the preference of a job near home. Married women were not being called up at present and married women with children would be the last to be called up'.[7] Mr Woodburn may have felt he was doing the right and fair thing in laying out this policy, but he got some flak from the local Trades Council who were alarmed at the idea that Alloa girls might be sent to England. His reply was that 'All Alloa women who are classified as "mobile" are being sent for training for employment in their own neighbourhood on important work' and that 'only one girl, at her own request, had gone to England'.[8]

With reference to the earlier point about going into farming, there was almost no information available concerning the role of the local Women's Land Army. The first reference in the press was in the *Circular* in June 1943 with the notification of the establishment of Woodside hostel in Cambus.[9]

WOMEN'S LAND ARMY

The Department of Agriculture for Scotland have taken a lease of Woodside, Cambus, occupied for so long by the late Mr Ralph W. Knox, and have converted it into a Hostel for the Women's Land Army. Accommodation is provided for 24 girls, who will be available for work on the land. The Land Army are doing excellent work and farmers are finding that the shortage of skilled labour, coupled with increased tillage, is making them indispensable on the farms. Farmers requiring the services of the girls are advised to apply to the Secretary of the Agricultural Executive Committee, 24 King Street, Stirling.

Alloa Circular 23rd June 1943

There was nothing else in the local press about these girls until June 1944 when the *Journal* reported that there had been a truck accident on the Alloa-Stirling road in which 7 Land Army girls were injured. They were on their way from Cambus to their various farms for their duties;[10] they may not though, have been Alloa girls. Other sources do give a picture of the life of these girls, especially Sadie Russell from Menstrie who was stationed at Woodside hostel.[11]

From 1942 onwards there are several press references to the importance of women in the workplace; the *Journal*'s editorial at the beginning of March 1942 praised women's service... 'The spirit with which women have already answered the call has provided a spontaneous demonstration of courage and self-sacrifice'.[12]

One interviewee in the *Alloa Docks Oral History Project* proudly remembered women's work at the yards... 'my wife, she was sent there into the shipbuilding. She was a welder. I'd say about 85% of the welders were women... they only got six weeks training. They were really good'.[13] Another interviewee was proud of her achievement but felt something was wrong with attitudes... 'We were in the welding school for a fortnight and then the foreman of the welders came to watch and we had to do a test for him. The first job I got when I went down was down the overhead lap under the boat, the tank landing craft, and you had to do three rows of welding. It was an hourly rate and we were paid weekly. I felt that I was doing the same job as the time-served men but I wisnae getting the pay he was getting'.[14]

At the end of December 1943, the *Circular* had a long editorial giving a glowing endorsement of the role of women in the war effort, under the heading 'Home Front Heroines'[15] which started with the comment that 'In years to come we shall look back at the dark days of total war and say 'we couldn't have won it without the women''. After much fulsome praising of almost

THE call to national service has introduced many 'thousands of men and women to unfamiliar work demanding the maximum output of effort and energy. It is part of that national duty to maintain a standard of health and fitness fully equal to the task.

In achieving this purpose delicious 'Ovaltine' will prove a great help. Prepared from Nature's best foods, 'Ovaltine' provides easily assimilated and revitalising nourishment to body, brain and nerves.

Taken at mealtimes or during morning and afternoon 'breaks,' 'Ovaltine' quickly helps to renew strength and energy and guard against undue fatigue. 'Ovaltine' at bedtime is the world's most popular aid to the enjoyment of restful, restorative sleep.

For these reasons make 'Ovaltine' your constant stand-by. If milk is not available it can be made with water only as 'Ovaltine' itself contains milk. 'Ovaltine' also has the advantage of being naturally sweet so that there is no need to add sugar.

Here's the Extra Energy you Need

Ovaltine
Restores Strengthens & Sustains

Prices in Gt. Britain and N. Ireland, 1/1, 1/10 and 3/3
P.6071a

Alloa Circular 27th January 1943

every wartime role that women could possibly have, it ended 'Let us vow to never forget the part they too have played in the defence of all we hold sacred'. From a modern perspective it looks rather propagandised but as a New Year's message for 1944 it was probably well meant. Its message was not that far away from a letter printed in the *Journal* in November 1945, when the war really was over. It was a farewell letter from B.W. Silverwood who for the past 2½ years had been in charge of Kelliebank Shipyard Welding School. He referred to the last three years of the war when he wrote 'approximately 300 of your County's girls have achieved the difficult task of transforming themselves from clerks and typists into experienced and highly skilled welders in from one to three weeks...

I shall always remember the excellent contribution to the common war effort made by Scottish girlhood'.[16]

It was always going to be difficult finding detailed information about the role of any specific Alloa women in the military side of the actual war effort, but the Imperial War Museum does have a collection of undated pictures taken by the RAF Official Photographer. These highlight the work of 'Leading Aircraftwoman S. Harrison of Alloa', a flight mechanic who prepared fighter planes for action. The caption further noted that 'She formerly worked in a fireclay factory'.[17]

In all the evidence in the local press, there were few signs of moral judgements on the behaviour of any of the people of Alloa during their wartime struggles, as there sometimes had been during the First World War; maybe the accusation made in January 1944 about the previous year's rise in juvenile criminality being due to poor parenting was a rare example. Equally, many Alloa women remembered the war as a time of opportunity and gaining new respect in the work place; but there were no reports of any decline in their morals. The single reference to this issue was in the *Alloa Docks Oral History Project*, where one interviewee claimed about Harlands that 'You had a lot of women working on night shift and day shift. A lot of things went on that some of the women's husbands wouldn't like to know about'.[18] Then, with so many Polish soldiers stationed in the area, it was no surprise that connections were made with local girls and marriages were registered. The local press never took a moral tone over this.

Alloa also had a few 'GI brides'; where Alloa women had gone off elsewhere in the UK to help the war effort and met foreign servicemen who they then married; who then went home themselves and their bride followed. No-one was keeping a count of these but a few got into the local press. The first was on 23rd February 1946 when the *Journal* noted the story of 'Alloa's GI bride'. She was Peggy Combs [nee Seton] originally from 237 Ashley Terrace who 'with her nine-month old baby boy, was among 1,700 GI brides who recently boarded the 81,000 ton *Queen Mary*, bound for the United States'.[19] She had been in the WAAFs, had met her husband [a lieutenant in the 9th US Air Force] and married him in St Mungo's Church in March 1944. Three months later the *Journal* reported on another Alloa girl who was a GI bride, this time going to Canada.[20]

It's clear that many Alloa women moved out of their traditional roles and played a vital part in helping win the war; but not many people asked the question about what their future post-war role might be. One group that did was the newly-founded Alloa and District Business and Professional Women's Club. This was set up in December 1944 with 37 founder members. Among its very modern-sounding aims were encouraging in businesswomen a realisation of their responsibilities in their own country… and the removal of sex discrimination in employment opportunities, promotion and pay. They believed they were not an 'aggressive feminine organisation' but wanted to play their part in the everyday affairs of the country.[21] Alloa's MP Arthur Woodburn was present at the inaugural meeting and the *Circular* reported his view that 'The present war has shown that they can do and have done men's jobs in the office, factory and shop, as well as running their own homes at the same time'. He further added that organisations like this one 'were going to be of great value in the post-war era'.

The twice-monthly meetings of this club showed how much Alloa's women were indeed concerned about the post-war future of Scotland. In December 1944 they invited the Clackmannan County Planner Mr Shearer to give a talk on future local housing developments[22] and had further discussions in February and March 1945 about the housing types and locations, the types of flooring, water supply and quality of building.[23] The Club was also very concerned about promoting the case for Prestwick Airport to become the aerodrome for international flights from Scotland; and also about when a Forth Road Bridge might be built.[24] They clearly had a firm idea of women's importance in shaping developments in post-war Scotland.

In April 1945, The *Circular*'s editorial raised this same issue of women's future role, and expressed the view that 'To women particularly, VE Day will bring fresh duties and responsibilities'[25] which maybe optimistically suggested the *Circular*'s recognition of the post-war continuation of women's new role and importance in society. Unfortunately the editorial then rather ruined its progressive tone by continuing with the comment that 'women may claim to have little interest in the broader political issues – but few will be uninterested in their homes, in the health and education of their children. On these subjects they not only have the right, but the responsibility, to make their views known'. So that's the *Circular* put them right back where it thinks they belong then; looking after the family!

Alloa lost two of its female citizens as civilian casualties during the Second

WAR CASUALTIES

KILLED IN LONDON

Nurse Margaret Johnstone

Intimation was received last Saturday morning by Mr Thomas Johnstone, 5 Clackmannan Road, Alloa, that his sister, Nurse Margaret Johnstone, had been killed by enemy action over London. Before going to London, Nurse Johnstone carried on a small dressmaker's business in Clackmannan Road. The funeral was of a private nature and took place on Wednesday afternoon to Sunnyside Cemetery. Rev. Dr. C. Robson conducted the service in the house and Rev. W. Francis Gibbons, B.D., officiated at the graveside. There were many wreaths and flowers sent by relatives and friends.

Alloa Circular 9th October 1940

Margaret Johnstone's grave in Sunnyside Cemetery. Her name was added on to her parents' gravestone where she was referred to as Meg, and the date of her death is given.[26]

World War: the names of both are inscribed at the end of the Second World War panels on Alloa's War memorial.

Nurse Margaret Johnstone was a civilian casualty in London. She was 43 years old when she was killed in an air raid on 28th September 1940. Details of her death were in the *Advertiser* and *Journal* of 5th October 1940. The *Journal* was more detailed; that she came from 6 Clackmannan Road, had volunteered as a nurse in 1939 'for the duration' and was serving in London. There was an air raid that seemed to last all night and between five and six o'clock in the morning, shortly before the 'All Clear' was sounded a bomb dropped on the clinic where she was serving, penetrating the roof and upper floors of the building. She and five other people were sheltering on the ground floor and she was the only casualty. 'She was killed in her sleep and never recovered consciousness'.[27] She was buried at Sunnyside Cemetery on 2nd October 1940. She was a member of Moncrieff Church in Alloa and her name is on their memorial to the members of the congregation who were lost in the Second World War.

The cemetery's grave register records that she was killed in 'West end Hospital, London' and that she was buried in the same lair as her parents, both of whom pre-deceased her.

Detail from funeral/grave registers at Sunnyside Cemetery

Detail from funeral/grave registers at Sunnyside Cemetery

Elizabeth Hatch Boyd was a civilian casualty of the Blitz in Birmingham. She was born on 16th August 1918 and lived at 33 Mitchell Crescent. She went to South School then Alloa Academy [Admission No. 2952, joined the school on 1st September 1931]. She was only at the Academy for 2 years; the admissions register recorded that she left because she had obtained a 'situation'.

Alloa Academy Roll of Honour

KILLED IN AIR RAID.—Mr and Mrs W. J. Boyd, Mitchell Crescent, Alloa, have received intimation that their daughter, Elizabeth, was killed during an air raid on Birmingham on Monday. Previous to going on munition work some months ago, Miss Boyd was in the employment of the Alloa Co-operative Society, Limited, first in the fruit shop in Drysdale Street, and latterly in the confectionery shop in Mill Street.

Alloa Journal 1st August 1942

The *Journal* on 1st August 1942 noted that 'Elizabeth Boyd was killed in an air raid last Monday'. The *Circular* was a little more detailed; recording of the death, that it was 'At Birmingham, on 29th July, as a result of enemy action, Elizabeth Hatch Boyd, aged 23'.[28] Her name is on the Roll of Honour of Birmingham People killed in the Blitz; the Commonwealth War Graves Commission also lists her death as a civilian casualty.[29] The raid on the night of 27th April 1942 was the last significant raid on Birmingham. It was carried out by between 60-70 German bombers, and bombs were dropped on 12 named areas of Birmingham including Bordesley Green, an inner-city area, about 2 miles east of the town centre. This area contained factories like Mulliners Cars [which later made ammunition] and BSA [Birmingham Small Arms]. CWGC records claim that she died at 29 Marchmont Road, a residential area of Bordesley Green. This suggests a possibility that she died where she was living, not whilst she was actually working in a munitions factory itself.

Elizabeth Boyd's grave in Sunnyside Cemetery

In fact, the smaller *In Memoriam* stone in front of her main gravestone suggests that her work was in military motor transport rather than munitions; it states

Detail from funeral/grave registers at Sunnyside Cemetery

Detail from lower stone at Elizabeth Boyd's grave in Sunnyside Cemetery

'She endeared herself to her newfound friends who sorrowfully mourn her passing. Morris Commercial Cars Ltd, Birmingham. 28th July 1942'. There was no specific reference to her funeral in the local press, but she was buried at Sunnyside Cemetery. The cemetery's grave register records the burial occurring on 1st August 1942 and gives the cause of death as 'War Operation'.[30]

ENDNOTES

[1] Violet, Countess of Mar died on 16 December 1938 aged 70. Her husband the 13th Earl of Mar was 74 at the start of the war... he died aged 90. Dr Cassie accepted a permanent post as MOH in Leith, because Alloa Burgh Council, knowing that they were obliged to re-employ Dr Finlator after his war service, was unable to offer her a permanent position.

[2] *Alloa Advertiser* 19th April 1941

[3] *Alloa Advertiser* 21st June 1941

[4] *Alloa Journal* 6th September 1941

[5] *Alloa Advertiser* 30th August 1941

[6] *Alloa Advertiser* 8th November 1941

[7] *Alloa Circular* 10th December 1941

[8] *Alloa Circular* 30th September 1942

[9] *Alloa Circular* 24th June 1943

[10] *Alloa Journal* 7th June 1944

[11] *Our War* (2006) p48-49. The Matron of the hostel was Rena Rankine; who gave a talk on her work to the Alloa and District Business and Professional Women's Club. See the minutes of 11th June 1945

[12] *Alloa Journal* 7th March 1942

[13] Alloa Docks Oral History Project 1987; William born 1920

[14] Alloa Docks Oral History Project 1987; Jean born 1925

[15] *Alloa Circular* 29th December 1943

[16] *Alloa Journal* 10th November 1945

[17] Imperial War Museum CH12070 and CH12071

[18] Alloa Docks Oral History Project 1987; Mr D. born 1908

[19] *Alloa Journal* 23rd February 1946

[20] *Alloa Journal* 14th May 1946

[21] *Alloa Circular* 6th December 1944

[22] Alloa and District Business and Professional Women's Club minutes 11th December 1944

[23] Alloa and District Business and Professional Women's Club minutes 12th February 1945 and 12th March 1945

[24] Alloa and District Business and Professional Women's Club minutes 12th February 1945

[25] *Alloa Circular* 25th April 1945

[26] Sunnyside Cemetery register of graves gives her grave reference as Section 12 Grave 181

[27] *Alloa Journal* and *Alloa Advertiser* 5th October 1940.

[28] *Alloa Circular* 5th August 1942

[29] *Alloa Journal* 1st August 1942. She wasn't forgotten; The 31th July 1943 issue of the *Alloa Journal* contained *In Memoriam* notices to Elizabeth Boyd, put in by her sister and a friend

[30] Sunnyside Cemetery register of graves gives her grave reference as Section 13 Grave 380D

CHAPTER 6

DAILY LIFE IN THE WAR

At the time of the Second World War, Alloa had three weekly newspapers; the *Advertiser*, the *Journal* and the *Circular*; the same three that had existed in the Great War. To some people it may be surprising that the major international wartime events got so little coverage in the local press; for instance, there was nothing in them on D-Day or the dropping of the atomic bombs on Japan. It must be recalled though that the Alloa population had clear access to all the daily papers in the national press and this [and the wireless] would have been their first port of call for day-to-day information; after all, the Alloa local press only came out weekly, the first two on Saturday, the *Circular* on Wednesday. Alloa Burgh Council also kept minutes of all its meetings, although its letter books for the time of the Second World War seem to have gone missing. Many other smaller organisations or groups kept records of their meetings and events during the war and this is the chapter where these groups have their say. If they took the trouble to record, at that time, how the war impacted their lives, then I can take the trouble to let their voice be heard. So, the local press, the Burgh Council and the records of a variety of smaller groups are the chief sources used here to create a picture; a miscellany really, of the changing daily life for the people of wartime Alloa. To try to provide a bit of structure to such a diverse and unchronological chapter; it is divided into two sections; the first dealing with all those aspects of a domestic nature, and the second dealing with aspects that had more of a connection with military matters.

DAILY LIFE: ASPECTS OF A DOMESTIC NATURE

ALLOA BURGH COUNCIL

In addition to the areas referred to in Chapter 1, the Burgh Council took a strong interest in organising the town and all its amenities to be run effectively in a state of war. Just as it had been in the Great War, the Town Hall was requisitioned by the military authorities and just as before, the Town Clerk expected payment of debts to the Council.[1] In December 1939 he reported that he had asked the army for compensation for lost income [which was, on average, £424 per year].[2] In what looks a bit like a counter-claim, in April 1940 the Council received a letter from the military authorities asking if they would reconsider the price of gas that they charged to the large number of premises that were occupied by troops. The Council agreed on a flat rate of 2 shillings and 8 pence per 1,000 cubic feet.[3]

In March 1940 the Council had letters of complaint from two badminton clubs who had, for the previous 15 years, used the gymnasium halls. These halls were now being rented out to 'another party for dancing'. What had happened was that there was now a shortage of halls [due to the Army taking over some of those belonging to the Council or local churches] and the badminton clubs found themselves 'priced out' due to the rise in hall rental charges. In essence they were objecting to the Council's attempt to cash in on the demand for halls by putting the prices up.[4]

In March 1940 the Council dealt with a request from the military authorities to use part of the ground immediately south of Gartmorn Dam as a practice range for 2 inch mortars. This was agreed to, as long as the military put up warning notices and posted men to warn people when there were practices.[5]

The Council led the way in the collection of scrap iron for munitions purposes. In September 1939 its Works Committee was told to organise the collection of railings for scrap iron.[6] Then, in March 1941 the Burgh Surveyor was told to really get moving on the salvaging of the scrap iron from railings on all Council properties and 'any voluntary surrender of railings from householders'.[7] By January 1942 there was some evidence of an attempt to increase the effectiveness of local salvage campaigns for both metal and paper[8] and in February 1942 the Council put notices in the *Advertiser* about the requisitioning of unnecessary railings.[9] There was an article in the *Journal* in

January 1942 which painted an optimistic picture of the success of the salvage campaign so far, noting an increase in the amount of paper, scrap metal, glass and bones that the Council had collected, and that it was round about 2 tons per 1,000 of the Alloa population.[10] It went on to note that 'Mr Cairns, the Surveyor, his staff and the public are to be congratulated on this highly satisfactory increase'. However, you do get the impression that the Burgh of Alloa's salvage record was actually not that impressive. In January 1944 the *Advertiser* reported that a total of £4,738 had been raised so far through salvage.[11] This was made up of £489 in 1940, £795 in 1941, £1,690 in 1942 and £1,771 in 1943. This figure was rising annually, but didn't seem very high compared to the figures for other burghs.

WAR SAVINGS

The people of Alloa had made a terrific contribution to National War Savings during the Great War; they had even been rewarded with the gift of a tank for their efforts. They made great savings efforts in the Second World War also, prompted partly one suspects by the memory of their earlier success, but also by the constant barrage of propaganda for savings in the local press. In December 1939 the *Advertiser* had a great big advert for National War Savings; half of page 5 was taken up with it.[12]

Then in the first months of 1940 the *Advertiser* had a regular series of war savings posters; often quite varied in their approach and appeal.[13]

THE NATION'S WAR SAVINGS CAMPAIGN

The Chancellor of the Exchequer announces the issue of two Gilt-Edged Securities

[I]

A NEW INVESTMENT
3 per cent.
DEFENCE BONDS

(Post Office and Trustee Savings Banks Issue)

On sale in denominations of £5 and multiples of £5. The Bonds bear interest at the rate of 3 per cent. per annum: Income Tax is not deducted at the source. They are repayable 7 years from date of purchase at par plus a premium of £1 for each £100 nominal value with interest accrued since the last half-year's payment.

On 6 months' notice holders can claim repayment at par with interest due to date. In case of urgent need repayment can be arranged on special terms within a few days. Individual holdings are limited to £1000. On sale at Post Offices and Banks.

Alloa Advertiser 2nd December 1939

ABOVE: War Savings Week in Alloa 1940
RIGHT: *Alloa Journal* 6th April 1940
BELOW: *Alloa Advertiser* 20th July 1940

It was during this mid-1940 period that the local press does give the impression that the country was going through a bad time; the Government's National Savings propaganda poster at the end of July had the less-than-optimistic 'Grimly Determined' heading.[14]

In the big annual one-off appeals for savings, the Council generally led the way. It decided in February 1941 that it would promote a 'War Weapons' week and began to make arrangements for military marches, National Savings promotional literature, procuring war weapons for everyone to see etc. To start off with its target was a savings/investment of £100,000. It had heard that Kirkcaldy had procured a shot-down Messerschmitt and was determined to do something similar for Alloa.[15] By the beginning of March it had confirmed that such a plane would be available, plus the possibility of a bren-gun display.[16] The Council now began to get more ambitious and more than doubled its target for the County to £250,000.[17] The *Advertiser* editorial on 22nd March was concerned that the Clackmannanshire people were going to be the victims of the Council's excessive pride in asking for more than could be delivered. It made the best of it with the double-edged comment that '30,000 people held to ransom for a cool quarter-million. It's the biggest hold-up in history, but freedom's cheap at the price. Pay up and smile'.

The *Journal* took a slightly more positive stance, acknowledging that 'a quarter of a million is a big sum of money...' but 'Clackmannan County has an opportunity this week to make history and maintain its reputation for patriotism'.[18]

In March 1941 the Council agreed to support the fund-raising with the purchase of £10,000 worth of government bonds. £7000 was to come out of the Gas Account and £3,000 out of Burgh funds.[19] The Messerschmitt was placed in the playground of South School and people were charged 6 [old] pence per visit; this raised over £40. The *Advertiser*'s reporter was surprised that there was little attempt to stop hundreds of school boys from clambering all over it and said 'he formed the impression that the disintegration – begun in the air – would be vastly accelerated on the ground before the week was out'.[20] There were military marches and parades, displays of weapons in the gas showrooms and speeches in the West End Park and the use of a cinema van. By the end of

CLACKMANNAN COUNTY

WAR WEAPONS WEEK

SATURDAY
22nd MARCH
TO
SATURDAY
29th MARCH

●

AIM:

£250.000

●

Alloa Journal 15th March 1941

the campaign the Council's ideas on financial targeting had been proven to be more than right. The *Advertiser*'s headline was 'War Weapons Week – a Brilliant success' followed by 'Magnificent response in town and county – £262,886 subscribed in 5 days'. That all helped towards an Alloa and Clackmannanshire total of £336,336 for that week.[21]

In November 1941 the Council agreed to support 'Warship Week' during the following April 1942; it had hoped to be able to 'adopt a warship'[22] but by February 1942 its new target was to raise enough to adopt a submarine.[23] In March 1942 the Council agreed to contribute to 'Warship Week' with an investment of £5,000[24] and agreed that the County target should be £200,000[25] which was raised to £250,000 two weeks later.[26]

Amongst the fund-raising events were a 3-day display of a Fleet Air Arm Swordfish aeroplane with torpedo attached in Mar Place, South School hosted a naval exhibition and there were daily lectures by naval personnel and a cinema van. Another fundraiser was to try to get 'a mile of pennies' on the pavement; starting at the war memorial and heading into town then up Primrose Street. This would be guarded by the scouts.[27] The

Alloa Advertiser 22nd March 1941

ABOVE: *Alloa Journal* 4th April 1942
RIGHT: *Alloa Journal* 11th April 1942

following week's paper revealed it raised £73... which was in fact nowhere near the notional figure for what a mile should actually have raised, but it was 'a very satisfactory financial result and a worthwhile experiment'.[28] Another gimmick was to have a big barometer of savings in front of the municipal buildings, where a local dignitary, once a day, adjusted the figures to show what had been saved.

(l. to r.) Mr A. R. Proctor, Mr G. Izatt, Mr J Lennox, Mr R. W. Knox, Mr A. C. Marshall (Organiser), Mr J. W. Napier (Chairman), Mr C. A. Atchley, Provost McKinlay, Alloa, Provost Scott, Dollar, and Mr J. Paterson.

THE ·DAILY BAROMETER.

The giant barometer in front of Alloa Municipal Buildings has recorded the total realised day by day. The figures were: —

Saturday,	... ...	£68,993.
Monday,	... ...	£107,374.
Tuesday,	... ...	£175,553.
Wednesday,	...	£226,216.
Thursday,	... ...	£259,147.

ABOVE: *Alloa Journal* 18th April 1942

LEFT: *Alloa Journal* 29th March 1942

BELOW LEFT: *Alloa Journal* 18th April 1942 in front of the war memorial

BELOW RIGHT: *Alloa Advertiser* 20th April 1942

COUNTY WARSHIP WEEK

THE OPENING CEREMONY

Magnificent Daily Response

£250,000 TARGET SMASHED BY THURSDAY

The Clackmannan County Warship Week, which closes to-night has been a magnificent success, the augmented target of £250,000 having been smashed by Thursday.

Opening Ceremony—Lord Mar Takes The Salute.

Left to right—Rear-Admiral Benson, D.S.O., Lady Balfour of Burleigh, Lord Balfour of Burleigh. Mr J. W. Napier, M.B.E. (*Chairman*), The Earl of Mar & Kellie, K.T., Viscount Younger of Leckie, D.S.O., Mr Arthur Woodburn, M.P.

Alloa special constables on parade (Allen Barnett)

A very peaceful looking Alloa in 1943, right in the middle of the War

'Warship Week' raised £259,000 within the County in its first five days and by the time it was over the *Advertiser* proudly announced that a total of £391,000 had been reached.[29] In May 1943 a short article in the *Advertiser* noted that HM submarine *Ultimatum* was the one adopted by the County after 'Warship Week'.[30]

The big savings campaign for 1943 would be 'Wings for Victory' week; the Council agreed this would have a £250,000 target.[31] There would be an RAF grand football match, concerts, a dance, plus an RAF exhibition.[32] The people of Alloa and Clackmannanshire responded with their typical enthusiasm; £235,000 was subscribed in the first 5 days[33] and the final figure for the County was all but £402,000.[34]

Alloa Circular 31st March 1943

Alloa Advertiser 28th March 1943

The pupils of Sunnyside School committed savings of £1,170 which was more than every other primary school in the burgh added together. In October 1943 there was a big meeting where the Air Ministry sent a delegation to thank Alloa for its 'Wings for Victory' total.[35] It was estimated that £400,000 represented the cost of ten 4-engined bombers and eight 8000 pound bombs.

"WINGS FOR VICTORY" WEEK

The Opening Ceremony

NEARING TARGET ON THURSDAY

The Clackmannan County "Wings for Victory" Week, which closes to-night, has been well supported in all parts of the County and it is certain that the target of £250,000 will be well smashed.

PHOTO BY CUMMINGS, ALLOA.

Left to Right—PROVOST McKINLAY, CAPTAIN J. P. YOUNGER, SHERIFF MACONOCHIE, Mr ARTHUR WOODBURN, M.P., Mr A. C. MURRAY, (Chairman), THE EARL OF MAR AND KELLIE, K.T., CAPTAIN J. LINDSAY, R.N., GENERAL DUCH, COLONEL WZACNY.

Alloa Journal 10th April 1943 in front of the war memorial

Wing Commander Edge from the Air Ministry presented the Burgh Council with a plaque but over the years it seems to have been mislaid. Similar plaques given to nearby Larbert for its war savings efforts still hang in the Dobbie Hall… where is Alloa's?

Certificate of honour for the Kilncraigs Savings group

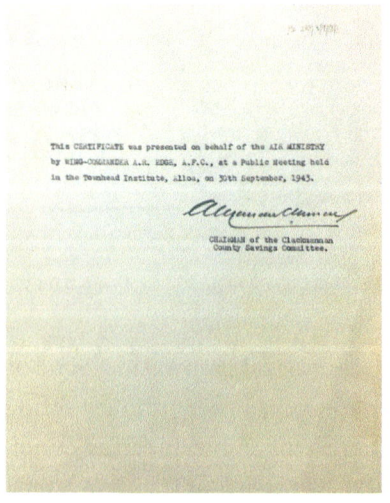

Obverse of certificate

1944's big savings effort was directed towards 'Salute the Soldier' week. Buoyed up by their over-achievement in the earlier savings efforts, the Council this time took the decision to try to raise £400,000; that would be the cost of equipping a battalion of the Argylls for one year.[36] In March 1944 the Council agreed to support this campaign with a contribution of £7,500, taken from the Burgh Department Sinking fund; it was to be invested in 2.5% National War Bonds 1952-54.[37]

Alloa Advertiser 18th March 1944

Alloa Advertiser 18th March 1944

There was the normal range of marches and processions but a highlight was the display in the gas showrooms where viewers could see twin bren-guns, a Vickers machine gun and a 4.2 inch mortar which had a range of 2 miles. Things went well with the fund-raising; by the end of the 5th day it reached £368,291.[38] On 10th April 1944 it was reported to the Council that £461,082 had been raised within the County during this week.

Alloa Advertiser
18th March 1944

Alloa Advertiser 25th March 1944

RATIONING

With that knowledge that comes from having lived through one war already and knowing what has to be done, the issue of rationing did not take long to appear. The *Circular* noted in the first week of the war that there was a 'Ban on Food hoarding – Offence to purchase more than a week's supply'.[39] Within a fortnight of the start of the war the *Journal* noted that petrol rationing would start on 16th September,[40] and within less than a month after the outbreak of war, the *Advertiser* commented that the question of food rationing 'is now looming on the horizon of war economy'. It stated that 'While in some cases attempts have already been made to anticipate the government's order, the official view is that rationing will not commence until the compilation of the National Register has been completed'.[41] The issue of ration books was to be under the charge of local Food Control Committees.[42] In early November 1939 there was a warning in the *Advertiser* that the Food Minister W.S. Morrison had said rationing would start but not before the middle of next month. It would be introduced in instalments... but butter and bacon would be two foodstuffs high on the list for rationing since mostly it came from northern Europe.[43]

Alloa Advertiser 4th November 1939

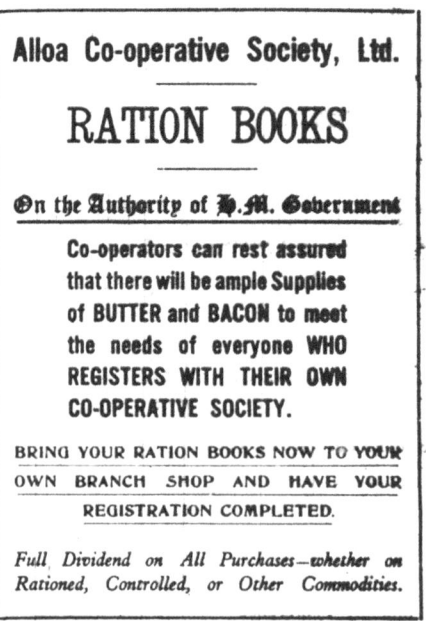

Alloa Journal 18th November 1939

In January 1940 meat rationing was ready to begin and everyone was told to register with a butcher. There was a big advert on the front of the *Advertiser*.[44] It was stoical about the impact of rationing, noting in its editorial that 'ration books are now presumably bereft of their first coupons... the transition to the dictatorship of the coupon has been effected with smoothness... rationing is a necessary part of the war economy and it should accepted with due philosophy...'[45] Butter, sugar and bacon were the first three goods that were rationed.

Alloa Advertiser 6th January 1940

Alloa Circular 13th March 1940

Alloa Advertiser January 1940

However, things could get tough; In February 1940, even before meat rationing actually began the *Journal* noted that 'this week there has been a decided shortage of beef in the town. On Thursday, 20 cattle were allocated to the county, to be divided between 28 butchers. There is also plenty of mutton'. The shortage was caused partly by the state of the roads in the iced-up conditions which stopped cattle reaching the market.[46] On 9th March the *Journal* had a big poster advising that meat rationing was to begin fully on 11th March. Adults were to get 1 shilling and 10 pence's worth of meat a week; children were to get 11 pence's worth.[47] Then in July the *Journal* announced that 'margarine and cooking fats would be the next things to be rationed... starting on Monday'.[48]

Clothes rationing with a points system was introduced on 1st June 1941 and almost seemed to go through without comment from the local press. In August the *Advertiser* reported that the 'experience of traders in the area indicate that there has been no rush for the new clothes ration cards. The numbers issued since they became available last week have been small and reflect a large measure of voluntary rationing even if the original allocation of 25 coupons for the first eleven weeks of the scheme was generous…'[49]

There seemed more concern about the threat of the tightening up on petrol rationing. The *Circular* noted in May 1940 that 'The Nazi invasion of Holland and Belgium has killed motorists' hopes of getting extra petrol. Planes and tanks are using thousands of gallons every day and naturally the Ministry of Mines will do everything possible to conserve supplies at home'.[50] Things worsened; there had been a warning in mid-1941 that the ration would be halved,[51] but by November came the threat that petrol rations would be likely to be abolished altogether.[52]

Indeed, on the rationing front things got worse in every direction. In July 1941 it was reported that 'the supply of coal to domestic consumers is now limited to one ton a month'.[53] By July 1942 there was a major push on economising on coal with a big notice on the front page of the *Advertiser* explaining 'Why We Must Save Coal Now'.[54]

The *Journal* chipped in with the view that 'it takes 250 tons of coal to turn out one heavy tank… multiply these 250 tons by the number of heavy tanks we need… and the necessity of the fuel economy drive becomes obvious'.[55] Two months later there was a massive poster on page 4 about meeting targets for fuel consumption… 'The demands of total war make it essential that we should use less fuel in our homes'.[56]

Alloa Advertiser 4th July 1942

Things continued to worsen; soap rationing had started on 9th February 1942, the *Journal* claiming that 'the oils and fats used in soap manufacture occupy much shipping space and some of this must be saved for food'.[57] Then in April came the introduction of the new wholemeal 'National Bread' and the view that 'it was generally being well received by the local people, despite its darker colour'.[58]

April 1942 also saw a warning that there was going to be a cut in clothing coupons.[59] The *Journal* confirmed this, saying that new clothes rationing books would be coming out and that the new scheme would start on 1st June, because 'war conditions have made necessary a reduction in your clothing ration; and your new supply of 60 coupons is for 14 months'.[60] There was a big notice on the front page of the *Advertiser* about this change in the value of clothing coupons.[61] It did seem that the government slightly relented in September when it showed a recognition that older children might need extra coupons; there was a poster on the *Advertiser*'s front page acknowledging this.[62] The *Journal* gave more detail in its 'Extra coupons for older children are now ready' notice with its allocations to different age groups; basically an entitlement to 10, 20 or 30 extra coupons.[63]

On the food front, the beginning of 1943 saw the announcement that 'there will be less cheese from 7th February when the ordinary ration will be reduced to 4 ounces a week'.[64] The start of 1943 also saw a form of 'rationing' spread into a new part of household life; the *Advertiser* contained its first advert for utility furniture.[65]

The Council must have been happy with the handling of any rationing issues by the Food Control Committee [or whoever] because curiously, for almost the entire war, there was no reference to rationing in the minutes of the Burgh Council. The only reference was in July 1945, when the war in Europe was over, when the Council noted that there had been a complaint about the distribution of new ration books.[66]

A LITTLE LOCAL DISPUTE

Within 9 months of the start of the Great War, there had been a single outbreak of anti-German feeling with the attack on Becher's pork butcher shop in the High St. and the large riotous mob which occurred on 15th May 1915. In a distinct echo of that, within 9 months of the start of the Second World War,

Alloa saw an outbreak of anti-Italian feeling with attacks on 4 Italian shops/cafes in different parts of the town on 10th June 1940. The violence was prompted by the knowledge that Italy had just joined the war on Germany's side. The *Journal* just had a brief report on anti-Italian demonstrations and 'disorderly scenes'[67] but the *Advertiser* really weighed in with a detailed report and some trenchant views about the ignorance of the mob. The *Circular* took a similarly robust view about the actions of the demonstrators; claiming that 'the law does not recognise the right of a self-styled 'patriot' to heave a brick through an alien's shop window'.[68]

The trouble seemed to have been started by a gang of children assembling outside Sibaldi's shop in Castle Street who started by being abusive. This threat 'was soon augmented by a dangerously disposed adult element and with excitement and mob hysteria mounting, the windows of the shop were smashed and considerable damage done to the premises'.[69] J. Pellici in the Mar Place Café suffered a similar but less hostile demonstration where 'various fittings were damaged'. Later that evening there was 'further rioting outside the premises of Flavio Toma in the High Street which was dispersed by the police'. At the same time there was a small demonstration outside J. Fusco's shop in Mill Street.[70]

The *Advertiser* in its editorial showed that it had no time for this sort of thing. It called it 'gangster belligerency', argued that it was 'unruly elements' conducting a 'kind of blitzkrieg' and that 'such methods are more appropriate to the enemy we are trying to overthrow'. It argued that the demonstrations were unpatriotic, that mostly the damage was done by 'mere hooligans' and, in a prescient comment, noted that it would have to be paid for by insurance companies or ratepayers.[71]

A fortnight after the first incident, a local

Alloa Advertiser

SATURDAY, 15th JUNE, 1940.

Anti-Italian Demonstrations

Up till Monday evening of this week Alloa and district might have been termed an ordinary peaceful section of the home front but events on that evening and also later in the week appear to have qualified it for the status of "gangster belligerency." We refer, of course, to the undesirable repercussions which followed Italy's entry into the war, an event which seems to have persuaded some unruly elements in the neighbourhood to conduct a kind of blitzkreig against shop premises occupied by Italians. Such methods are more appropriate to the enemy whom we are striving to overthrow than to British citizens; they are not merely undesirable but also unjust and unpatriotic. They are undesirable because they make an unwelcome addition to the heavy responsibilities of the police who are speedily rounding up all aliens whose behaviour has given any ground for suspicion. They are unjust because the great majority of Italians in this country, many of them being long resident and law-abiding citizens, have more sympathy with the Allies than with the enemy and if they had had any influence would have used it against Italy's intervention. Fifth columnists there may possibly be, but a mob, bent only on blind destruction, is hardly likely to be the most discriminating body to conduct investigations in such matters. The demonstrations are also unpatriotic because they are contrary to the British tradition that private vengeance should not be wreaked by individuals. Finally— if more material considerations must be cited—the outrages are foolish because the mischief done in the course of them —much of it by mere hooligans—will be a liability either to insurance companies in this country or to ratepayers. Belligerency can surely be exercised in more laudable ways or reserved for more appropriate occasions.

Alloa Advertiser 15th June 1940

miner was prosecuted for putting his fist through the window of Flavio Toma's restaurant in 49 High Street. The miner was Hugh Hamilton Watson from East Castle St and he pleaded guilty to the charge of malicious damage. He was fined 21 shillings or 14 days in prison.[72] However, the *Advertiser*'s earlier observation about who would pay came true in October 1940 when the Council considered a claim against them for reparation for damage done through 'riotous and disorderly conduct' on 10th June, the cause being 'the entry of Italy as a belligerent on the side of Germany into the World War'. The claimants were Flavio Toma and Catherine Boyle [recent purchaser of Sibaldi's business]. The claim was for almost £9 damage to windows and £90 worth of theft/destruction to the two shops. The Council was told that a number of persons had already been dealt with in court for the offences, but that was irrelevant to this issue; the Town Clerk said that if either claim could be proved then basically the Council had to pay up.[73] The *Circular* reported in early November that 'In connection with the above claims submitted, it was agreed that a sum of £70 should be paid as a full settlement in the claim by Catherine Boyle. The claim at the instance of Flavio Toma was regarded as being reasonably stated at £8.16/11 and it was agreed that it should be paid in full'.[74]

It was still the case however, that members of the Italian community in Alloa were not treated like other citizens. In October 1941 an Italian restaurateur was fined 30 shillings for offences against the Aliens (Restrictions of Movement) Order. He had been outside of his own residence between the hours of 11 pm and 6 am and was prosecuted. He argued that he had married a Scotswoman in 1912, that he had a son in the RAF, another son in the RA and a daughter in war industries, but this did not count enough in his favour; he had to pay up.[75] Both the *Advertiser* and *Journal* had full reports on this trial and both respected the man's anonymity in their reporting; although surely, given the specific nature of the information that he had used in his defence, it could not have been hard to work out who he was?

ENTERTAINMENT

Alloa had three cinemas during the years of the Second World War; the Gaumont, the Central Picture House and the Pavilion. The Gaumont was opened in April 1939 and was built on the site of the Scala cinema which was there during the Great War from January 1916 onwards.[76] They all put on full selections of all the latest films throughout the war; the most well-advertised was the arrival of *Gone with the Wind* at the Pavilion Theatre in September 1944.[77] All three cinemas were also used as venues for reviews, stage shows, dances, musical events and public lectures and ceremonies.

Other entertainment highlights during the war years were 2 visits to the town hall by Sir Harry Lauder and his concert party. The first was in November 1939 when the *Journal* reported of Harry Lauder that 'for 45 minutes he held his audience...'[78] The *Circular* noted that 'A special treat was served up to the local servicemen on Monday evening when Sir Harry Lauder brought along his Concert Party... The main feature was, of course, Sir Harry himself, who despite the passing of the years stands supreme as Scotland's greatest comedian'.[79] Then in January 1940 he visited again; both the local papers reported on this.[80] The *Advertiser* noted that 'Sir Harry Lauder and his concert party came to Alloa town hall and did a performance for servicemen, to a capacity audience on 4th January 1940'. The vote of thanks was given by Colonel Mitchell, one of the directors of the Alloa Coal Company who was also the County Welfare Officer.

Alloa Circular 15th May 1940

In January 1943 there was a concert in the Pavilion by 'a talented company of Polish soldier artistes'.[81] The *Journal* noted that the concert had pieces from a pianist and also bands and choirs.[82] It also commented that there 'was a very large audience and the building was filled to capacity' and that 'The programme was sustained entirely by Polish talent'.

On 24th April 1943 the Glasgow Orpheus Choir came to Alloa under Sir Hugh Roberton and performed at the Pavilion.[83] The *Journal* commented that 'They had a large and appreciative audience...'[84] The report in the *Circular* was ecstatic; calling it a 'brilliant programme', 'An exquisite rendering', 'sustained brilliance' and 'a memorable evening in the musical experience of the County'.[85]

On 26th September 1943 there was a concert by the Polish Army choir in the Gaumont. This was very well reported in the *Journal* the following week where it gave almost a piece-by-piece commentary on the entire programme.[86] This in-depth reporting of the repertoire now became the standard response by the local press. In April 1944 there was another concert by the Polish Army string quartet and soloists at the Gaumont which was well received.[87] The *Journal's* full report was enlivened by the inclusion of what I think was the cleverest joke that the local press referred to in the entire war... 'Lieut. Makowicz, the breezy compere... told a story of how Paderewski, the great pianist and composer, arrived at a house party to find the company being entertained at the piano by a man who was more renowned as a polo player than a pianist. As soon as he saw the great musician the pianist stopped and apologised for his amateurish efforts. "That's alright" said Paderewski, "You're just a poor soul who plays polo: and I'm just a poor Pole who plays solo!"

In October 1944 there was a public notice in the *Journal* about a Norwegian concert to be held on 29th October. This was noteworthy because it was going to be the first

---

PAVILION THEATRE, ALLOA

SUNDAY, JANUARY 17th

Polish Concert

(in aid of Scottish Branch of British Red Cross Society and Polish Forces Educational Fund)

Concert by :

Solo Pianist - **Lieut. M. BLASZCZYNSKI**

POLISH 1st BRIGADE MILITARY BAND

and

POLISH SOLDIERS' CHOIR

" BOGACZY "

Doors Open 6-30 p.m.   Commence 7 p.m.

Admission - Balcony (Reserved) 2/6; Stalls 2/- & 1/-

Tickets may be obtained at the Pavilion Theatre.

Alloa Circular 9th January 1943

NORWEGIAN CONCERT
(In Aid of British Red Cross)
ALLOA TOWN HALL
TO-MORROW (Sunday), 29th October
Doors Open 7-30 p.m.   Commence 8 p.m.

The programme will be sustained by :

Professor HELMER DAHL
Born 1916. Graduated from Technical University of Norway, 1932. Lecturer, in Electrical Communication Engineering at Technical University, Norway, 1940-41. Escaped from Norway and joined Norwegian Forces in Great Britain, Spring 1942. Now at The British Research Establishment. Will talk about Norway and show Lantern Slides.

Madam SOFFI SCHOENNING
Famous Norwegian Singer, will render selection of Grieg Songs. Leading parts in many operas at the National Theatre in Oslo. Many concerts in B.B.C. Numerical Concerts for Norwegian and British Audiences in Great Britain. Concerts with the London Philarmonic Orchestra in Albert Hall, London.

DANIEL KELLEY
Will render Pianoforte Solos.

SIGMUND GJELSTAD
Will give Violin Solos.

GUDRUN BARLAUP
Norwegian Actress, will recite Norwegian Poetry. Leading Parts in Classical Plays—mainly of Henrik Ibsen. Has given Talks in B.B.C.

NORWEGIAN MILITARY BAND
Will render selections.

Seats (Reserved & Booked), 4/-; Reserved but not numbered, 3/- & 2/-

Tickets can be had at Mr J. B. Rae's, Primrose Street, Alloa, or at the Door.

Alloa Circular 28th October 1944

use of the de-requisitioned town hall. The 'concert' was a mixture of talks with lantern slides, singing and poetry; the money raised went to the Red Cross.[88]

HARLANDS DISPUTE

In Chapter 1 we saw a reference to the expectation that Harland Engineering Company would expand its labour force as a result of wartime contracts; and this would lead to an increased demand for housing that Alloa Burgh Council would have to deal with… It's surprising how this turned into a long-running spat between the Council and Harlands. This was partly because the Council was aware, from the advice of its Medical Officer, that the quality and stock of housing in Alloa was not really up to scratch anyway, and that they were being asked/required to provide more housing accommodation for a local industrial employer who then became quite picky about what houses they would be prepared to accept! In March 1941 the Council received a letter from Harlands saying they needed more of the Council's houses to be made available for their 'employees in the airframe factory'; that 20 houses had been promised but only 9 provided.[89] The Council Convenor pointed out that the problem was that in 2 of the original 9 cases, the man had left the employment of Harlands [joined the forces?] but 'had left their wives and children in possession of the houses and they declined to leave because they could not get houses elsewhere'. The Council agreed in March to try to re-possess these two houses but then changed its mind. This was all sufficiently fractious for the *Journal* to print quite a long article in April covering some aspects of the issue of Harlands housing and families not leaving.[90] On 28th April it was agreed by the Council to **not** repossess these houses, but to take them out of the agreement with Harlands, which would now only amount to the provision of 18 council houses.[91] There were more letters to Harlands and in July it was agreed with them that only married employees of Harlands should get houses, and if they stopped being employees then the houses **must** revert to the Council.[92] By January 1942 it was all getting rather acrimonious; particularly because the Council didn't like having the houses that it offered being rejected. By then Harlands had occupied 12 and rejected 5 of those offered. The Council called it a day and said that's all you're getting. Basically they objected to Harlands picking and choosing what houses they wanted. However, it was reported to the Council in October 1942 that Harlands had taken up 20 houses and were happy with them.[93] It looks like the Council had given way; but when Harlands asked for 9 more houses in December 1942 the Council refused.[94] In what looks suspiciously like a counter-claim, Harlands then asked for a reduction in their gas price in early 1943. This was also refused.[95] In September 1943 Harlands made a big appeal for more housing, asking for at least 22 houses of which 10 were urgent. It provided the Council with lots of statistics on just how big a local employer Harlands had become; but they got no more houses.[96] You do get the impression that Harlands just wouldn't let this grudge rest over their housing shortage. In March 1946 the Managing Director of Harlands wrote to the Council complaining about their pathetic progress in building houses; saying that even now the war was over 'the Council had only got 60 houses under construction… and the waiting list for our employees alone reaches about that figure'.[97]

It really was a continuing source of worry for the Council about where/how they could get more houses. In August 1942 Sir William Arrol and Company had also asked for housing for key married workers who were being transferred into Alloa 'to take charge of work of the highest Admiralty priority'. They were turned down by the Council.[98] You can see why these companies felt justified in keeping on tackling the Council about providing them with housing. A note in the *Journal* in October 1942 rather gave the game away here when the Housing Factor for the Burgh Council stated that of all the houses that had been built in Alloa under the government's various housing acts since 1919, 'By December 1941 approximately one half of the houses within the Burgh were owned by the Alloa Town Council'.[99]

With the clear inflationary rise in the cost of local privately rented property, the Council was the natural first place to look by these companies. In October 1942 the Town Clerk somewhat alarmingly told the Council that he expected 'between 600 and 700 transferred war workers would be coming into the town before next March'[100] but there is no evidence that this actually happened.

However, the Council did have to face up to the issue of where to house any incoming workers and the *Advertiser* reported by October 1942 that the Council accepted that voluntary billeting for incoming essential workers had failed and now there would be compulsory billeting.

The Town Clerk said 'he was handling a most delicate situation and one which would entail considerable worry and a certain amount of resentment amongst the ratepayers'. He reminded the councillors that the Government would not sanction building accommodation huts whilst there was still an available stock of spare rooms.[101] This had its inevitable consequence; in May 1943 an Alloa man in Tullibody Road was fined £5 for failing to billet a war worker. He had billeted one earlier but when that one left he refused to take in another.[102] Three weeks later another Alloa man was fined £14 for failing to billet two female war workers in his house in Alexandra Drive. He probably didn't endear himself to the magistrates when he said that he hadn't bothered to appeal against the original billeting notice because 'that would be a waste of shoe leather'.[103]

Transferred War Workers

THE result of the appeal for Lodgings has been disappointing. All householders having accommodation are urgently requested to make it available for transferred War workers, and they should forthwith give their names, addresses and details of accommodation to the Town Clerk, Town Clerk's Office, Alloa. If sufficient accommodation is not found voluntarily it will be necessary to exercise the compulsory powers.

Alloa Journal 18th April 1942

THE LOCAL MAGISTRATES

The magistrates in Alloa in the Second World War deserve a mention because they did keep minutes of all their wartime meetings and they did have to take decisions on some war-related issues. The usual attendance at the magistrates meetings was the Provost, four Bailies and the Chief Constable. It was the case that their traditional areas of [non war-related] business just went on as usual; they spent their time licensing cinemas, agreeing on Sunday openings, applying the law on house-to-house collections, debating whether public meetings should go ahead etc.

In some ways the magistrates, all of whom were councillors, provided the legal justification to back up other Council decisions. Thus, in May 1940 when there was the issue concerning evacuation, of whether the Burgh Council should go down the road of compulsory billeting if it was required, the magistrates took the moral hard line and said that the Council should appoint an Evacuation Officer who was prepared to enforce this as a part of his duties.[104] They also felt that there were plenty of teachers who would be prepared to enforce this hard line and agreed to get in touch with the Director of Education to pick one.

On a more humdrum note, concerns were expressed to them about dangers of the blackout in October 1940.[105] This was due to the fact that the three local cinemas all attracted large audiences and at night the queues stretched out into the street. In the blackout this was considered dangerous. The magistrates came up with a solution by 21ˢᵗ October; they suggested 'the provision of danger lights at the head, centre and rear of the queues', and this was put into operation.

The magistrates already had the right to take decisions on slum clearance of unsanitary houses, but the Government's Fire Watchers Order of 1940 let councils take action against properties considered to be fire risks in the light of a possible attack by German bombers. In the magistrates' view, some premises in Mill Street were 'hopelessly unsatisfactory from the point of view of fire protection' and they advised that the police were to take action 'to have the premises rendered suitable'.[106]

In May 1942 the magistrates had a run-in with the Alloa branch of the Communist Party, who had applied to hold meetings within the Burgh and at places other than the Public Park.[107] The Provost, Town Clerk and Chief Constable agreed to go to a meeting to hear their views but at the next magistrates' meeting on 8ᵗʰ June, 'it was unanimously agreed not to grant permission to hold meetings on the public streets'. It is a bit surprising, from our later perspective, to see this mistrust of the Communist Party at the very same time as Communist Russia was making a major contribution towards winning the war; and even Winston Churchill had come round to praising their strengths as a vital ally against Nazi Germany. But the magistrates did not budge. Even when the Alloa Communists re-applied on 31ˢᵗ August 1942 for permission for a radio van to go round the streets and to distribute party pamphlets, the magistrates again agreed that permission would **not** be granted. I think they felt that since the Communists had been granted permission by the Council to hold public meetings in the park on summer evenings; that should be enough.

As the war went on into 1943 and 1944 you get the impression that the magistrates were kept quite busy by their need to judicially respond to the increasing disregard shown by the Alloa citizens for the war-time regulations which should have controlled their conduct. This comes out in the local press, where, week after week the magistrates imposed a surprising number of fines / imprisonments for infringements against breaking the blackout, not turning up for or leaving essential work, members of the home guard not turning up for duty, and house-owners refusing instructions on the billeting of essential war workers. The magistrates did not let up; they even fined a cyclist for riding without a rear light in October 1944 when dim-out was in operation.

CRIME

In January of each year, the Chief Constable of the County gave a report of the crime figures for the previous year. This was always reported, at some length, in the local press. In February 1940, admittedly referring to the 12 months of 1939 that only had 4 months of being at war in it, he was able to report a decline in crime… in 1939 297 persons were convicted, a decrease of 62 on the previous year.[108] He was not able to repeat this good news about the County's criminality for the next 2 years! In February 1941 he reported that the number of crimes in the County in 1940 went up by 36 to 576.[109] Then in February 1942 he reported that it had gone up again; there had been 651 crimes in 1941, an increase of 75.[110]

Luckily, in February 1943 he was able to report a 'Substantial reduction in crime in 1942' and that 'a particularly gratifying feature is the reduction in the number of juvenile offenders'. There were 462 crimes, a decrease of 189.[111] However, things certainly didn't last. His report for 1943 noted that there had been 479 crimes in that year, an increase of 17.[112] The *Advertiser*'s opening editorial in January 1944, whilst it was very optimistic about the progress of the war abroad,[113] was less than happy about things in the crime picture on the home front; it was forced to report a substantial increase in juvenile crime in the previous year. There had been 85 cases in 1943 compared to 50 in 1942 and 92 in 1941. It blamed it on lack of parental control.[114] Things deteriorated dramatically; with virtually a crime wave over 1944. The Chief Constable's report for 1944 [issued in February 1945] noted that there had been 744 crimes in 1944, an increase of 265.[115] However; the *Circular* in February 1945 explained the reason for this; noting that it was more than accounted for by the earlier 'crowd scene' at Alloa sheriff court with a big increase in the number of people breaking the Regulated Area [No 2] order of 1944 to do with the carrying of identity cards. Basically there had been 'a police round-up of people not carrying their identity cards' and this had produced an unexpectedly large catch.[116]

ALLOA BRASS BAND

Its proper title was Alloa Instrumental Band and Mr Muddiman was still the band master, just as he had been throughout the years of the Great War. The band really was an Alloa institution and was sponsored by the Burgh Council; it was expected to play at the bandstand in the Public Park on weekends for the enjoyment of the Alloa citizens. Its instruments and uniforms were at least partly paid for by Council funds, and every year the band got a grant from the Burgh Council. In the years before the war and in 1939 this amounted to about £130 pa. But from 1940 onwards, there was a payment to Mr Muddiman of between £25 and £30 a year to keep the band practices going, but nothing else.

Things had been going so well for the band in 1939, it's a pity the war came because that absolutely ruined everything. The band leader reported to the Council and had a meeting with them every June. At the 1939 meeting, Mr Muddiman reported that 'the band has attained a higher standard of efficiency than in any one of the past 32 years during which he had acted as Bandmaster'.[117] Thereafter it was all downhill. By June 1940 he sadly reported that the band had intended to build a Band Hall on ground offered by Patons and Baldwins at the old Springfield Mills, but due to the war this plan has been allowed to drop. He then went on to point out that 'Under present war emergency conditions, it would be impossible for the Band to provide the usual weekly performances in the Public Park during the summer'. He added that although he was training up young people 'to replace those who had joined the Forces or were unable to attend the practises by reason of their being employed on munitions or other government work', they wouldn't be of a standard to put on public performances.[118] He repeated this view in June 1941, 'that there was still little likelihood of the Band being able to give public performances'. It was for these reasons that the Council [and Mr Muddiman] agreed that the Council's grant should stop; and that Mr Muddiman should just be paid a small fee to try and keep training up a few new bandsmen. The Council didn't forget that it really had 'rights of possession' over the band's equipment and uniforms, and it noted its concern in June 1943 that 'a number of instruments are still in the hands of players who are now on Military Service'. It was agreed to try and get these instruments and uniforms back so they could be stored in the Municipal Buildings.[119] Even by the time of his annual meeting with the Council in June 1944, Mr Muddiman could make no better promise for the future of the band than that 'a few junior members of the band had been called to HM Forces, but others had come forward to take their place'.

So that was the big difference: during the Great War Mr Muddiman, despite adverse circumstances, had managed to keep the Alloa Brass Band playing for every summer season of the war; in the Second World War he was not able to do it at all.

However, not all was lost for the brass band music lovers of Alloa because someone else managed to do it! In October 1940 the *Journal* reported on the formation of a new brass band in Alloa, founded by Alloa Coal Company, with 18 players. The instruments were donated by Colonel Harold J. Mitchell, one of the directors. It was to be known as Alloa Colliery Band.[120] The *Circular* noted that 'Many of the personnel are members of the Home Guard and we understand that the band may probably be used in connection with Home Guard activities and parades'.[121] The band appeared at the Polish 'International' football match at the Recs in the last days of December 1940, all dressed in Home Guard uniforms. Mr Cook was band leader. By the time of a report in the *Journal* in early March 1941, it does seem that the band actually now styled itself as the Home Guard's band, not the ACC's band.[122] The *Journal* confirmed this in June 1941 when it reported that 'by kind permission of Colonel Spens, the Home Guard band will play in the Alloa Public Park each Wednesday evening until further notice. The band is wholly recruited from the Alloa Coal Company platoon'.[123] It was also the case that a variety of military brass bands from different regiments that were passing through Alloa played in the Public Park on different occasions. For those that liked something different; there was even an occasion in August 1942 when the *Journal* reported, under a heading of 'Music at Pleasure Grounds', that 'On Wednesday evening, Simpsons radio van discoursed a musical programme for the benefit of those in the Pleasure Grounds. The announcement that this was to be done brought a good crowd to the grounds'.[124]

THE MASONIC LODGE

Lodge of Alloa No. 69 kept very good minutes of all its meetings; these show just how busy and successful the Lodge was right through the war; there was a constant stream of new members to be inducted. Just as in the Great War, Alloa Lodge No. 69 found that its premises were taken over for military purposes at the start of the war, even though, in August 1939, 'In view of the crisis and to meet the requirements of the authorities, arrangements were made to have the windows in the hall and anterooms darkened'.[125] They were hoping to hang on to the use of their premises but in early September 1939, 'The Master intimated that although not officially advised, he understood the hall and anterooms had been taken by the military authorities and in consequence he was unable to state where the next meeting would be held'.[126] In fact, just as in the Great War, the Lodge held all the rest of its wartime meetings in Kilncraigs Hall.[127]

During the war years, the income of the Lodge steadily grew. It must be pointed out though, that the Lodge was, to a great extent, a benevolent society looking after the health and welfare of its members and their families; its financial assets were therefore, in effect, the members' insurance. The Lodge generally had two funds, the Ordinary Fund and the Benevolent Fund; figures for both were clearly recorded in the minute book, as were disbursements.[128]

		Ordinary Fund	Benevolent Fund
Sept.	1939	£297	£156
Sept.	1940	£394	£154
Sept.	1942	£691	£119
Apr.	1943	£750	£114
Nov.	1944	£1,040	£113
Nov.	1945	£1,051	£114

The Lodge did, therefore, have the financial ability to invest in war savings. In March 1942, 'In connection with local 'Warships Week' next month, it was agreed to recommend the investment of £100 from the Ordinary Fund in 3% Defence Bonds'.[129] Then in March 1943, 'In connection with the 'Wings for Victory' campaign in April, it was agreed to recommend investing £150 in 3% Defence Bonds'.[130]

It also kept a keen eye on the welfare of Lodge members in the armed forces; in January 1940 it agreed to keep a record of all current members serving in HM Forces[131] although it did not think that there should be any exemption of Lodge fees for any serving members.[132] In time for Christmas 1940 the 'Committee agreed to recommend that a postal order for 7/6 be sent to each member of the Lodge at present serving in HM Forces'.[133] This particular act of benevolence was not repeated, but the Lodge did take a much greater and more sustained interest in one small group of its members; those who were prisoners of war. In September 1942 the Committee commented that 'As far as it was known, 3 members of the lodge were prisoners of war and with a view to sending them something, a collection will be taken at the regular meeting on 1st October 1942' [It only raised about a guinea but a second appeal for donations in November raised another guinea].[134] In January 1943 'It was agreed that 15/- be handed over to the relatives of the four members of the Lodge who are known to be prisoners of war'.[135] The Lodge had another collection in November 1943 which amounted to 2 guineas, then another collection almost a month later which raised a further £2.[136] This money was supposed to be handed over [£1 each] to the relatives of 4 named POWs [Bros D Liddell, Adams, Pyper and Gordon Dennett] in April 1944 but was forgotten about until November 1944 when the Committee agreed to do this… 'it having been overlooked'.[137] The last act of benevolence to serving members was in March 1945 when a motion was unanimously accepted that there should be a 'War Service Thanksgiving Fund' which would be able to recognise the duty, nobly done, of the Lodge members who had been in the Services.[138] By November 1945 this fund had just over £10 in it.

By late 1944 the Lodge had become aware that their hall and premises were about to be de-requisitioned… they appointed a committee to 'deal with matters which would arise in connection with this'.[139] There had been extensive damage to the property 'and much of it was malicious'.[140] The Lodge pursued its claim for damages and got just over £756 from the Government by August 1947. This sum did not cover the true cost of the restoration of the premises where much damage had been done to the storeroom roof and furnishings through damp. The Government refused to pay for this.

The Lodge meeting of 16th August 1945 was the first full meeting after the end of the War. The minutes soberly noted that, 'This being the first meeting since the cessation of hostilities, a 2 minutes silence was observed in memory of members of the Lodge who had made the supreme sacrifice- the members being upstanding'.

WAR CHARITIES

In addition to the more centrally organised National Savings campaigns; there were many examples of local involvement in charitable savings for particular aspects of the war effort. One example that didn't quite come off occurred in the late summer of 1940, following the surrender of the 51st Highland Division at St Valery, leading to the sudden creation of a lot of prisoners of war with an Alloa connection. Around Alloa there were a lot of 'back-green' concerts and sales to raise money for the families of the soldiers who were now in POW camps. The *Advertiser* was so impressed with these fund-raising efforts that it thought it could be developed further into 'An Alloa Spitfire?' fund. It had seen Stirling doing something similar and thought Alloa could match it.[141] BUT this was at the very same time as concerns arose about unlicensed collections for so-called war charities. There was a concern in the Government that some people might go round making charitable collections for what they claimed was a war-related good cause, but in reality it was a fraud which exploited the good will of the unsuspicious donors.[142] The War Charities Act of 1940 was therefore introduced to stop charity collections for any war purpose unless they had been officially vetted first. Every war charity now had to get permission from the local council and fill in an application certificate stating its aims. It then had to have its accounts audited on a yearly basis. In September 1940 the Burgh Council agreed to implement this;[143] which naturally made it impossible to continue with the much more informal Spitfire fund. By mid-September the *Advertiser* noted that 'the Spitfire project was side-tracked'[144] although some local people still supported it.[145] The Council put a big notice in the *Advertiser* on 7th September warning that collections for war charities were being 'prohibited by law'. In the war years there were 3 or 4 charities in Alloa[146] which fulfilled the government's requirements; the one with the clearest, fullest records was St Mungo's Roman Catholic War Charities Fund.

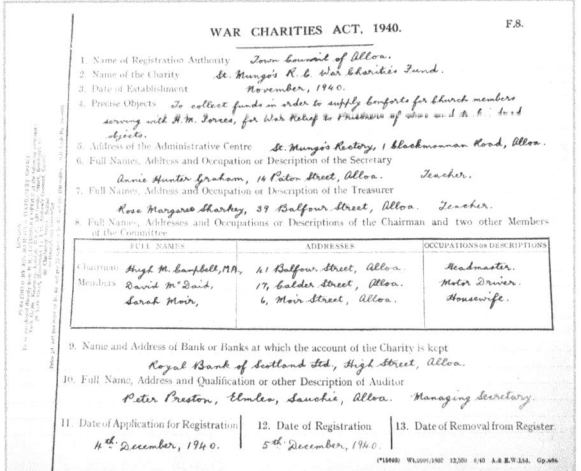

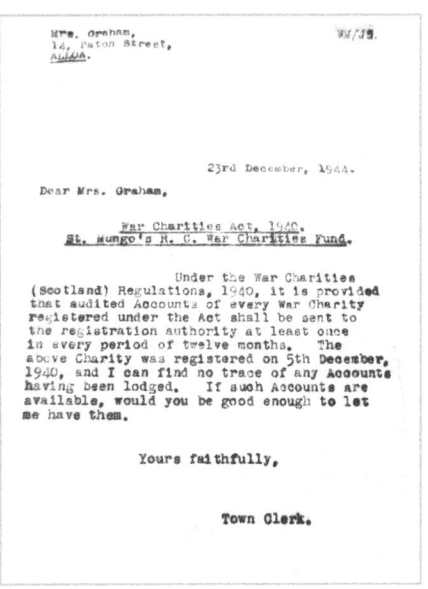

This charity was set up in November 1940 for the provision of soldiers' comforts. It tended to raise its money by individual contributions, church collections and church socials. Like the other local war charities it received a rather abrupt letter from the Town Clerk in December 1944, asking why it had never submitted audited accounts. However, it was able to produce a good and clear set of accounts for each year of the war. From their neatness and similarity of presentation, one suspects they were all written at the same time, probably in December 1944, in compliance with the Council's request! These accounts showed the following charitable gifts / actions:-

Dec 1940-Nov 1941	Sent out parcels of socks and cigarettes to servicemen £43 worth of cash was distributed through the parcels
Dec 1941-Nov 1942	£53 worth of postal orders sent out to servicemen
Dec 1942-Nov 1943	Paid for masses for deceased soldiers £51 worth of postal orders sent out to servicemen
Dec 1943-Nov 1944	Gave 139 gifts of 5/- in postal orders to servicemen On 31.10.44 gave gift of £5 to a returned POW (G. Currie)
Dec 1944-Nov 1945	Held Welcome-Home Social for POWs and gave 9 POWs £5 each

As a postscript to this particular section; the *Journal* printed a nice report of the Welcome-Home Social and Dance referred to above, which took place on 31st May 1945 in the Co-operative Hall. Hugh Campbell, the chairman of this charity presided over the event, Father Matthews congratulated the boys on their safe return, and 'in a very happy little speech' Private W. Donnelly, one of the returning POWs, thanked everyone for their kind support.[147]

ROYALTY VISITING ALLOA

Alloa had only been graced by the presence of royalty twice during the Great War; and they were fairly minor royals at that.[148] In the Second World War that was well surpassed when both the King and the Queen came to Alloa on 29th July 1943 to visit Harland Engineering Company. Out of all Alloa's schools, only Sunnyside School log book noted that, 'The whole school assembled at the Whins Road to see the King and Queen as they passed on their way to

KING AND QUEEN IN THE COUNTY

Their Majesties Surprise Visit En Route to War Factory

Cheering Crowds Give Royal Reception

Scenes of great enthusiasm were witnessed in Alloa on Thursday forenoon when the occasion was the supreme honour of a visit from Their Majesties, The King and Queen.

The Royal visit had been a closely guarded secret until Thursday morning when loud speakers announced the forthcoming auspicious event, but thereafter crowds soon assembled along the route and cheered the Royal car on its progress through the district. At a Classic Burgh in the vicinity the Provost and Magistrates, accompanied by a detachment of the Home Guard, took up their stations at the Municipal Buildings and gave the salute as the King and Queen passed, to the accompaniment of vociferous cheering.

At the town which was one of the objectives of the visit the streets were beflagged and lined with spectators who greeted the Royal Party with patriotic fervour.

Visit To War Factory

Proceeding then on their journey to a factory in Southern Scotland, the King and Queen were welcomed by the local Provost and his wife, and Mr C. A. Oakley, Regional Controller of a War Ministry, Mr Oakley then presenting the Managing Director of the Works which were being visited.

The King wore naval uniform and was attended by Colonel Kavanagh and Sir Eric Mieville. The Queen looked charming in a two-piece suit on powder blue, with a hat the same colour trimmed with fine blue veiling, caught into a cluster in the crown, and with long scarf ends. In her coat was pinned a diamond thistle brooch and her simple dress was adorned with a corsage of sequins and a triple row of pearls. Lady Hambleton was in attendance on Her Majesty.

The Royal Party was also accompanied by Lord Rowbery, Regional Commissioner; Sir Steven Bilsland, District Commissioner; and Mr Hector Neill, District Deputy Commissioner.

Following the introductions to the Royal visitors, the party was conducted to the staff dining room, where tea was served and where the Provost presented the County

Convener and his wife. The Managing Director then presented his wife, and also the following members of the staff of the firm—the Works Director; the Secretary; the Works Manager of the main factory; the Works Manager of an auxiliary section of the factory; and the Welfare Superintendent.

At the conclusion of these proceedings the King and Queen were conducted on a tour of the factory, the King being accompanied by the Managing Director, and the Queen, in addition to the Welfare Superintendent, by the Provost and his wife.

Their Majesties took a keen interest in the various aspects of the work, and conversed with many of the employees, who explained the particular duties on which they were engaged.

Talks With Shop Stewards

One talk, which lasted some time, was with Mr J. Carruthers, shop steward convener, and Mrs Graham, senior shop stewardess, in the main factory.

The King asked their union and was told the Amalgamated Engineering Union.

"Are relations between the employers and yourselves harmonious?" inquired His Majesty.

"Yes," was the answer. "We have our differences, of course, but they are settled round the conference table."

"Is the Production Committee working satisfactorily?" was the King's next question.

"Oh, yes," Mr Carruthers replied.

In the auxiliary section of the factory, Mrs Wright, who took out the first check in the establishment, and Mrs Shearman, whose daughter is also among the workers, were presented as the shop steward officials, and described working conditions. The Queen remarked, "All the girls are doing marvellous work."

Other Interviews

Other employers who were interviewed by Their Majesties were—Mr J. Michie, senior foreman, who has 40 years' service; Mr W. Craven, office employee with the longest service (38 years); and Mr J. Hunter, who

has had the longest service as operative employee (40 years).

In one of the informal talks the principals were the Queen and Laurie Buchanan, an 18-year-old apprentice, who was hard put to it to retain his composure when his work-a-day task became the focus of the Royal limelight.

On emerging from the factory, after a most interesting and instructive tour, the Royal visitors were received with outbursts of cheering from the assembled work people who had by this time (it was now 12.15 p.m.) resolved themselves into a vast and enthusiastic reception committee. The penultimate stage of the tour, had, however, now been reached and amidst repeated ovations and through a concourse of employees—hardly kept in check by the intimidating presence of their own unit of the Home Guard the King and Queen proceeded to the Royal car and were given a rousing send-off as they entered upon the next stage of their journey.

Notes and Incidents

Every group of cottages, every road-end on the "Royal route," had its waving group, and the workers in the fields paid their tribute with doffed hat.

Near to a farm served in the Sauchie district a motoring party of four were given a Royal salute all to themselves—an unexpected honour which they duly reciprocated.

Mr Andrew Sharp (an Alloa business man) and his parents were the recipients of a similar honour at a quieter section of the Royal itinerary.

School children had produced a surprising profusion of flags, and one gathering, evidently unable to draw upon old stock and not to be outdone in patriotism, had improvised flags with cardboard and coloured crayons.

Two workers at one point held up between them a large V-sign with "Good Old 51st" inscribed between the arms of the letter.

"The Orel Bulge"

Nor was the Russian front forgotten! At the junction of Candleriggs and Mill Street, when there was a period of threatened congestion, an Alloa police-sergeant's good-humoured counter-attack on the advancing

horde was accompanied by the wise-crack—"What's all this—the Orel bulge?"

Actually it was a patriotic "break"—but not a break-through!

Which brings us to our final note—that police arrangements in the County section of the Royal tour were under the capable supervision of the Chief Constable—who was later presented to Their Majesties—and were irreproachable in every way. With efficient direction at every point—even at Orel!—there was not the semblance of a hitch from start to finish.

ROYAL PRESENTATION OF COOKERY PRIZES

Alloa Girl in Forefront Episode

A very happy function was held in the College of Domestic Science in Edinburgh on Thursday. Some 200 invited guests were present in a lecture room to see Her Majesty handing over prizes to the winners of the oatmeal and potato cookery competition. There were present members and officials of Education Authorities, Domestic Science Supervisors and parents of the competitors. Clackmannan County was represented by Baillie and Mrs Brown, Mr A. C. Marshall, Director of Education, Miss M. H. Scott, Domestic Science Teacher, Miss Jemima Scott, Inch of Ferryton, Clackmannan, pupil of Alloa Academy, and Miss Margaret Snaddon, Gartmorn Road, Sauchie, pupil of Sauchie School, along with their mothers.

The Secretary of State introduced the royal party with a happy reference to a previous King who had something to do with oatcakes—the well-known story of King Alfred. Then Her Majesty, before presenting the prizes, made a most delightful and homely speech with the fine delivery that we all enjoy hearing on the radio.

Their Majesties also chatted to the girl prize-winners about the dishes they had cooked, specimens of which were on view. Queen to Jemima Scott, of Alloa Academy, while the inspection was being made.

"Yours look lovely dishes," remarked the Queen to Jemima Scott, of Alloa Academy, while the inspection was being made.

Her Majesty was given a book of the recipes used by the entrants in the competition and she promised to try some.

Alloa Journal July 1943

C. A. A. was a proud and happy man when Their Majesties King George and Queen Elizabeth visited B.E.P. Works in July, 1943. The Company had long been heavily engaged in war work; management and employees alike regarded the Royal visit as appreciation at the highest level of their contribution to the national effort.

Harland Magazine printed in Autumn 1966

visit the works of the Harland Engineering Company. Their Majesties passed at 11.30 and the pupils were dismissed…' No other school referred to it in any way [even though two of them were virtually next door to Harlands], nor was there a single reference in the minutes of Alloa Burgh Council. But, the *Advertiser* was jubilant, giving a full report on 31ˢᵗ July 1943 in a big article on page 3 about the surprise visit of the King and Queen '*en route* to a war factory'.[149]

However, the *Advertiser* and *Journal* were both very coy about giving specific details of the actual engineering works or the names of any of the top personnel that were presented to their majesties. Censorship obviously played a part here in the reporting of the local press.

Alloa also had a visit from Mary, the Princess Royal [the sister of King George VI] in August 1942 when she 'passed through Alloa on Thursday afternoon [20ᵗʰ August] on her way to an east of Scotland destination'.[150] At a slightly lower level of royalty; Alloa had already received a visit from Princess Alice, the Duchess of Gloucester in October 1940. She was the wife of Prince Henry, the third son of George V; she was therefore royalty by marriage. This was a private visit at the invitation of John Forrester-Paton to inspect the arrangements for the welfare of the troops at the YMCA's Mar Street premises.[151]

POST-WAR HOUSING ISSUES

It was painfully clear to the Council, even in 1939, that Alloa's housing stock was inadequate, but there was not really much they could do about it during the war years. The Council however did listen to advice about what a post-war world might have to be like and in late 1943 it appointed Mr Shearer, as the County Planner,[152] to be in charge of planning for the future and the implementation of the Town and Country Planning Act of 1943. The *Circular* reported his appointment under a heading of 'Planning for Posterity', which certainly showed an optimistic outlook.[153] However, from late-1944, when it began to appear as though the war could soon be won, planning for the future became a really live issue among the councillors, especially discussing what improvements in the provision of housing might be possible once victory was achieved. The first time that this idea was minuted, was in October 1944, but thereafter, there was some sort of discussion at almost every Council meeting. In October the discussion was over possible post-war housing sites such as Arns and Bowhouse and also looking into 'Factory Made Temporary Houses'.[154] In November 'it was agreed that the Arns site was the only possible site available and suitable for immediate development...' and there should be 'partial development to the extent of 100 houses...'[155] Things looked good when at the end of that month the Dept. of Health notified the Council that they had been allocated 110 temporary homes[156] [what we would nowadays call prefabs]. The Council even had a say in what type of houses they were to receive; it was agreed that the Arcon Mark 5 Bungalow was the most suitable of the different temporary houses that the Dept. of Health was offering, and that the Council would apply for them.[157] The first decision was to erect them on the Bowhouse site[158] but they realised it was going to cost the Council £15,000 to prepare that site [George Wimpey made the lowest estimate],[159] so they decided that some should go on the Arns site and some at Hutton Park, which were partially prepared. They also discussed whether to utilise ground in East Castle Street and Grant Street.

So the provision of prefabs was going to be of some help to Alloa's housing needs; but the Council also moved on to discussion of where the sites for permanent housing should be; in other words, which private builders would be contracted to provide the Council with more council housing. In July 1945 the Council decided that 20 Swedish timber houses would be put up at Hutton Park, and 40 houses would go up in Forbes Street 'where the work of servicing the site, by German prisoners of war, has proceeded very satisfactorily'.[160] The *Journal* was aware of the creation of this new labour force and had reported on the plan for 3 months' worth of work by German POWs at Forbes Street.[161] These prisoners would be transported in each day from their prison camp at Comrie, Perthshire[162] 'but will of course be under guard'. The Council had been given a government instruction about the use of POWs, and Alva Council had picked up on it first. The *Advertiser* in June 1945 reported on the use of German POWs to clear the Alva site 'west of Coblecrook' for its temporary housing, and that Alva Council was the first local authority in Scotland to do this. Clearly, by the end of July Alloa Council had followed suit since there were so many advantages; 'they could get as many as required' and 'the prisoners would come from the nearest camp each morning and no responsibility would rest with the local authority re food, lodging etc...'[163]

The *Circular* reported that 20 German POWs will start work on Monday

Prefabs just after the war in
Smithfield Loan

Prefabs in early 1950s near Forbes Street
[middle top of photo]

on 'site preparation for the servicing of the Forbes Street housing scheme'.[164]

The chance of getting all this new housing led the Burgh Council to take the ambitious step in June 1945, of considering the appointment of a full-time burgh architect at a salary of between £500 and £750 pa.[165] The *Journal* reported by August that there had been 42 applications and a short leet of 5 names was drawn up.[166] The appointment was then made; but not before an unseemly row between the councillors! At the interview stage Bailie Procter wanted to ask the candidates what their religion was and was criticised for this by Councillor Mulholland on the grounds that it could have no bearing on the qualifications needed for the job.[167] However, Provost Stanton said Bailie Procter could ask whatever questions he liked, basically pointing out that two candidates had already been asked whether they went fishing so why shouldn't they be asked what church they went to!

DAILY LIFE: ASPECTS WITH A MILITARY CONNECTION

HOME GUARD

In May 1940 the Home Guard was set up; the *Advertiser* noted that 'In response to Anthony Eden's broadcast on Tuesday evening, men between the ages of 17 and 65 have been steadily enrolling in the Local Defence Volunteers [LDV]. Alloa, as might be expected, gave a lead to the County, both in readiness of response and numbers enrolling'. It continued that 'the new force, which is voluntary and unpaid, is designed to supplement, from forces yet untapped, the home defences of the country'.[168] The *Journal* echoed this, stating that

Eden's appeal had led to 'an exceptionally satisfactory response' from Alloa and the County.[169] The Commander of the LDV area which included Alloa, Clackmannan, Cambus and Tullibody was Major J. Kennedy Tullis.[170] He quickly put a call out for people to contribute shotguns, rifles, ammunition etc. which were urgently required to equip his new force.[171] The local press was quite disparaging about the abilities of the Home Guard. They were very sceptical about whether they could defend the nation against a well-armed force; especially of enemy paratroopers. The *Advertiser* noted that '...the function of the LDV can only be to represent subsidiary aid to a strongly armed counter-attacking defence force' and thought that the LDV would probably only be called on to act as 'scouts and observers'.[172] Be that as it may, local men had shown their willingness to join, and by August 1940 the *Advertiser* was proudly displaying a big poster noting that there were now enough men to make up four companies of the 2nd (Clackmannanshire) Battalion of the Home Guard.[173]

HOME GUARD

2nd (Clackmannanshire) Battalion

So gratifying has been the response throughout the County to the call for Volunteers to serve in the L.D.V. Company that HIS MAJESTY'S ARMY COUNCIL has given permission for this Company to be enlarged to a BATTALION known as the 2nd (CLACKMANNANSHIRE) BATTALION of the HOME GUARD. There are, at present, some vacancies for men between the ages of 17 and 65 of reasonable physical fitness, who will have the privilege of selecting the Company most convenient to their homes, in which to serve. Conditions of Service are the same as those for the L.D.V. and intending Volunteers should enrol without delay if they wish to avoid being placed on the waiting list.

A. COMPANY—Alloa District.

B. COMPANY—Alva, Menstrie, Tullibody and Cambus Districts.

C. COMPANY—Dollar, Tillicoultry Coalsnaughton and Devonside Districts.

D. COMPANY—Kilbagie, Kennet, Clackmannan, Forest Mill, Sauchie and Alloa Districts.

Give your name and address at the nearest Police Station and arrangements for your enrolment will be made immediately.

Applications will be taken strictly in rotation.

"First Come, First Served"

ABOVE: *Alloa Journal* 10th August 1940

RIGHT: *Alloa Advertiser* 10th August 1940

HOME GUARD

2nd (Clackmannanshire) Battalion

SO gratifying has been the response throughout the County to the call for Volunteers to serve in the L.D.V. Company that HIS MAJESTY'S ARMY COUNCIL has given permission for this Company to be enlarged to a BATTALION known as the 2nd (CLACKMANNAN-SHIRE) BATTALION of the HOME GUARD. There are, at present, some vacancies for men between the ages of 17 and 65 of reasonable physical fitness, who will have the privilege of selecting the Company most convenient to their homes in which to serve. Conditions of Service are the same as those for the L.D.V. and intending Volunteers should enrol without delay if they wish to avoid being placed on the waiting list.

A. COMPANY—ALLOA DISTRICT.

B. COMPANY—ALVA, MENSTRIE, TULLIBODY and CAMBUS DISTRICTS.

C. COMPANY—DOLLAR, TILLICOULTRY, COAL-SNAUGHTON and DEVONSIDE DISTRICTS.

D. COMPANY—KILBAGIE, KENNET, CLACK-MANNAN, FORESTMILL, SAUCHIE and ALLOA DISTRICTS.

Give your name and address at the nearest Police Station and arrangements for your enrolment will be made immediately. Applications will be taken strictly in rotation. "FIRST COME FIRST SERVED."

You just get the feeling that the councillors were also not very enthusiastic about the Home Guard; the first reference to it in the Council minutes was in July 1940 when they recorded that No. 2 Platoon of the Local Defence Volunteers [Home Guard] was run by Colonel Grant. He had told the Council that there he had selected several points around Alloa as good defensive points 'in the event of an invasion'... but needed help in digging trenches etc. The Council was a bit dubious about offering labour and suggested the matter be brought before the allotments committee![174] In December 1940 the Home Guard wanted to hold 'a competitive shoot' over the Christmas period and asked the Council to support it with a donation to its prize fund. The Council agreed to give 2 guineas out of the Common Good fund, which was about the same as it gave Alloa Academy every year as a contribution towards its prize giving.[175]

HOME GUARD ON PARADE

Sauchie Home Guard Marching to Remembrance Day Service.

Alloa Circular 20th November 1940

Alloa Journal 1940 Alloa Home Guard miniature rifle shooting cup team

SHOT BY HOME GUARD

SAUCHIE MAN SEVERELY INJURED

LEG AMPUTATED BELOW KNEE

A tragic episode apparently arising from failure to comply with a Home Guard's challenge to halt took place in the southern part of Alloa on Monday evening and resulted in a Sauchie man receiving injuries which have since necessitated the amputation of a leg below the knee.

The victim of the untoward occurrence, Alexander Waddell, 34 Schawpark Avenue, Sauchie, was cycling to his work about 10 p.m. on Monday when a Home Guard on sentry duty called upon him to halt.

Waddel, for some reason, appeared to have failed to comply with the injunction (which, it is stated, was twice repeated) and was proceeding on his way when, it is reported, the sentry raised his rifle and fired.

The cyclist was shot in the leg, and, following his removal to the County Hospital, it was found necessary to amputate the limb below the knee.

Waddel is a married man with a family of three.

Alloa Circular 18th December 1940

Harlands had their own company of the Home Guard; 'A' Company of the Alloa Battalion, with about 50 members.[176] An interviewee in the *Alloa Docks Oral History Project* from 1987 remembers being in a platoon of that company guarding the railway bridge over the Forth; 'they had a trench dug just by it'.[177] General public support for the actions of the Alloa Home Guard would hardly have been increased by the following accident; in December 1940 the *Advertiser* reported on the sad case of a Sauchie man who lost his leg when cycling to work in a southern part of Alloa at 10 pm. The Home Guard shot him when he didn't stop when ordered to, and the leg had to be amputated.[178] This event, which happened outside Harlands, was well remembered by another interviewee[179] who said 'he came down and started cursing and kept on cycling and they shouted 'Halt' and he never halted and the boy fired to the ground and it hit his leg and he had to get his leg off'. This was the story of one Harlands employee being shot by another one!

During the years from 1941-1944 the *Advertiser* contained plenty of reports of the effectiveness of the local Home Guard doing its military exercises and mock attacks around the County.[180] One of the highlights must have been a military display on 16th May 1943 that it put on at part of the Schawpark golf course. The *Advertiser* carried advance notice that the golf club would host a Home Guard exercise with displays of grenade throwing and the use of spigot projectors etc. Its report a week later showed how impressed it was that the 'climax was the explosion of 4 anti-tank mines and 4 barrel flame traps'.[181]

It looked like the local Home Guard knew their existence was coming to an end in September 1944 when the Council noted that the Clackmannanshire Home Guard were going to hold a drumhead service;[182] that is usually taken as a sign of a celebratory pat-on-the-back. Sure enough, in December 1944 the local battalion of the Home Guard was dissolved. In a ceremony at the town hall convened by the Earl of Mar, the County Home Guard was thanked for its efforts and officially stood down.[183] The Earl of Mar's 'Stand-down' speech included a thank you message from the King for their 'patient, ungrudging effort',[184] it was also when the Earl of Mar made incidental reference to the bomb which fell near Alloa, helping to verify the occurrence. He said 'we have been singularly fortunate, for only once or twice did enemy planes pass over the County on their way to and from Clydebank, dropping a few bombs on the way home, and I remember seeing an enormous crater on the Schawpark golf course'.[185]

CONSCIENTIOUS OBJECTORS

In the Second World War the British Government and people did not take the same harsh attitude towards conscientious objectors that they had in the Great War. C.O.s did not have to appear before local 'kangaroo court' tribunals and get publicly shamed; they were simply recorded as such and allowed to go on their way. Since conscription had already been introduced, all men of different age groups had to register at the local labour exchange, and that would then let the military authorities decide where to send them. So the *Circular* in May 1940 stated that "26's Register at Alloa' and that 'Included in the number were four conscientious objectors, representing slightly under 2 per cent of the registrations'.[186] Then again, in July 1940 the *Advertiser* stated that '1907 class registered at labour exchange... 221 in Alloa of whom 2 were conscientious objectors'.[187] That was it; no identification of particular individuals and no public vilification. C.O.s who registered as such had to put their objections to military service in writing within 14 days and appear before a tribunal which had a much more thoughtful and considerate composition than the often militarily dominated tribunals of the Great War.

In December 1941 it was the turn of the youngest age group that it was possible to register at that time; those who were 18 years and 6 months old.[188] It was understood that for this group, they would not be sent overseas until they were 19. For the Alloa group that registered, there were no conscientious objectors.

However, don't think that everything was totally fine for C.O.s; there were still 'issues' with some people. In November 1944 the Education Committee got itself into a bit of a pickle over whether to award a grant to a student from the County who wanted to go to the Royal College of Medicine in Edinburgh. The student was a conscientious objector and his grant application had been refused. One of the councillors supported this by saying that 'they would be up against the rate payers if they made such an award'. Councillor Miller however was outraged; commenting that normally this lad 'would have been lauded to the skies for what he had done...' (ie getting the entrance qualifications through all his hard work) and that 'this was the sort of case that the Committee are out to help'. He then took the moral high ground, arguing that the lad 'was granted unconditional exemption' by the tribunal and that the Council was now acting as if it had higher authority. However, no vote was taken and the issue was sent back to the sub-committee to reconsider.[189]

POLISH TROOPS IN ALLOA

Trying to pin down what exactly was the connection of the Polish forces to Alloa is very difficult. There clearly was a strong link, after all, the exiled Polish president came to the town twice, and there is plenty of evidence in the local press of their close cultural and sporting connections through the concerts and football matches.

In June 1943 there was even a notice in the *Journal* on the proposed formation of a Clackmannan County branch of the Scottish-Polish Society, with a meeting at the Townhead Institute.[190]

BUT... where is the actual military **detail**? How many Polish troops were there, where exactly were they stationed, how long were they in Alloa for? The local press was full of generalised information about when they left but never mentioned their arrival; and much of what they could say about their purpose during their time in Alloa was probably classified information anyway. The website 'Polish Forces in Scotland in World War Two' gives a breakdown of where some of the Polish military groups were stationed but is not specific about dates. It has Alloa as the HQ of the 1st Independent Rifle Brigade, Tillicoultry as having one field artillery regiment and one infantry battalion, and Clackmannan as having 'elements of a medium artillery regiment'. In all these cases it is difficult to get an idea of exactly how many men were involved. In trying to pin down more exactly their local placement, we can say that Polish soldiers were billeted at Kennet House, Clackmannan. Also that some Polish troops were stationed at Middleton and Oak Mills areas of Tillicoultry; the ground where Firhill ski slope is was used as a military training area.[191] In terms of social facilities; evidence suggests that, at different times, Polish troops used the Liberal Club in Mar Street and were billeted above a garage at the bottom of Fenton Street, the Polish sergeants mess was in St Andrew's Church hall,[192] and Chalmers Church hall was used as a club/mess for Polish officers.[193] But surely there was more than that?

The Polish armed forces camera unit definitely took some photographs of their troops during their time in Alloa. These are held by the Imperial War Museum and are only in negative format.[194] Their catalogue lists them under vague headings such as 'Strips 90-93 Photos of Alloa town', 'Strip 96 Troops by a milk cart in Alloa', 'Strips 98-99 Alloa in 1943'.

By September 1944 with the prosecution of the war having moved to occupied Europe, the Polish forces pulled out of Alloa in order to take part in the fighting. The Council was informed of this and decided they were going to give 'the Polish Armoured Grenadier Division which had been billeted within the Burgh' a shield and illuminated address.[195] This happened quite quickly after the decision, and the *Advertiser* reported a few days later on the exchange of shields with Polish soldiers after their 'period of stationing in the town'. It was noted that the Polish Armoured Grenadier Division had been in the area for 20 months, previously having been stationed in Biggar.[196] In September 1944 the Polish forces held their farewell concert in the YMCA hall.[197]

REACTIONS IN ALLOA TO SPECIFIC BIG EVENTS IN THE WAR

Dunkirk and loss of many local soldiers; killed and taken prisoner

The evacuation of British troops from Dunkirk [27th May-4th June 1940] and the surrender of much of the 51st Highland Division at St Valery on 12th June, soon showed its effect in Alloa. The fact that so many local men were in the 7th Battalion of the Argyll and Sutherland Highlanders which was in the 154th Brigade of the 51st Highland Division, meant that the town was hard hit. There was a time-lapse in getting really accurate information. For instance, the *Advertiser* only reported on 22nd June that there were a lot of local men missing and even on 19th August, 2 months after the surrender, it was only reporting on events from before that surrender date. This was the same with the *Circular* which had a headline on 14th August 1940 of 'County Argylls' Heroic Part in Somme campaign'.[198] The *Advertiser* noted the heroic fighting of the Argylls in the withdrawal from the Somme area back to St Valery, commenting that '... naturally the resistance entailed heavy losses'.[199] This certainly prepared its local readership for the fact that things did not look good. By the following week the *Advertiser* was beginning to print big lists of the Alloa men who were prisoners of war.[200]

In writing about Alloa's prisoners of war, there is something of an 'urban myth' that Alloa's most famous POW was Lieutenant J.E.M. (Jimmy) Atkinson, of the 7th Argylls. He was captured at St Valery in 1940 and became celebrated for his writing of the country dancing steps to *The Reel of 51st HD* over the winter of 1940-41 while he was a prisoner at Oflag VII-C near Salzburg. This is dealt with at length in *Our War* which argues that 'it was conceived by Alloa man Jim Atkinson'.[201] Supporting this view, Michael Young in *Reel of 51st Division* (1983), an article found on-line in the *Box and Fiddle Archive*, says Jimmy Atkinson 'had done a little country dancing in his home town of Alloa before the war...' However, the patchy evidence on Jimmy's background suggests that he only came to Alloa from maybe about 1947, and that his story, famous though it has become, has no direct relevance to any account of Alloa during the war years.[202]

North Africa Campaign and 51st Highland Div.

The 51st Highland Division was reconstituted after its losses in 1940.[203] After two years of re-training and home-defence service, by 1942 it was serving in North Africa and was involved in the Battle of El Alamein in October-November 1942. The 7th Argylls were still in that division. The *Advertiser* tried its best to keep up home morale with stories of the success of what was still seen as Alloa's local battalion. In November 1942 there was a long article under the heading 'The Argylls in Africa: epic story of gallantry',[204] then in January 1943 a picture of 2 soldiers, one from Alloa, reading the *Advertiser* at El Alamein.[205]

"ADVERTISER" AT EL ALAMEIN

Alloa Advertiser 2nd January 1943

The war progressed and the *Advertiser* in mid-1943 carried a morale-boosting article entitled 'With the 51st Division in Sicily'.[206] In January 1945 the *Advertiser* reported on the publication of *The 51st Highland Division in North Africa and Sicily* by Capt. James Borthwick, expecting a wide local interest.[207] The book does not contain anything which specifically relates to Alloa.

Clydebank Blitz in March 1941

Apart from the recognition in St Mungo's Primary school log book that there was an influx of new evacuees from the Glasgow area in May 1941, there was nothing in the local press which would have caused alarm in Alloa about the impact of German bombing on urban areas. There had been an air raid alert in Alloa throughout the night of 13th March 1941 and Grange School fire-watchers had been on duty, but the *Advertiser* on 15th March merely noted that

'Two units of Alloa's AFS were involved in fighting the blitz of Clydebank the previous Thursday evening'.[208] The *Circular*, under a headline of 'Fighting the Blitz', noted that Alloa had also sent a 'rescue and demolition squad' which 'had remained in the bomb-devastated area until late on Saturday night' and also that 'A YMCA mobile canteen from this district was also on duty at Clydeside over the weekend'.[209]

The local press might not have found much to report about Alloa's reaction but the following week, St John's Church held a 'Retiring Collection for the Lord Provost of Glasgow's Air Raid distress fund' and raised '£6. 9/6 which was sent direct'.[210]

1942-43

Of all the local press, it was the *Circular* which kept writing something in its editorial for longest, and which also made the most wide-ranging commentary about the state of the war. In early January 1942 for instance, recognising that the German bombing of Britain had become a decreasing threat, it commented that 'At home, thanks largely to the fury with which the Russian people have met the Germans, our towns and cities have so far been spared a repetition of the grim ordeal they underwent last winter'.[211] The *Circular* at least knew where the credit should be given! In the same edition, Arthur Woodburn MP was prepared to give our defensive abilities more credit; he noted in a front page article that 'The bomber got through all right... but often he did not get back. If Germany has not destroyed our towns in these two years it is not because she did not want to, and therefore it seems logical to conclude that it is because she could not'. While Woodburn was talking up our defence, the *Circular* was occasionally prone to talking up our offence! In March 1943 its editorial praised the virtues of 'Round-the-Clock Bombing' where, in the light of Bomber Command's heavy casualties in the middle years of the war, it made the spectacularly unjustifiable assertion that 'Our pilots are adept at night-flying and their long experience of anti-aircraft fire has taught them just how, when and where to fly and to bomb when operating over vital enemy targets in the darkness'.[212] If only! The same editorial also commented that 'US bombers, flying over enemy targets by day, have been found to have surprisingly little need for fighter protection'; another wildly unjustified statement to make.

In August 1942 the *Circular*'s reporting showed one of the many ironies of wartime life. It had a big advert on page 2 for the Regal cinema in Stirling which was showing the film *Dive Bomber* starring Errol Flynn... yet on page 3 was a long article by Arthur Woodburn justifying why Britain was spending so much money on long-range heavy bombers and refusing to invest in dive bombers at all![213]

Over 1942 there was nothing in the local press about the two great Allied victories at Stalingrad and El Alamein, but it did seem that the tide of war had turned and that the people knew it. The *Journal* started off its editorial in its first 1943 issue with the rousing view that 'The years of stubborn defence lie behind us, the years of positive offensive achievement lie ahead... the time has come to take up fresh positions on the civilian battle front...'[214] It was to take more than 2 years for this victory to be achieved, but the local press in 1943 did give a sense of a more optimistic view on the progress of the war compared to the days of gloom in mid-1940

D-Day

There was nothing whatsoever in the local press giving information about the Allied invasion of Europe on 6th June 1944. Any researcher hoping for something on Alloa's reaction must be in despair on reading the best that the *Advertiser* could offer when it noted that a year previously, on 6th June 1943 a Sauchie baby had been born who was christened with the middle names of Churchill Roosevelt, and what a coincidence it was that a year later, on 6th June 1944 there had started the invasion of Europe with the armies of Churchill and Roosevelt.[215] Could it not have managed a comment of greater significance than that? The *Journal* contained nothing either; its first issue following D-Day was on 10th June; and the main local event coming up was Red Cross Week, so that made up the bulk of the news! The first reference,

Alloa Journal 24th June 1944

by implication, was on 24th June with the printing of a war savings poster asking people to 'Support the Invasion' because 'It was now past the Talking Point'. Well, it certainly was, the national press had been talking about it for a fortnight!

Dropping the Atom bombs

There was a sense of gladness and celebration in Alloa that the war was over with VJ Day on 15th August 1945. The *Journal* reported that 'In a dramatic midnight broadcast on Tuesday, Mr Attlee, the Prime Minister announced that with the surrender of Japan that day, the last enemy of the United Nations had been laid low'.[216]

There were street parades, bonfires and open-air dancing in Alloa, and groups of revellers, hundreds strong, paraded round the streets singing lustily. There were VJ Holidays on 2 days and a VJ Day service in St Mungo's Church.[217] In all this reporting however, there was no clear reference to the fact that victory had been brought about by dropping atomic bombs. The closest that came to it was in a part of the sermon by Rev. Pitt Watson in the evening church service... 'Towards the end of his discourse the preacher referred to the latest achievement of science, so closely, terribly and hideously linked with this victory, and resounded a solemn note of warning with regard to the same'. Presumably all the necessary information about the bomb was already in the national press; and greater information must have soon been around locally, because on 7th September 1945, the topic for debate at the Alloa Academy Literary and Debating society was 'That the use of the atomic bomb is morally justified'.[218]

The King's Call to Thanksgiving
on the occasion of
THE SURRENDER OF JAPAN
and
the RESTORATION of PEACE
_____
A United Service
will be held in
ST. MUNGO'S PARISH CHURCH,
on SUNDAY, 19th AUGUST,
at 6.30 p.m.
Printed Orders of Service provided.
Collection for United Aid to China Fund.
REV. G. G. CAMPBELL will preside.
REV. ALEX. CHISHOLM and REV. W. D. MACGREGOR will conduct the service.
REV. J. Pitt WATSON will preach.
Subject:
VICTORY IS CRISIS.

Alloa Journal 18th August 1945

Nearest bomb dropping

The *Circular* printed an interesting article in December 1939 which asked 'Is Alloa A Safe Area?'[219] It asked this question because it noted that 'An Aerial view of the ammunition works at Alloa on the Firth of Forth was published in the national press on Monday. It is claimed by the Germans to have been made by one of their pilots during recent reconnaissance flights over Scotland'. The photo, taken in October 1939, shows what are supposed to be a storehouse for ammunition and two munition factories.

With permission from the National Collection of Aerial Photography, Historic Environment Scotland. ncap.org.uk

It's difficult to know if the people of Alloa were right to be concerned; the photograph seemed more interested in anti-aircraft positions up-river at the naval armaments storage base at Bandeath than in Alloa itself.[220] I personally don't think the photo should be taken to mean that Alloa was ever considered to be a military target. However, Harlands may have thought differently because an interviewee for the *Alloa Docks Oral History Project* remembered that he 'was taken on in 1940 to camouflage the roof'.[221] So how close did the bombing come to Alloa? The *Journal* at the end of June 1940 reported that 'shortly after midnight on Wednesday, German raiders, flying at a great height, came over the midlands of Scotland'. It continued that 'five of the raiders were accounted for' and 'that bombs were dropped in several districts', without being specific where they were.[222]

The *Circular* was slightly more detailed and offered more clues. It noted that 'About thirty incendiary bombs were dropped within and around a village which could not possibly have been the true object of the attack'. It continued that 'A bomb also fell in the gardens of the Parish Church Manse, while four dropped in open spaces between houses. Several are also believed to have fallen on an adjacent golf course and on the slopes of a range of hills a few miles distant'.[223] I wonder if this could have been the event referred to by two interviewees in the *Alloa Docks Oral History Project* of 1987. They claim to remember that incendiary bombs fell on Sauchie; but neither gave a date. One of them stated 'There was stick of incendiaries dropped right across Sauchie; Main Street, Beechwood, Schawpark Avenue and the field between Gartmorn Road and Jellyholm'.[224] Another interviewee also remembers the incendiary bombs dropped on Main Street, Sauchie.[225]

In regard to other nearby bombings; on the night of 19th July 1940 two bombs fell on Stirling, 6 miles away as the plane flies. One fell on waste ground and did no damage but the other fell on the Forthbank football ground where Stirling King's Park football team played [in 1945 they became Stirling Albion]. The bomb severely damaged the stands, causing an 18 feet wide crater. The blast was felt in neighbouring streets and a nearby cottage was almost completely destroyed. Shops in the town, more than a quarter of a mile away, had their plate-glass windows blown in. This may have been reported in the press without the actual location of the town being revealed at the time, but there was no specific reference in Alloa's local papers.

I think there is enough evidence to suggest that the closest that major enemy action came to Alloa was on Thursday 24th October 1940 at 3.15 in the morning, when a single German high explosive bomb [possibly a parachute mine] fell on the 8th fairway of Schawpark golf course, the home of Alloa Golf Club [See Chapter 4 also]. The *Advertiser* on Saturday 26th October, without specifically naming the town, printed the following article on the extent of the damage, and that the only casualty was a solitary hen.

One of the saddest war-related tragedies that came upon the people of Alloa was at 6pm on Tuesday 28th July 1942 when the Jellyholm Road Explosion occurred.[226] 'This distressing occurrence' involved 3 Alloa boys, and left one of them dead and two seriously wounded, one of them needing to have a leg amputated. The *Journal* on 1st August 1942 identified them as Charles Smith of East Castle St, Charles Scotland

Air Raid over Central Scotland

Bomb Damages Farm Steading

About 3.15 on Thursday morning enemy aircraft passed over Central Scotland and dropped a high explosive bomb on a golf course about a mile to the north-east of an industrial town.

Damage was done to a farm steading about two hundred yards distant. Windows were shattered and two heavy doors of a byre were torn from their iron frames.

Animals Terror-Stricken

Inside the byre the animals were terror-stricken and it was some considerable time before they could be quietened. One of the cows, which was in an outhouse, had not risen from the ground nearly twelve hours after the explosion, though it was to all appearance unhurt. Actual casualties, however, were restricted to one hen which was killed by a flying fragment of stone.

Boulders Riven by Explosion

The crater caused by the bomb measured 25 yards in diameter and was about 15 feet deep. Huge boulders riven by the explosion were torn from the earth and lay scattered over a radius of a hundred yards.

A number of other explosions were heard in the district but these bombs appear to have fallen in outlying country areas. No damage to property has been reported.

In a field adjoining another golf course, near to the country residence of a London M.P. another bomb was dropped and left a crater about 30 feet in diameter and five feet deep. There were no casualties.

Alloa Advertiser 26th October 1940

of Calder St and Alexander Robertson of East Castle St, but does not give their ages or say which school they attended, although their addresses suggest Park School. Charles Smith was the boy who died. Since local schools had already broken up for their summer holidays on 11th July, none of the Alloa school log books mentioned anything about this event. The press had very little information as to what may have caused the explosion; just blaming it on 'some unknown reason' and they made no guesses at the time. The *Circular* reported that the boy was killed 'as a result of a mysterious accident' in the vicinity of the Gartmorn Dam'. It sadly continued that a local farmer had heard the explosion and he had found the boys, and that 'the fathers of the boys are serving with the forces'.[227] It was only about 2 months later, when a similar but even more tragic event happened near Tillicoultry, that some claims were then made which may have had a strong element of truth. In the Tillicoultry event, some boys had discovered an anti-tank bomb and an incendiary grenade on a military training area at Firpark in Tillicoultry.[228] They later took these munitions with them to play with more of their friends at the disused Devonside Brickworks, which was being used as a coup [rubbish area]. These munitions somehow came into contact with each other and they blew up, killing 4 of the children and wounding three more.[229]

Even though there were obvious military secrecy implications, this sort of event could really not be hushed up. The *Circular* had a big article reporting what it thought had happened and even named all the victims.[230] To start with, no-one knew how such devices came to be there... nor why some sort of explosive device had been in Jellyholm Road; but pointed comments were now made about the possibility that the military authorities had been careless with clearing up their munitions on both occasions. This was clearly the case at Firpark and, after all, Jellyholm Road was a back road leading to the Gartmorn Dam where the armed forces also had training facilities. Arthur Woodburn MP asked a question in parliament about 'the serious accidents involving children as a result of misadventure in handling projectiles left by military forces'[231] so he was certainly prepared to point the finger at where he thought the blame lay. He was somewhat brushed off by the government's reply but he did get in the comment that he thought the two accidents were connected.

In terms of nearby military action, other sources[232] show that there were two sets of major military air disasters in the Ochil Hills, within 6 miles of Alloa, during the war years, but **none** of this was reported in the local press, although surely some of the local people must have known/heard about them. On 10th December 1941 a Liberator bomber of 120 Squadron failed to clear the top of Tarmangie Hill while *en route* from Aberdeen (Dyce) to Nutts Corner (County Antrim). It crashed at 4.40pm and all five crew were killed. Then three Spitfires crashed into King's Seat Hill on 16th January 1943. The two Canadian pilots died instantly, the Australian pilot survived. Another serious crash of a bomber was on 6th July 1943 when an Avro Lancaster Mark 1 [ED548] from 12 Squadron dived into the River Forth at the entrance to the Powburn, just upstream from the Kincardine Bridge. It had exploded in flight. All the crew were killed.[233] Grangemouth Aerodrome was the home of 58 Operational Training Squadron from 1940 onwards. Internet records[234] of their aviation losses record that at least 6 planes, mostly Spitfires, crashed within 6 miles of Alloa, including locations in Bogside [June 1942], Bengengie Hill, Alva [September 1943] and Sheardale, Tillicoultry [December 1943]. Not one of these fatal crashes was reported in the local press at the time.

ENDNOTES

[1] Alloa Burgh Council minute book 26th December 1939. The minute for 8th July 1940 confirmed that the Army was prepared to pay a sum of £300 per year for the use of the town hall. The minute for 27th October 1944 shows that the Council accepted a figure from the valuer of £645 as compensation for military use of town hall and that this figure would be submitted to the military authorities. The *Alloa Journal* for 16th December 1944 noted that the War Office offered £645 7/- compensation for their use of the town hall. The Council minute for 12th March 1945 shows that the War Office and Council agreed on this figure and the War Office would pay it

[2] The Council was quite good at getting its due compensation. There is only one extant set of full financial accounts for the Burgh, those for 1942. These had an end-section called Emergency War Services. This reveals that £235 was spent by the Council on various expenses to do with evacuees and Alloa's share of the joint ARP Committee's expenses; and that the government, through different grants, reimbursed this money

[3] Alloa Burgh Council minute book 29th April 1940

[4] Alloa Burgh Council minute book 11th March 1940

[5] Alloa Burgh Council minute book 25th March 1940

[6] Alloa Burgh Council minute book 8th September 1939

[7] Alloa Burgh Council minute book 31st March 1941

[8] *Alloa Advertiser* 24th January 1942

[9] *Alloa Advertiser* 21st February 1942

[10] *Alloa Journal* 10th January 1942

[11] *Alloa Advertiser* 15th January 1944

[12] *Alloa Advertiser* 2nd December 1939

[13] At this time the *Advertiser* also had quite a lot of blackout warning posters, many versions of those quite well-known posters about taking in evacuees, and also quite a lot of big Ministry of Food posters. One suspects the Government was putting some serious effort into influencing people's wartime behaviour

[14] *Alloa Advertiser* 27th July 1940

[15] *Alloa Advertiser* 8th February 1941

[16] *Alloa Advertiser* 1st March 1941

[17] *Alloa Advertiser* 15th March 1941

[18] *Alloa Advertiser* 22nd March 1941

[19] Alloa Burgh Council minute book 10th March 1941

[20] *Alloa Advertiser* 22nd March 1941

[21] Alloa Burgh Council minute book 31st March 1941

[22] *Alloa Advertiser* 29th November 1941

[23] *Alloa Advertiser* 28th February 1942

[24] Alloa Burgh Council minute book 30th March 1942

[25] *Alloa Advertiser* 28th March 1942

[26] *Alloa Advertiser* 11th April 1942

[27] *Alloa Journal* 18th April 1942

[28] *Alloa Journal* 25th April 1942

[29] *Alloa Advertiser* 25th April 1942

[30] *Alloa Advertiser* 15th May 1943

[31] *Alloa Advertiser* 27th February 1943

[32] *Alloa Advertiser* 27th March 1943

[33] *Alloa Advertiser* 10th April 1943

[34] *Alloa Advertiser* 17th April 1943

[35] *Alloa Circular* 6th October 1943

[36] *Alloa Advertiser* 22nd January 1944

[37] Alloa Burgh Council minute book 27th March 1944

[38] *Alloa Advertiser* 8th April 1944

[39] *Alloa Circular* 6th September 1939

[40] *Alloa Journal* 16th September 1939

[41] Everybody was to receive a National Identity card, once they had submitted their personal details and registered as of Friday 29th September 1939. It could take quite some time after that to collate all the information, before it would be possible to then issue ration books

[42] *Alloa Advertiser* 30th September 1939

[43] *Alloa Advertiser* 4th November 1939

[44] *Alloa Advertiser* 8th January 1940

[45] *Alloa Advertiser* 13th January 1940

[46] *Alloa Journal* 3rd February 1940

[47] *Alloa Journal* 9th March 1940

[48] *Alloa Journal* 20th July 1940

[49] *Alloa Advertiser* 30th August 1941

[50] *Alloa Circular* 22nd May 1940

[51] *Alloa Advertiser* 30th August 1941

[52] *Alloa Advertiser* 22nd November 1941

[53] *Alloa Advertiser* 12th July 1941

[54] *Alloa Advertiser* 4th July 1942

[55] *Alloa Journal* 25th July 1942

[56] *Alloa Advertiser* and *Alloa Journal* 29th August 1942

[57] *Alloa Journal* 14th February 1942

[58] *Alloa Journal* 25th April 1942. According to an internet source, 'the National Loaf was grey, mushy and unappetising; only one person in seven preferred it to white bread, which became unavailable. The government insisted on it because it saved space in shipping food to Britain and allowed it to better utilize its existing stock of wheat'

[59] *Alloa Advertiser* 25th April 1942

[60] *Alloa Journal* 23rd May 1942

[61] Alloa Advertiser 28th June 1942

[62] *Alloa Advertiser* 5th September 1942

[63] *Alloa Journal* 5th September 1942

[64] *Alloa Journal* 30th January 1943

[65] *Alloa Advertiser* 9th January 1943

[66] Alloa Burgh Council minute book 9th July 1945

[67] *Alloa Journal* 15th June 1940

[68] *Alloa Circular* 12th June 1940

[69] *Alloa Advertiser* 15th June 1940

[70] *Alloa Advertiser* 15th June 1940

[71] *Alloa Advertiser* 15th June 1940

[72] *Alloa Advertiser* 22nd June 1940 and *Alloa Circular* 26th June 1940

[73] Alloa Burgh Council minute book 28th October 1940

[74] *Alloa Circular* 13th November 1940

[75] *Alloa Advertiser* 14th October 1941. He was not named in the article

[76] *Alloa Journal* 6th May 1939 had a big report on its opening

[77] *Alloa Journal* 9th September 1944

[78] *Alloa Journal* 18th November 1939

[79] *Alloa Circular* 15th November 1939

[80] *Alloa Journal* and *Alloa Advertiser* 6th January 1940

[81] *Alloa Advertiser* 23rd January 1943

[82] *Alloa Advertiser* 9th January 1943

[83] *Alloa Advertiser* 1st May 1943

[84] *Alloa Journal* 1st May 1943

[85] *Alloa Circular* 28th April 1943

[86] *Alloa Journal* 3rd October 1943

[87] *Alloa Journal* 15th April 1944 and 22nd April 1944

[88] *Alloa Journal* 28th October 1944

[89] Alloa Burgh Council minute book 31st March 1941

[90] *Alloa Journal* 19th April 1941

[91] Alloa Burgh Council minute book 28th April 1941

[92] Alloa Burgh Council minute book 14th July 1941

[93] Alloa Burgh Council minute book 26th October 1942

[94] Alloa Burgh Council minute book 28th December 1942

[95] Alloa Burgh Council minute book 25th January 1943

[96] Alloa Burgh Council minute book 27th September 1943

[97] *Alloa Journal* 2nd March 1946

[98] Alloa Burgh Council minute book 31st August 1942

[99] *Alloa Journal* 31st October 1942

[100] Alloa Burgh Council minute book 12th October 1942

[101] *Alloa Advertiser* 17th October 1942

[102] *Alloa Advertiser* 8th May 1943

[103] *Alloa Advertiser* 29th May 1943 and *Alloa Circular* 2nd June 1943

[104] Meeting of Magistrates minute book 13th May 1940

[105] Meeting of Magistrates minute book 14th October 1940

[106] Meeting of Magistrates minute book 30th December 1940. *Alloa Advertiser* 27th July 1940 noted that Alloa Burgh Council issued a notice to all householders giving orders to clear lofts and roof spaces so as not to have anything that incendiary bombs might set fire to

[107] Meeting of Magistrates minute book 25th May 1942

[108] *Alloa Advertiser* 24th February 1940

[109] *Alloa Journal* 1st February 1941

[110] *Alloa Journal* 7th February 1942

[111] *Alloa Journal* 6th February 1943

[112] *Alloa Journal* 5th February 1944

[113] *Alloa Advertiser* 8th January 1944

114 *Alloa Advertiser* 22nd January 1944

115 *Alloa Journal* 24th February 1945

116 *Alloa Circular* 21st February 1945

117 Alloa Instrumental Band minute book 9th June 1939

118 Alloa Instrumental Band minute book 5th June 1940

119 Alloa Instrumental Band minute book 14th June 1943

120 *Alloa Journal* 26th October 1940

121 *Alloa Circular* 23rd October 1940

122 *Alloa Journal* 1st March 1941

123 *Alloa Journal* 28th June 1941

124 *Alloa Journal* 8th August 1942

125 Alloa Lodge No. 69 minutes 28th August 1939

126 Alloa Lodge No. 69 minutes 7th September 1939. The minute for 27th August 1940 reveals that the military authorities were paying the Lodge £110 per year for the use of the hall

127 Lodge meetings were held in Kilncraigs Hall from 20th October 1939. It was not until 22nd January 1946 that the first meeting was held back in the Masonic Hall in Church Street

128 There is a good set of records for Alloa Lodge No. 69 in the Archives, but no minute book exists for 1941

129 Alloa Lodge No. 69 minutes 13th March 1942

130 Alloa Lodge No. 69 minutes 29th March 1943

131 Alloa Lodge No. 69 minutes 19th January 1940

132 Alloa Lodge No. 69 minutes 5th September 1940

133 Alloa Lodge No. 69 minutes 25th November 1940

134 Alloa Lodge No. 69 minutes 28th September 1942

135 Alloa Lodge No. 69 minutes 4th January 1943

136 Alloa Lodge No. 69 minutes 18th November 1943

137 Alloa Lodge No. 69 minutes 27th November 1944

138 Alloa Lodge No. 69 minutes 15th March 1945

139 Alloa Lodge No. 69 minutes 27th November 1944

140 *The History of the Lodge of Alloa No. 69* p106

141 *Alloa Advertiser* 31st August 1940

142 There had been a Wartime Charities Act in 1916 which was basically now being amended. In the 1940 reading of the new Act in the House of Lords they were concerned to save the public from a situation like in 1916 where 'it was clear that some charities existed mainly for the benefit of ingenious promoters' [*Hansard* 11th June 1940]

143 Alloa Burgh Council minute book 2nd September 1940

144 *Alloa Advertiser* 14th September 1940

145 *Alloa Advertiser* 13th December 1941 noted that there was a concert '… in aid of the Spitfire fund held in Paton's sports pavilion'

146 The other three were Clackmannanshire War Relief Fund (Earl of Mar & Kellie was chairman and Captain Younger was a member), Clackmannanshire Warmth for Warriors Scheme (registered to a Mrs Cameron at National Bank House on the High Street) and Burgh of Alloa Welcome Home & Commemoration Fund (Provost William Stanton was chairman)

147 *Alloa Journal* 9th June 1945

148 HSH Prince George of Battenberg, whose mother was a granddaughter of Queen Victoria, in April 1916; and HRH Princess Christian, the third daughter of Queen Victoria, in September 1916. It is fair to point out that royalty did also visit Alloa at other times. The St Mungo's Primary School log book noted on 16th April 1938 that the children were taken by their teachers to see the Queen Mother as she passed through the streets of Alloa. Alloa Academy Magazine [1939 issue] noted that the pupils were

given a half day when Queen Mary visited Alloa House in September 1938

[149] *Alloa Advertiser* and *Alloa Journal* 31st July 1943

[150] *Alloa Advertiser* 22nd August 1942 and *Alloa Circular* 25th August 1942

[151] Alloa Advertiser and *Alloa Journal* 5th October 1940

[152] Alloa Burgh Council minute book 31st January 1944

[153] *Alloa Circular* 29th December 1943

[154] Alloa Burgh Council minute book 9th October 1944

[155] Alloa Burgh Council minute book 6th November 1944

[156] Alloa Burgh Council minute book 27th November 1944

[157] Alloa Burgh Council minute book 26th December 1944

[158] Alloa Burgh Council minute book 29th January 1945

[159] Alloa Burgh Council minute book 12th March 1945

[160] Alloa Burgh Council minute book 30th July 1945

[161] *Alloa Journal* 21st July 1945

[162] Valerie Forsyth put forward reminiscence evidence that these German prisoners came from 'Camp 21 at Comrie'. This would have been Cultybraggan Camp where only the more seriously Nazi Category A prisoners were housed. No wonder they were 'under guard' when they came out on their work parties!

[163] *Alloa Advertiser* 16th June 1945. Alloa Burgh Council was still using German POWs almost a year later and there was concern that those working on its building sites were not getting very well fed for their 12-hour working day. The Council agreed that it would write to the appropriate authorities. See *Alloa Journal* 4th May 1946

[164] *Alloa Circular* 18th July 1945

[165] *Alloa Circular* 6th June 1945

[166] *Alloa Journal* 4th August 1945

[167] *Alloa Circular* 1st August 1945

[168] *Alloa Advertiser* 18th May 1940

[169] *Alloa Journal* 18th May 1940

[170] *Alloa Advertiser* 1st June 1940

[171] *Alloa Journal* 1st June 1940

[172] *Alloa Advertiser* 15th June 1940

[173] *Alloa Advertiser* 10th August 1940

[174] Alloa Burgh Council minute book 8th July 1940. The minute book of Alloa Burgh Council's Allotment Holders Association is still in the archives; they make no reference to this request.

[175] Alloa Burgh Council minute book 9th December 1940

[176] Alloa Docks Oral History Project 1987: George: born 1899

[177] Alloa Docks Oral History Project 1987: Peter born 1912

[178] *Alloa Advertiser* 21st December 1940

[179] Alloa Docks Oral History Project 1987: Jock born 1921

[180] *Alloa Advertiser* 9th August 1941

[181] *Alloa Advertiser* 22nd May 1943

[182] Alloa Burgh Council minute book 4th September 1944

[183] *Alloa Advertiser* 9th December 1944

[184] *Alloa Circular* 6th December 1944

[185] *Alloa Journal* 9th December 1944

[186] *Alloa Advertiser* 1st May 1940

[187] *Alloa Advertiser* 27th July 1940

[188] *Alloa Advertiser* 20th December 1941

[189] *Alloa Journal* 4th November 1944

[190] *Alloa Journal* 19th June 1943

[191] See Valerie Forsyth article in *Alloa Advertiser* 28th September 2018

[192] Reminiscence evidence from Helen Wingate

[193] Chalmers Church Deacons' Court Minute Book 12th October 1943

[194] Imperial War Museum Negative Albums 9-11

[195] Alloa Burgh Council minute book 4th September 1944

[196] *Alloa Advertiser* 9th September 1944

[197] *Alloa Journal* 2nd September 1944

[198] *Alloa Circular* 14th August 1940

[199] *Alloa Advertiser* 19th August 1940

[200] *Alloa Advertiser* 26th August 1940

[201] *Our War: Clackmannanshire and Stirlingshire During the Second World War* (2006) p69

[202] An article in the *Herald* gave his date of birth as 14th July 1912. ScotlandsPeople records that there were 3 James Atkinsons born in 1912. One with the middle name of Low was discounted. The other two did not have middle names recorded in the summary of information, but their places of birth were Greenock East and Old or West Kilpatrick. There were no James Atkinsons born in Alloa between 1910 and 1915. Thanks to Susan Yule for this piece of research

[203] The *Mapa Scotland* website states that 'This Division was reconstituted overnight by simply renaming the 9th Scottish Division, thenstationed at home, as the 51st Highland Division'. Wikipedia more accurately explains that 'in August 1940 the 9th Highland Infantry Division (the 51st (Highland) Infantry Division's 2nd line Territorial Army duplicate, which it had helped form) was re-designated as the 51st (Highland) Infantry Division.

[204] *Alloa Advertiser* 28th November 1942 and *Alloa Circular* 25th November 1942

[205] *Alloa Advertiser* 2nd January 1943

[206] *Alloa Advertiser* 21st August 1943

[207] *Alloa Advertiser* 6th January 1945

[208] *Alloa Advertiser* 15th March 1941

[209] *Alloa Circular* 19th March 1941

[210] St John's Church Service Book 23rd March 1941

[211] *Alloa Circular* 7th January 1942

[212] *Alloa Circular* 10th March 1943

[213] *Alloa Circular* 19th August 1942

[214] *Alloa Journal* 2nd January 1943

[215] *Alloa Advertiser* 10th June 1944. The *Alloa Circular* on 16th June 1943 had reported the christening of the Sauchie boy with those middle names.

[216] *Alloa Journal* 18th August 1945

[217] *Alloa Journal* 18th August 1945

[218] Alloa Academy Literary and Debating Society minute book 7th September 1945

[219] *Alloa Circular* 20th December 1939

[220] This photograph is picture 27 in the catalogue of the National Monuments Record of Scotland. It was taken in October 1939

[221] Alloa Docks Oral History Project 1987: George born 1899

[222] *Alloa Journal* 29th June 1940

[223] *Alloa Circular* 17th July 1940

[224] Alloa Docks Oral History Project 1987: Jimmy born 1924

[225] Alloa Docks Oral History Project 1987: Ina born 1923

[226] *Alloa Journal* 1st August 1942

[227] *Alloa Circular* 5th August 1942

[228] *Alloa Advertiser* 23rd September 2018 article by Valerie Forsyth

[229] *Alloa Journal* 26th September 1942

[230] *Alloa Circular* 30th September 1942

[231] *Alloa Circular* 14th October 1942

[232] See *Our War: Clackmannanshire and Stirlingshire During the Second World War* (2006)

[233] This information can be found on the website www.britmodeller.com

[234] This information can be found on the website www.gairney.plus.com

CHAPTER 7

CHURCHES AND THE WAR

The story of Alloa's churches and how they and their congregations responded to the impact of the Second World War would be a pretty thin one if the only evidence to be utilised were the minutes of the churches' own Kirk Sessions or Deacons' Courts. In many cases these records say little or nothing about the effects of war on their spiritual life or everyday business. If you look at Greenside Church[1] for instance; apart from a reference on 11th September 1939 to a discussion by local ministers on the impact the blackout might have on the timing of Sunday services; their Kirk Session minutes contain NO other mention of the war. The minutes of its Management Committee additionally record that they agreed to donate £2 towards the cost of blackout materials and that on 28th June 1943 they agreed 'to assist soldiers of our own congregation', and that was it; two references to the war. This was the extreme example but even with some of the other churches it was not untypical that a whole year could pass with no war-related reference in their Session minutes. In fact, as another example, none of the local churches paid any written recognition in their Session minutes to either the fact that a war had started in September 1939, or that it had ended in May 1945.[2] The only qualification to that comment is that, in the case of St John's Church, they also kept a weekly *Service Book* which was a register of when the service was, who gave the sermon, how much was in the offertory etc.[3] This book had the following note written in it on the very day that war was declared: 'September 3rd; Trinity xiii the Prime Minister's statement on a state of War existing between Britain and Germany broadcast in Church at 11.15'.

This same book also noted that 8th May 1945 was 'VE Day' and that a service

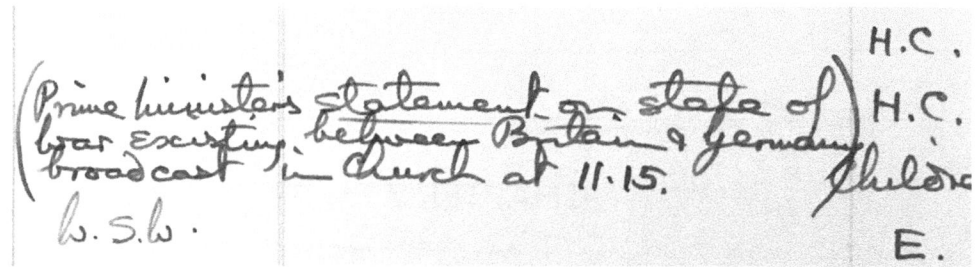

St John's Church Register of Services entry on 3rd September 1939

was held at 7.30 pm. With so little to go on in the various churches' minutes, it's a good job that the local press was able to provide a little extra evidence to fill in the broader picture of the impact of the war on church life. However, looking at it from a study of church records, it does seem that there were four common threads to the issues that the local churches had to deal with in their wartime situation: Coping with the Blackout, Preparation for air-raids, Events with a military connection, and Caring for congregational members in the Armed Forces.

COPING WITH THE BLACKOUT

We have already noted that within a week of the start of the war, local ministers held a meeting to discuss the effects of a blackout on the times of services. The Minister of St Andrew's[4] told his Session that local Ministers had met and agreed that 'commencing Sunday 17th September would be new times for church services'.[5] On 12th September 1939 at Chalmers Church, 'discussion on darkening of windows in the hall and ante-rooms took place and it was agreed to have this done'.[6] By July 1940, Chalmers Church became concerned both about how to black out their stained glass window and how to protect it; the Deacons' Court ordered the spending of £3.4/- on material to black out the Rose window with wood and felt.[7] St Mungo's was still worrying about blackout a year later when in July 1941, the Moderator had a meeting with the Chief Constable 'in connection with the blackout of the church, and he was sure there was a scheme whereby the Church could be dimmed'.[8] In the case of St John's, it was not until December 1943 that they took steps to protect their stained glass windows. Their Vestry Committee minutes in December 1943 noted that they had 'decided to see Captain Younger about protection for the Hallan window on the south side of the chancel'.[9]

PREPARATION FOR AIR RAIDS

Nothing much happened in the first 3 months of the war. It wasn't until December 1939 that St Mungo's Session Clerk reported that 'he had heard from the Dean of Guild informing him that an Air Raid Shelter was to be built on a piece of ground to the south east of the church hall property in Bedford Place.[10] There is no further reference to this in the Kirk Session minutes. In June 1940 most of the local churches took a sudden interest in air raid precautions. St Mungo's led the way when it was reported that they 'had ordered two stirrup pumps to be placed at each end of the church in case of an emergency'.[11] Then in St Andrew's the Minister suggested 'that some provision should be made to counteract fire in the event of an air raid and it was agreed to endeavour to obtain buckets and shovels' [to distribute sand].[12] It was only by September 1940 that Chalmers Church '… agreed to empower Mr Reid to obtain pails, rake and sand to be ready in case of incendiary bombs being dropped'.[13] Similar concerns were expressed in St John's where, under a marginal heading of ARP, 'the Secretary was instructed to see the Chief Constable to arrange for the necessary fire issues'.[14] In February and March 1941, both Chalmers Church and St Mungo's discussed what to do if an air raid alert sounded during the actual service.[15] In February 1941 St Mungo's set up a committee to decide on the operation of fire-watching procedures; they decided to make an appeal to young men in the Fellowship Class of the Congregation to actually do the fire-watching, but they only had 2 volunteers.[16]

Once the actual bombing of Scottish towns started in 1941, local churches became concerned about insuring their property under the War Damage Act 1941.[17] Chalmers Church valued its organ at £100 and the furnishings at £500. The annual cost of the premium for this insurance was about £28.[18] St Mungo's initial valuation of their insurable worth was £1,500. This was altered in May 1941 when they reckoned the Church at £2,000, £1,500 for the organ, £100 for the clock and £400 for the Church halls. From 25th April 1943 they increased the insurable total to £5,000.[19] At St John's in November 1941, the Treasurer reported that there had been 'a new charge of £10.10/- for War Damage Insurance'.[20] By June 1942 he reported that 'this war risks insurance was £30'.[21]

EVENTS WITH A MILITARY CONNECTION

The local churches were among the first to suffer from the irresistible demand from the military for space for their troops and stores. Within a week of the start of the war, St Andrew's Church hall had been requisitioned by the military at a rate of £3 a week in summer and £3.10/- in winter.[22] A month later, St Mungo's also lost the use of its hall to the military authorities.[23] Chalmers Church was able to keep the use of its church hall; by 1943 there was a reference in the Deacons' Court minutes to the creation of a club for Polish officers, using the hall on most nights of the week but not Sundays.[24] It maybe cost them £6 for its use but it is difficult to see what length of time the minute was talking about, and therefore how many months the club lasted. It seems the military had also been using Greenside Church's Park Lane hall but had given it up by 5th November 1943.

One small event with a military connection that seemed to run and run started in May 1940 when the Treasurer of Chalmers Church reported 'that damage had been done to the church railings by an army lorry. The officer commanding [the Argyll and Sutherland Highlanders] had accepted responsibility. Estimate for repair was £16.16/-'.[25] Further minutes for about the next two years show how the church adopted a slightly undignified pursuit of this money, how the army tried to wriggle out of paying it, how temporary wooden fencing was put up etc. You really would have thought that in the trying circumstances of the war they would all have had better things to worry about. It was all rendered irrelevant after three years when Rev. Gordon Campbell 'read a letter from the Ministry of Works stating that under the scheme for the collection of scrap metal it was proposed to remove the railings in front of the Chalmers Church'.[26] The church complained about this, maybe because the chance of getting its 16 guineas compensation had disappeared, but by 14th December 1943 the minutes noted 'that the railings in front of the church had been removed'.

St Mungo's lost the services of two consecutive Assistant Ministers to the call of military duties. In February 1941 Rev. Andrew Swan went off to the Orkneys with 'Huts and Canteens', a sort of church mission to the military, for 6 months.[27] His replacement Rev. Andrew Russell speedily followed his example by joining HM Forces in May 1941.[28] Unlike in the Great War, where there was quite a rush; no other local ministers gave up their duties to serve in the military.

The Session minutes did not report that in August 1942 Rev. Gordon M.B. Bennett, formerly an Assistant Minister at St Mungo's, but now Chaplain to the Forces; had become a prisoner of war of the Japanese.[29] He had left Alloa after 3 years to go to Catterick Camp in May 1939 and had ended up as Chaplain to the 2nd Battalion of the Royal Scots serving in Singapore when it surrendered, being one of 7 military chaplains to be captured. In October 1942 the *Journal* reported that they had good news about his situation: 'He is well and allowed to preach to the captives once a week. He can also write one letter home each month'.[30] He had almost 4 years of captivity, serving as Chaplain in Changi Camp.[31] Rev. G. Bennett's story did have a happy ending; in October 1946 he married Nurse Lydia Maclean from Clackmannan. Both had been POWs of the Japanese and they had met on the train home from the Far East.

In May 1940 the Minister of St Mungo's[32] reported 'that the CO of the Black Watch stationed in Alloa had asked permission to erect an Anti-Aircraft gun on the lawn at the back of the church'.[33] There was no further reference to this; one suspects that nothing came of it.

One of the few occasions during the war when there was any reference to the local unit of the Women's Land Army, was in October 1944 when they led the harvest thanksgiving service at St Mungo's.[34]

The last way that military affairs impinged on the church was in the sad references in the Kirk Session minutes to missing family, friends and colleagues within the various congregations, who had died in action. The fact that this was so rarely reported on [when surely a good percentage of Alloa's 125 military deaths would have been local church-goers?] suggests it was just seen as the 'accepted' consequence of war, and that the person who had died had to have a direct and personal contact with the upper levels of his church to have his death recorded in the Session records. This was certainly the case in August 1944 when the Minister of St Mungo's 'expressed the Session's deep and affectionate sympathy to Mr and Mrs Purgavie on the death in action of their son Captain David G. Purgavie MC'.[35] This was the son of the man who had been the Session Clerk until the end of 1943.

After the war was over, St Mungo's held a ceremony to unveil its stained glass memorial window in commemoration of those of the congregation who had lost their lives in the war. At this ceremony a wreath was laid by Mrs Purgavie 'on behalf of the kinsfolk of the fallen'.[36]

Having a connection to the upper levels of the church was even more the case in Chalmers Church in October 1944 when 'Mr Cuthbert [an elder] made moving reference to the great loss the Minister had suffered by the loss of his son George while on active service as Chaplain in HM Forces...'[37] On this occasion, the minutes of a fellow Church also acknowledged the loss; St Mungo's Kirk Session 'noted the death by an air accident of Rev. GAG Campbell'.[38] This death was also reported in the *Advertiser*.[39]

CARING FOR CONGREGATIONAL MEMBERS IN THE ARMED FORCES

You had a sense, in connection with the blackout, that plenty of church members in all the churches, would have remembered the lighting restrictions of 1916 in the Great War, and therefore it was no surprise to see them introduced again. This sense of a re-run of the past was even more clearly the case with the different attempts by congregations to support their members in the armed forces. In November 1939, Rev. Pitt Watson of St Mungo's reported to his Session that 'Some of the older members of the Women's Guild had mentioned to him that during the last war the Congregation had brought gifts which were later made into parcels for boys from the Congregation serving in HM Forces as Xmas gifts. It was agreed... a 'Gift Sunday' would take place on 3rd December'.[40] This obviously worked well because he later reported that 'a splendid response had been made by the Congregation to the appeal for gifts for members of the Congregation serving with HM Forces, and also the sum of £14 had been received. Parcels had been made up by members of the Women's Guild'.[41]

What we then see is that all the local churches followed much the same pattern of having special collections or gift services, and also whist drives and jumble sales in the case of Chalmers Church, to raise money for their 'Comforts Funds'.[42] In November 1940, St Mungo's agreed to repeat the gift service and Xmas parcels to members in the Forces, to be organised by the Women's Guild. They pretty well agreed to this procedure for the rest of the war. By November 1942 they had the names of 270 members of the congregation serving with HM Forces. They would all get a card and a 5/- postal order, but those serving overseas would have the money kept back for them.[43] St Andrew's followed the same pattern[44] but Chalmers Church was slightly more generous; in September 1942 they agreed to send a 10/- postal order with a greetings card to those men of their congregation serving overseas. If they were serving in UK it would be a 7/6 postal order. Chalmers Church Women's Guild also agreed to hold a party for the wives and mothers of the men on service on Wednesday 21st October 1942. They held these parties and sent the postal orders right through the rest of the war[45] and in April 1943 even sent 32 pairs of socks that they knitted to serving seamen.[46] There is no evidence from St John's that they produced Christmas comforts for the troops, but in February 1941 they had a 'Retiring Collection for Parcels for Prisoners-of-War' which raised £3. 2/6.[47] St John's also took part in the gift-giving to servicemen from their congregation; the Vestry Committee minutes in November 1941 noted that 'there were 70 members in service with HM Forces... and that gifts had been sent to all last Xmas and it was hoped to do the same again this year'.[48]

Information about the size of membership of Alloa's churches was much more fully available in the records for the time of the Great War. Only St Mungo's kept fairly full records during the Second World War. These show that its congregation stayed pretty steady at just over 2200 members. The number of members taking Communion at least once tended to vary; in 1939 was 67%, in 1940 it was 70%, in 1942 it was 54%, then in 1943 it was 60%. It does look like church attendance held up fairly well during the war years; maybe in St Mungo's case it was because the Minister had such an optimistic view about the progress of the war. He must have been confident of victory, even with eight months still to go, because in August 1944, he 'reported that a service would be held in St Mungo's Church on the evening of the day on which hostilities with Germany ceased'.[49] The Session minutes do not record whether this service was actually held although the *Advertiser* for 12th May reported that it was well attended.[50]

Alloa's churches during the war seem to have taken the view to chiefly focus on the needs of their own congregations; there were very few occasions where the Alloa churches, either individually or collectively, took a lead on providing uplifting moral guidance to the wider local population. During the Great War there had been several National Days of Prayer; these didn't get the same support in the Second World War; only St John's seemed to seriously observe these events on 1st October 1939, 26th May 1940 and 7th September 1941.[51]

One example where there was a collective church input was in July 1940 following the evacuation at Dunkirk and the subsequent surrender of the

51st Highland Division, with so many of its soldiers with an Alloa connection who then became prisoners of war. There was a real sense of gloom, so a big notice was put in the *Advertiser* which you suspect must have come from the local religious community because it had so many references to 'listening to God'. It was signed by all the provosts in the County and was all about keeping up morale. It itemised 6 things including 'forgetting yourself and helping your neighbours' and not spreading rumours.[52] The editorial in that issue also talked about not being alarmist or defeatist.

Moncrieff Church Kirk Session 1941

Another example of a local church taking a strong moral position occurred in March 1943 when, alone among Alloa's churches, Moncrieff Church expressed its horror 'at the German attempt to exterminate the Jews'. The Kirk Session unanimously adopted 3 resolutions; the first asking that the British government should try to offer asylum to more 'refugees from Nazi persecution as they may succeed in making their way' to safer territories. It secondly requested that the 'government should pledge themselves to provide for the ultimate settlement of the above-mentioned refugees in the post-war period', and thirdly that the government should consider all this as a matter of the greatest urgency.[53] This was the only reference in the Alloa press to Nazi persecution of the Jews that can be found during all the war years. The only other reference was in October 1945 when it mentioned that a Sauchie soldier, Sergeant J. Drysdale, was on guard duty during the war-crimes trial of Josef Kramer, the 'Butcher of Belsen'.[54]

There was a collective Alloa mission, starting on Sunday 18th September 1943 where there was a week of campaigning with all the local protestant churches collaborating in spreading the Christian message. The highlight was a meeting at the Gaumont cinema which was 'crowded to the utmost capacity, with several hundred people unable to gain admission'.[55] Another example of a local church providing spiritual uplift was in September 1944 when Moncrieff Church ran its own evangelical mission; the *Advertiser* reported that it was 'An Inspiring Week'.[56]

Alone amongst the local churches, St Mungo's did record its agonies of thought about how returning servicemen might respond to the Christian message, following their long brutal years

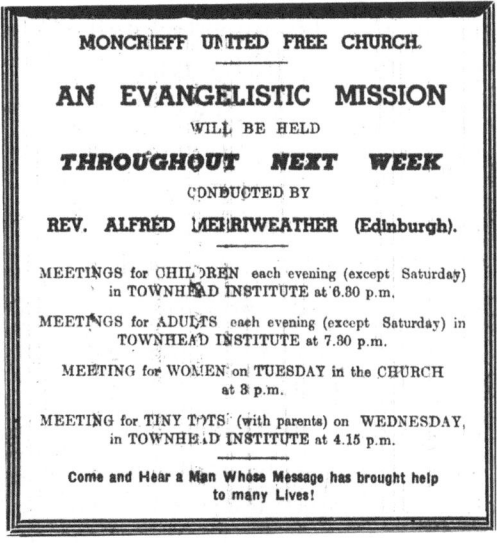

Poster advertising the Moncrieff Church mission *Alloa Journal* 16th September 1944

of war. In October 1944 they held a series of discussions called 'When they Return', leading to thought on how to best prepare the church and its ministry for the needs of returning soldiers. There was agreement to suggestions that sending out circulars and supplements to church magazines to still-serving soldiers would help to keep them in the fold, that there should be a men's club, and the church should have a clear and exact knowledge of which members had served, from which families etc. They then set up a group called Special Demobilisation Committee to come up with firm ideas.[57] Not much else was recorded about how these discussions went, but this does give us an insight into one of the few occasions, admittedly late-on in the war, where it seems the church was trying to give some sort of spiritual leadership within the community.

There were three more religious groups in Alloa during the Second World War who are very difficult to get any detailed information about; the Roman Catholic Church of St Mungo's, the Baptist Church and the Salvation Army. It is frustrating in the case of the Baptist Church because they kept good records during the Great War but nothing during the Second World War. All we know is that their Pastor was Rev. W.D. MacGregor.[58]

The lack of information about the Catholic Church is less surprising; they kept no records during the Great War and none in the Second. They did not advertise their church services in the local press; whose reporting of events in this church during the war years comprised of little more than a note on the comings and goings of some of the priests. At the outbreak of war the Catholic community in Alloa was led by Canon A.S. Roche. He had served in Alloa for 11 years but was promoted to St Joseph's Dundee. He was succeeded in May 1940 by Very Rev. Canon James Matthews[59] who had previously served in Lochee, Dundee and Arbroath. The rise in numbers of Catholics in Alloa during the war [possibly due to incoming war workers] led to the appointment of a permanent curate in 1942; this was Father Peter Foylan.[60] All three local papers carried an announcement of this appointment.[61] Now, another priest, Father O'Donoghue, must have joined this ministry at some time because in October 1946 he departed for Dundee. It was the function being held in his honour which led to the mention in the *Journal* that this was the first occasion that the recently de-requisitioned St Mungo's RC church hall could be used, so it was a double celebration.[62]

The only records kept by the Salvation Army of their wartime ministry in Alloa are from the Farewell Report of the outgoing Commander of the Salvation Army's Scotland Territory in May 1945. This was General George Lyndon Carpenter. He noted that Alloa had 36 members of congregation and an officer as minister; this was about the same size as Alva. His report said nothing of their activities over the war years, just that they had ownership of 'a property, referred to as 'Alloa' situated at Marshill House', used as a home of rest [donated by Mr Forrester Paton], and two other properties in Alloa [Alloa cottage and Alloa greenhouses] which were rented out. He also noted that 'Plans were in hand for a new hall but it had to be temporarily abandoned owing to war conditions'. This doesn't exactly fit with the evidence in the press which had slightly more to say about the Salvation Army than about the Roman Catholic Church. The *Journal* in December 1940 noted that the Salvation Army opened its new premises in Mar Street... on a site gifted by Mr J. Forrester Paton of Inglewood.[63] The *Circular* noted that this hall had been transferred from another site and was a temporary building because, although there had been plans for a permanent one, 'they had to be deferred owing to the war'.[64] The *Journal* in January 1942 reported that 'Captain and Mrs Jannels have completed two years in charge of the local corps',[65] and in May 1942 that they were moving to Dundee; the new leader would be Captain Alice Francis.[66] One of the highlights of the war years must have been the visit in November 1942 of Lt Col Wycliffe-Booth, grandson of the founder of the Salvation Army who came to give a talk in Alloa; 'He gave a vivid and engrossing account of his experience in France and Switzerland at the outbreak of the war...'[67]

ENDNOTES

[1] In the Great War, Greenside Church had been a Mission under the charge of Moncrieff Church. It became a separate charge of the United Free Church in 1921, joined the Church of Scotland in 1929 then merged with Alloa West in 1941. During the Second World War its minister was Rev. Alexander Chisholm

[2] This was quite different to the reaction in Alloa's schools where every single one of them recorded both events!

[3] The details in St John's Church Service Book were probably filled in by the Rector, Rev. William Wilson. He died suddenly in March 1942. The *Alloa Circular* reported on 25th March 1942 that 'his fatal illness was of a brief and sudden nature, and he had been carrying on his duties the previous day'. The new Rector was Rev. Canon GK Sturrock Clarke who started his duties on 1st August 1942

[4] The Minister of St Andrew's Church for all the war years was Rev. James Clark

[5] St Andrew's Kirk Session Minute Book 10th September 1939

[6] Chalmers Church Deacons' Court Minute Book 12th September 1939

[7] Chalmers Church Deacons' Court Minute Book 9th July 1940

[8] St Mungo's Kirk Session Minute Book 27th July 1941

[9] St John's Church Vestry Committee Minute Book 20th December 1943

[10] St Mungo's Kirk Session Minute Book 18th December 1939

[11] St Mungo's Kirk Session Minute Book 17th June 1940

[12] St Andrew's Kirk Session Minute Book 30th June 1940

[13] Chalmers Church Deacons' Court Minute Book 14th September 1940

[14] St John's Church Vestry Committee Minute Book 16th September 1940

[15] Chalmers Church Deacons' Court Minute Book 4th February 1941 and St Mungo's Kirk Session Minute Book 17th March 1941

[16] St Mungo's Kirk Session Minute Book 9th February 1941 and 17th February 1941

[17] The War Damage Act was introduced by Sir Kingsley Wood who said at the time [HANSARD, 17th

December 1940] that the Bill was an instrument of justice and an act of social solidarity spreading the burden of the war damage over the whole community. Incidentally, it reflected confidence in ultimate victory.

[18] Chalmers Church Deacons' Court Minute Book 19th May 1941 and 10th December 1941

[19] St Mungo's Kirk Session Minute Book 7th May 1941 and 18th May 1941

[20] St John's Church Vestry Committee Minute Book 9th November 1941

[21] St John's Church Vestry Committee Minute Book 16th June 1942

[22] St Andrew's Kirk Session Minute Book 10th September 1939

[23] St Mungo's Kirk Session Minute Book 16th October 1939

[24] Chalmers Church Deacons' Court Minute Book 12th October 1943

[25] Chalmers Church Deacons' Court Minute Book 14th May 1940

[26] Chalmers Church Deacons' Court Minute Book 4th July 1943

[27] St Mungo's Kirk Session Minute Book 9th February 1941

[28] St Mungo's Kirk Session Minute Book 18th May 1941

[29] *Alloa Advertiser* 1st August 1942

[30] *Alloa Journal* 17th October 1942 reported on the contents of a letter that his father had received

[31] Most of this information is from Rev. Gordon Bennett's article in the Royal Army Chaplain's Department Journal in 1969. This is referred to in several places in David G Coulter's Edinburgh University thesis of 1997 entitled *The Church of Scotland Army Chaplains in the Second World War* which can be read on-line. Also see *Alloa Journal* 12th October 1946

[32] The Minister of St Mungo's Church for all the war years was Rev. James Pitt Watson

[33] St Mungo's Kirk Session Minute Book 20th May 1940

[34] *Alloa Journal* 21st October 1944

[35] St Mungo's Kirk Session Minute Book 27th August 1944

[36] Information found in *St Mungo's Parish Church The Story So Far*, a history celebrating the bi-centenary of the church's foundation (2019)

[37] The Minister of Chalmers Church for all the war years was Rev. George Gordon Campbell

[38] St Mungo's Kirk Session Minute Book 8th October 1944

[39] *Alloa Advertiser* 7th October 1944

[40] St Mungo's Kirk Session Minute Book 15th November 1939

[41] St Mungo's Kirk Session Minute Book 18th December 1939

[42] Chalmers Church Deacons' Court Minute Book 11th June 1940, St Andrew's Kirk Session Minute Book 29th September 1940 and 30th October 1940

[43] St Mungo's Kirk Session Minute Book 3rd November 1940 and 29th November 1942

[44] St Andrew's Kirk Session Minute Book 12th November 1941

[45] Chalmers Church Women's Guild Minute Book 25th September 1942

[46] Chalmers Church Women's Guild Minute Book 9th April 1943

[47] St John's Church Service Book 16th February 1941

[48] St John's Church Vestry Committee Minute Book 9th November 1941

[49] St Mungo's Kirk Session Minute Book 27th August 1944

[50] St Mungo's Kirk Session Minute Book Sunday 19th August 1945 did record that a special Victory Thanksgiving Service was held in the church at 6.30 pm. This was after VJ Day, not VE Day

[51] See St John's Church Service Book

[52] *Alloa Advertiser* and *Alloa Journal* 27th July 1940

[53] Alloa Journal 20th March 1943 and *Alloa Circular* 17th March 1943

[54] *Alloa Journal* 13th October 1945

[55] *Alloa Journal* 25th September 1943

[56] *Alloa Advertiser* 22nd September 1944

[57] St Mungo's Kirk Session Minute Book 24th December 1944 recorded the first meeting of this Committee; curiously they thought a mixed club would be better!

[58] *Alloa Advertiser* 30th November 1940

[59] Alloa Advertiser 1st June 1940

[60] Information found in John Gallacher, *St Mungo's Alloa: 150 Years of Faith*

[61] *Alloa Journal* 8th August 1942, *Alloa Advertiser* 15th August 1942 and *Alloa Circular* 12th August 1942

[62] *Alloa Journal* 12th October 1946

[63] *Alloa Journal* 28th December 1940

[64] *Alloa Circular* 25th December 1940

[65] *Alloa Journal* 3rd January 1942

[66] *Alloa Journal* 30th May 1942

[67] *Alloa Journal* 7th November 1942

CHAPTER 8

LOCAL AND NATIONAL POLITICS

Right from the start of the war, there seemed to be a general consensus, echoing the situation during the Great War; that elections for local political positions should simply not be bothered with. It was crisply noted in the *Advertiser* in September 1939 that 'Preliminary discussions seem to indicate that municipal elections [for councillors] due to be held all over the country two months from now will not take place. The arguments for their cancellation require little elaboration and will readily commend themselves to a citizenship faced with greater issues'.[1]

However, Alloa had a bigger political issue than municipal elections because their local MP, Lauchlan MacNeill Weir for the Labour Party, had just died and there needed to be a parliamentary by-election.[2] The *Journal* predicted that 'In regards to the constituency vacancy, there is likely to be a party truce... no candidate will be set up to contest the seat'.[3] The *Advertiser* agreed, reporting that the same rule [for municipal elections] held true for parliamentary elections as well. It claimed that 'A by-election is considered undesirable... the parties have agreed to call a truce... and Arthur Woodburn [the Labour candidate] will 'automatically fill the seat without any opposition'.[4] Arthur Woodburn had an interesting past; he had been imprisoned as a conscientious objector in the Great War, but had risen to become the Secretary of the Scottish Labour Party from 1932 to 1939. He had stood for parliament on two losing occasions before he secured the nomination to the seat of Clackmannanshire and East Stirling.

The political truce was agreed to by the other parties. In October there was a notice on the front page of the *Advertiser* from Alan Stein, Chairman of

Clackmannan and East Stirling Unionist Association. He stated that 'At the beginning of the war the parties supporting the National Government agreed with the Labour and Liberal opposition parties not to nominate candidates in By-Elections for parliamentary vacancies, against the candidate nominated by the Party which held the seat at the time the vacancies occurred. In these circumstances the Unionist Party have not nominated a Candidate in the present By-Election'.[5] This noble truce however almost came to nothing when Andrew Stewart put himself forward as [an independent] candidate for the Anti-War Party. The *Journal* was somewhat short with him and his views, saying that 'Mr Stewart is the anti-war candidate. Mr Stewart is in favour of stopping the war because, he contends, it is absolutely useless'.[6] He was an assistant editor of the *Peace News* and saw himself as the representative of pacifism.[7] He had support from James Maxton, the veteran pacifist member of the Independent Labour Party and MP for Bridgeton who spoke up for him at a meeting in Sauchie. The *Circular* reported Maxton's views under a headline of 'Plea To Stop Insane Conflict'. Mr Stewart didn't accept the rules of the truce so there had to be an election campaign; just him against Arthur Woodburn.[8]

In the election there was only a 35% turnout.[9] The votes were counted and Arthur Woodburn got over 15,000 votes and Andrew Stewart got 1,000 and lost his deposit.[10] Stewart made an ungracious speech after his defeat, along the lines of 'I used to think the people of this constituency were half mad when I started this election campaign, now I know they are all mad', which didn't endear him to the *Journal*.

In May 1940 Lord Erskine, the Earl of Mar's eldest son became Conservative MP for Brighton... in an uncontested election; on the same terms as how Arthur Woodburn got in.[11]

Arthur Woodburn certainly believed in letting his constituents know who he was and what he stood for. He had a column in the *Advertiser* at least once a month which discussed a range of political issues. He also made visits to local industry to encourage the workers and tirelessly pestered the government to consider the merits of restoring shipbuilding to the derelict yards of Alloa. In April 1940 he visited Harlands and made a speech about the importance of engineers.[12]

He also made a point, in the first half of 1941, of visiting most of the local schools and addressing the pupils. Grange School log book for 14th February noted that he 'addressed pupils on 'Houses of Parliament' (with film strip)'. The following day he visited Alloa Academy,[13] and on 7th March he visited Sunnyside where the log book recorded that he 'gave a lecture on 'The Work of Parliament' to the senior pupils this afternoon. The lecture was illustrated by slides'. Basically he went all round the County, just about to every school, giving his slide-show lecture. The local press reported this again in May[14] and the *Journal* in July reckoned that, 'to date he has delivered his talk to over 3,000 County school children'.[15]

In February 1941 he was appointed Parliamentary Private Secretary to the Secretary of State for Scotland, Tom Johnston.[16] This was regarded as quite a promotion since Woodburn had only been an MP for about 18 months.

On 22nd June 1941 German Armies invaded Russia in Operation Barbarossa, and within less than a week Woodburn asked the Prime Minister in Parliament whether 'in considering means of helping Russia, he will, as a measure of mutual help, investigate the possibility of arranging free passage to Russia for skilled workers in the railway, transport, engineering and other civil or armed services, in cases where such workers are adherents of the Communist Party professing their first loyalty to Soviet Russia'.[17] It's difficult to know if this should be seen as a noble expression of Woodburn's socialist solidarity with a new ally or a less-than-subtle attempt to purge British socialism of its more extreme left wing elements! It might have been expected that Woodburn would hold the first view since he had been a keen member of Edinburgh's 'Hands Off Russia' campaign in the 1930s; but by May 1943 he was making more pointed comments about the 'underground menace' of the Communist Party... which led to refutations from the secretary of the local Communist Party a week later in the Alloa press.[18]

Things were not totally sweetness and light for Arthur Woodburn MP in Alloa, especially in early 1942. As we have seen, he was always very anxious to get out among his constituents and take advantage of modern technology, and what he had done on Tuesday 3rd March 1942 was to lead discussion on a national wireless broadcast where some of his guest speakers were Alloa children. One of them was a boy called Keith Irvine who, Woodburn admitted, some months previously 'had notified him that salvage was not being carried on in Alloa as enthusiastically as it might be'. The upshot of this was that Woodburn revealed on the radio that he had then approached the cabinet minister concerned who had then approached Alloa's Town Clerk. The result was that the Council had then launched the salvage drive which started in the first week of January 1942. Mr Woodburn went on to say that he thought it was an excellent demonstration of the way that democracy worked.[19] The Council naturally was outraged at this suggestion that 'an Alloa boy of from 8 to 10 years of age had influenced the Alloa Town Council to have a paper salvage week in the Burgh'.[20] They thought the boy was highly precocious, that 'no letter ever came to the Town Clerk from London' and that 'Mr Woodburn should be asked to withdraw what he had said'. A week later he replied to their complaint, saying the Council had got it out of proportion.[21] Mr Woodburn certainly wasn't prepared to give much ground; the *Circular* included a big article on 'Mr Woodburn and his broadcast' where he justified his position.[22] There was 'some feeling in the Council that the MP Mr Woodburn had unjustly maligned members of the Council in his radio broadcast about salvage', however, he had then expressed regret in two letters 'if his broadcast had carried any unjust reproach on the officials'. The Council expressed dissatisfaction at Mr Woodburn's replies but agreed to let the matter drop.[23]

In the Great War, the Prime Minister, David Lloyd George, dropped in to Alloa on one occasion. In the Second World War, Winston Churchill never came to Alloa, but his Deputy Prime Minister, Clement Attlee did. The *Advertiser*

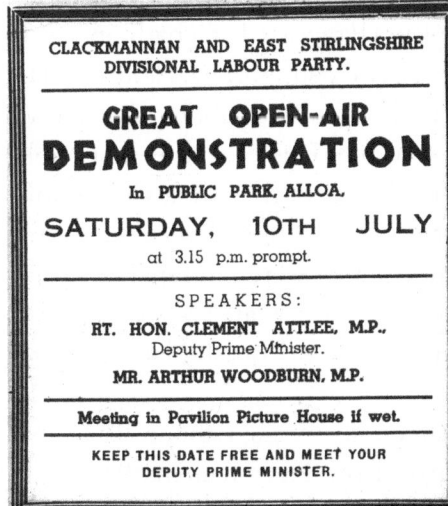

Alloa Circular 3rd July 1943

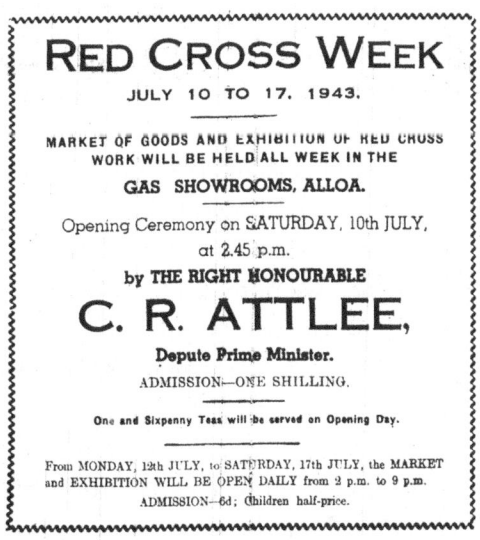

Alloa Advertiser 3rd July 1943

knew of this on 22nd May 1943 and it was first noted in the Council minutes of 14th June 1943 when the 'Provost reported that Rt. Hon C.R. Attlee, Deputy Prime Minister was coming to Alloa to address a Labour Party demonstration on 10th July at 3.15pm and he thought it fitting that recognition should be made of Mr Attlee's visit'. There were provisional arrangements made to entertain him to lunch with a civic reception, and Mr Attlee would then open a sale and exhibition at the Gas showrooms organised by the British Red Cross.[24]

All this went ahead and seemed to have gone off without a hitch, including his declaration of the official opening of Red Cross Week in Alloa. The *Advertiser* regarded his visit as 'a red letter day in the political and administrative history of Alloa'.[25] The *Journal* likewise approved and their report contained a long description of his speech in the Public Park quoting his rousing closing words on what would be the Labour Party's peacetime ambitions; 'We are going to defeat these barbarians but there is a danger we may relax when we have defeated them. In the less heroic atmosphere of peace we must bend our minds to the great task of winning the peace...'[26] The Council minutes for 12th July however, acted like it was all no big deal and just recorded that Provost McKinlay thanked various people for their efforts on the day.

There might not have been any elections in Alloa during the war years, but there still was democratic debate. Different political parties were authorised by the Council to hold public meetings, mostly in the West End Park, to put across their viewpoints. In August 1941 the *Journal* reported at length on a well-attended meeting in the Public Park, of Labour Party supporters... addressed by Sir Patrick Dolan, Lord Provost of Glasgow and Arthur Woodburn MP.[27] It then reported in February 1942 on the Scottish National Party and the 'first public meeting they had held in Alloa so far'.[28] In May 1942 the Alloa Communist Party was given permission to hold a meeting in the Public Park and use the bandstand. We noted in Chapter 6 that the Council were unprepared to give them any more democratic freedom of expression than that! This meeting was to be held on 20th September.[29] In late August 1942 the Scottish National Party was given the same permission.[30]

Then there was a bit of a dispute between the local Labour Party and the local Communist Party around the turn of the New Year in 1941-42. In December 1941 the Communist Party had made a call to 'all workers for a People's Mobilisation for Victory Meeting' but the Labour Party put a letter in the *Journal* basically arguing that the workers have already been fully mobilised and haven't got time to attend this sort of meeting because they are too busy winning the war.[31]

On 2nd July 1944 Arthur Greenwood, the deputy leader of the Labour Party, came to Alloa to speak at a party demonstration held in the Pavilion theatre.[32] He recognised 'the war was now entering its final phase' and that we should have our plans ready for legislative action as soon as the war was over since 'there would be no return to 1939'. He was laying down markers of the Labour Party's policies for the first post-war general election. He spoke approvingly of the Beveridge Report and what it offered,[33] of the need for 'a proper health service' and the absolute necessity of full employment. He received much applause for his comment that 'Of the new generation, millions have never voted yet they have borne the stress of war. We want to give that generation a fresh chance...'

Alloa did have a Men's Unionist Association supporting the Conservative Party, which met in the Unionist Rooms in Bank Street and it kept minutes of its Committee meetings right through the war. However, in reality it was largely a social club, not a dynamically active political meeting place. Members paid a subscription of 3/- a year to get access to social facilities like billiards and snooker, card playing and a lounge to read the newspapers. In fact this social aspect was their first connection with wartime issues; in October 1939 the Association agreed to limit the number of newspapers made available to the club as a wartime economy and it was also suggested that some of the soldiers coming to Alloa should be offered the use of the club facilities. It was proposed to write to the CO of the Regiment.[34] The Association was a bit short of money by 1941 and effectively increased its income by adding on a joining fee of 2/6 to the annual subscription in 1941.[35] The Chairman was not, however, downhearted by the lack of money or the state of the war, and at the AGM on 14th July 1941 he 'referred to the present crisis and the Premier's speech that day, and hoped the next AGM would be held under much better circumstances'.[36] There was nothing in the Committee minutes for almost the next 4 years that referred to the war! That is, until February 1945, when the war looked like it was almost won, and the prospect of the first peace-time parliamentary General Election was in the offing. The Alloa Unionist Association was asked to consider a suitable candidate to represent the

Conservative and Unionist Party in the Clackmannan and East Stirlingshire constituency at this election. The Committee wondered if Captain JP Younger, the former Provost, would consider standing as a prospective candidate... and agreed to approach him on the matter.[37] This news obviously got out into public circulation and the *Advertiser* reported breathlessly on the 'rumours that Capt. Younger would be Conservative candidate'.[38] However, a week later it noted that Sir John Gilmour had been given the candidacy. He had been a director of Calder's brewery since 1937, his father was a former Secretary of State for Scotland, he was aged 32 and was presently serving in the army.[39] Gilmour had come home on 7 days leave to accept his nomination as Unionist candidate;

MAJOR SIR JOHN E. GILMOUR, BART., D.S.O.

Alloa Journal 23rd June 1945

that came roughly at the same time as the news that he had been awarded the DSO. He was commander of a tank squadron and the long citation started with the comment that 'Major Gilmour has commanded a squadron throughout the campaign and has shown outstanding courage and leadership'.[40] In the actual election campaign which started in July 1945, there was no evidence that his heroic celebrity gave him any advantage.

It all seemed a very gentlemanly sort of election campaign. Major Gilmour argued for some sort of National Coalition rather than 'party politics', so that the government would be able to 'consolidate the victory' and he pushed the view that Winston Churchill, having won the war, could be trusted to win the peace. Gilmour also spoke in favour of the Beveridge Report, which he said figured prominently in the Conservative Party's housing and social service programme. For the Labour Party, their candidate, the sitting MP Arthur Woodburn, neatly argued that 'the future prosperity of this country was not got by shuffling about the honey that was already in the pot, but by getting more honey in the pot'. This meant production had to be increased and that workers should be better respected. He argued that the elected MPs would have to 'build a new kind of world, where people will get a new deal, a fair deal and a square deal...';[41] he certainly had more of a way with catchy phrases than Gilmour.

None of the local papers dwelt too much on what were the policy differences of the two candidates; talking vaguely about the 'political situation'[42] and how busy both candidates were in addressing their many meetings. One of these meetings, which wanted to find out exactly what the policy differences were, was organised by the recently established Alloa and District Business and Professional Women's Club. It was held in the Co-op Hall on the evening of Saturday 30th June. The attendance of 120 members and friends heard the two candidates give their answers to three prepared questions: - on their policy towards the manufacture of armaments for private profit, their policy towards equal pay for equal work, and their policy towards men and women paying equal National Insurance contributions and getting equal benefits.[43] The Club's minutes of that meeting did not express any comment about how satisfied they were with any of the answers they received.

The *Circular* noted that in the closing stages of the election campaign, 'The Party Big guns were brought into action'[44] and guest speakers came to Alloa for both parties. The Conservatives welcomed Major Sir Ralph Glynn, who had won this seat for them in 1918; and the Labour Party welcomed Herbert

Mr Arthur Woodburn.

Alloa Journal 23rd June 1945

Morrison, ex-Home Secretary who 'gave a powerful address'. The local press talked of this 'last lap in the General Election' and a 'strenuous eve-of-the-poll period' but they never got to grips with explaining in depth what the candidates for the two parties stood for; maybe that was left to the national press. The *Advertiser* noted that the counting of votes was going to be in Alloa Academy on 25th and 26th July and that polling looked to be heavy... on average 80%.[45] It got that wrong because when the result was announced there had been only a 73% turnout and Woodburn gained 24,622 votes, Gilmour gained 14,522 votes ... a majority of just over 10,000 for the sitting candidate.[46]

Sir John Gilmour's loss in the 'Labour Landslide' was obviously felt within the Alloa Unionist Association; in January 1946 'The Chairman in his remarks referred to the great change which had taken place in the political world but he was sure that if everyone who believed in Conservative policy would make a special effort, we could reverse things in the near future'.[47]

Mentioned purely because of the local connection; one of the younger sons of Viscount Younger of Leckie, Major Kenneth Younger, stood as a Labour candidate in the 1945 election and won a parliamentary seat in Grimsby. He served as a Labour MP until 1959, rising to be deputy Foreign Minister under Ernest Bevin.

With the General Election out of the way, it was now the turn, in October 1945, for the first municipal elections in Alloa for over 6 years. In the 4 Alloa wards, amongst the 16 candidates, were 2 women both representing the Labour Party; neither was elected.[48] Then Clackmannanshire held its County Council elections for the landward part of the County in November 1945.[49] By the start of 1946 therefore, the democratic status of Alloa was back to its pre-war normality!

ENDNOTES

[1] *Alloa Advertiser* 16th September 1939
[2] *Alloa Circular* 23rd August 1939 noted that he died on 18th August
[3] *Alloa Journal* 16th September 1939
[4] *Alloa Advertiser* 9th September 1939
[5] *Alloa Advertiser* 7th October 1939
[6] *Alloa Journal* 7th October 1939
[7] *Alloa Circular* 4th October 1939
[8] Alloa Academy Rector's log book for 13th October 1939 noted that the school was closed on Friday due to the Parliamentary election
[9] *Alloa Journal* 14th October 1939
[10] Arthur Woodburn served as the local MP until 1970. He became Secretary of State for Scotland from 1947-1950 in Attlee's post-war Labour government
[11] *Alloa Advertiser* and *Alloa Journal* 11th May 1940
[12] *Alloa Advertiser* 13th May 1940
[13] This is referred to in Alloa Academy Magazine 1941
[14] *Alloa Advertiser* 24th May 1941
[15] *Alloa Journal* 5th July 1941
[16] *Alloa Advertiser* and *Alloa Journal* 22nd February 1941
[17] *Alloa Journal* 28th June 1941
[18] *Alloa Circular* 26th May 1943
[19] *Alloa Journal* 7th March 1942

[20] *Alloa Journal* 14th March 1942

[21] *Alloa Journal* 21st March 1942

[22] *Alloa Circular* 18th March 1942

[23] Alloa Burgh Council minutes 30th March 1942

[24] Alloa Burgh Council minutes 14th June 1943

[25] *Alloa Advertiser* 17th July 1943

[26] *Alloa Journal* 17th July 1943

[27] *Alloa Journal* 2nd August 1941

[28] *Alloa Journal* 7th February 1942

[29] Alloa Burgh Council minutes 25th May 1942

[30] Alloa Burgh Council minutes 31st August 1942

[31] *Alloa Journal* 3rd January 1942

[32] *Alloa Advertiser* 8th July 1944. In the article he was entitled 'Labour Party leader' but that was incorrect since the leader was Clement Attlee. However, Greenwood did have the title of 'leader of the opposition' since Attlee was a member of the coalition government holding power

[33] *Alloa Circular* 3rd March 1943 also had a long article by Arthur Woodburn speaking up in favour of the Beveridge Report. This Report, issued in November 1942, was properly entitled 'Social Insurance and Allied Services'; it was a blueprint for a radical overhaul of the way national insurance, pensions and health care would be organised and paid for

[34] Alloa Men's Unionist Association Committee minutes 11th October 1939

[35] Alloa Men's Unionist Association Committee minutes 14th July 1941

[36] This was a reference to Churchill's 'You do your worst – and we will do our best' speech

[37] Alloa Men's Unionist Association Committee minutes 13th February 1945

[38] *Alloa Advertiser* 3rd March 1945

[39] *Alloa Advertiser* 10th March 1945

[40] *Alloa Journal* 7th April 1945

[41] *Alloa Journal* 7th July 1945

[42] But even when talking about the 'political situation' the local press did not mention key national factors that could have had an effect on the local voting outcome; such as the role of the 'forces vote' or the significance of Churchill's 'Gestapo speech'

[43] Alloa and District Business and Professional Women's Club minutes 30th June 1945

[44] *Alloa Circular* 11th July 1945

[45] *Alloa Advertiser* 14th July 1945

[46] *Alloa Advertiser* 28th July 1945

[47] Alloa Men's Unionist Association Committee minutes 29th January 1946

[48] *Alloa Journal* 27th October 1945

[49] *Alloa Journal* 17th November 1945

CHAPTER 9

THE END OF THE WAR AND COMMEMORATION

The liberation of Occupied Europe by the Allied forces started with the Normandy landings on D-Day, the 6th June 1944. It is an interesting point to ponder on just exactly how soon after that was the moment when people in Alloa began to think that the Allies genuinely were on the road to victory. It could well be argued that the Alloa press had expectations of victory well before D-Day! The rousing editorial in the *Journal* on 8th January 1944 showed they were well aware that 'in company of all the other nations ranged against Germany, they await the grandest assault of all... 1944 has already become, in our minds, the year of victory in Europe'. In this view, D-Day was only a point on the road to victory rather than being the starting point. The first time that Alloa Burgh Council was that optimistic was in late November 1944 when they established the 'Welcome Home and Commemoration Fund' and set up sub-committees to consider how to raise the money.[1] By late December the local press was reporting that 'Alloa was preparing its welcome home celebrations' and that it had exemption from the War Charities Act to try and raise as much funding as it could by public donations.[2] The *Advertiser* in late January 1945 noted that the fund had been inaugurated and the minimum target was £10,000.[3]

By late April 1945, with victory over Germany only a matter of a few weeks away, the Council had discussions on what sort of celebrations there should be to recognise the Victory in Europe; accepting 'that VE Day may not see the end of hostilities and that the war in the Far East would still be proceeding'. It said that schools and businesses etc. could give half holidays.[4] By early May the Council was clearly aware that VE Day was coming up but didn't know exactly when. It agreed not to overdo the celebrations for VE Day because of its worries about the fighting still going on against Japan so they suggested that citizens could display flags and bunting and there would be a service of thanksgiving. Its view was that 'Thanksgiving was more appropriate than celebration'.[5]

When VE Day arrived (Tuesday 8th May 1945), the *Advertiser* (4 days later) had a big report on how the town had celebrated; noting that 'grey skies and pouring rain did nothing to encourage a celebrant mood, but in the evening a focal point was provided by the service of thanksgiving at St Mungo's Church which attracted a large congregation'.[6] The *Journal* didn't mention the rain but commented that 'one could sense a certain restraint borne of the feeling that much yet remains to be done in the Far East...'[7] However, it did give much more detail of 'the profusion of flags and bunting', the improvised pipe band in Ward Street, large numbers dancing in the streets, and a large bonfire at Castle Street.

The generally low-key nature of the occasion was continued in the days that followed; we have already referred to the lack of any note about VE Day in all of the local churches' minutes of meetings, although almost all the school log books mentioned it; maybe because the pupils and staff got 2 days holiday. Then, the first Council meeting after VE Day was on Monday 14th May 1945 but there was no reference in its minutes to the end of war in Europe. There

Feast for Forbes Street Children

Alloa Advertiser 1st September 1945

Greenfield Street Backlands VJ Party
Alloa Circular 12th September 1945

was only a reference three months later to VJ Day once it had passed; saying it was pleased the celebrations went off well. The Council may have been low-key about the final victory, but the Alloa public definitely were not; there was a whole series of street parties throughout September 1945 to celebrate the end of the war.

Alloa Circular 19th September 1945

Calder Street VJ celebrations

Alloa Circular 26th September 1945

The local press, towards the end of April and into May 1945 had a steady stream of articles about and lists of the returning local soldiers who had been prisoners of war. The highlight of the *Advertiser*'s reporting was the note that 'Lt Col E.P. Buchanan, CO of 7th Argylls returned home on 26 April, liberated by the Americans after 5 years of captivity. He had been captured at St Valery in 1940'.[8]

At a more local level the *Journal*, as early as September 1944, under a heading of 'Alloa Prisoners of War Return' had reported that 'four Alloa men in the Argylls were among those repatriated from Germany via Sweden last weekend...' and 'they got a cordial welcome from their relatives and townspeople...'[9] A week later it noted that there had been a 'welcome home' cabaret and dance for these 4 men at the town hall with an attendance of over 1000 people.[10] One 'welcome home' which got a particular mention in the *Journal* was the return of one of the Chalmers boys, the second eldest, in February 1945.[11] The local press was well aware of the uniqueness of this family, with its 7 sons in military service, and was happy to report that 'Flags were flying and pipes playing last Friday evening at 5 Carron Street, Alloa, when a happy party of relatives and friends met to welcome home Warrant Officer Chalmers, who came from Italy a few weeks ago...'

COUNTY EX-P.o.W. AT "THE MAYFAIR"

A further company of 100 prisoners of war were entertained by the P.o.W. Association (County Branch) at "The Mayfair" on Tuesday when a festive evening was spent.

Returned POWs being entertained at the Mayfair.
Alloa Journal 12th May 1945

As the *Journal* said in April; 'Prisoners of war who have been recently liberated are arriving home almost daily and are receiving a warm welcome...'[12] Right through May and June there were lists of returning POWs in the *Journal* just about every week, often amounting to 10-15 men each time.

The local press didn't have that much to say at the time about the conditions that these returning POWs had faced in their camps, but this must soon have come out to the families once they had returned, and helped shape their attitudes towards their defeated enemies. In September 1945 came the first news of Alloa servicemen who had been POWs in the Far East, where, under a headline of 'Liberated From Japs', the *Journal* gave a list of 14 names of local men.[13] A week later was a list of another 10 names, then on 6th October, a list of another 11, including a nurse, Mrs Dorothy McDonald, formerly of Coningsby Place.[14] The press reported little more than a general sense of disbelief about the treatment of POWs in the Japanese camps but this must have been evident in the condition of the returning survivors. The *Journal* reported that Driver John (Jack) Gallacher [Service No. 66964] from 119 Bristol Street had become a POW of the Japanese in Java in 1942.[15]

He was in their POW camps for the rest of the war and his post-internment debriefing report lists these camps.

POSTED MISSING.—Mrs Gallacher, 119 Bristol Street, Alloa, has received word that her son, Driver John Gallacher, R.A.S.C., who was serving with the Forces in Malaya, has been posted missing since 15th February. Driver Gallacher enlisted previous to the war.

Alloa Journal 21st March 1942

He was hospitalised on several occasions, suffering from dysentery, pleurisy, bronchitis and malnutrition, and possibly malaria and beriberi. His return was not listed in the local press in 1945, but he did make it home. However, a family memory belies what should have been the happiness of this occasion; 'a special welcome had been arranged for Jack when he returned to his home town of Alloa by train. They had a welcome party, welcome home signs, and lots of people there etc. However when he saw what was waiting as the train pulled up, he jumped off the other side of the train and ran off because he looked so emaciated and felt so embarrassed, that he didn't want them to see him like that'.[16]

Jack Gallacher's post-internment debriefing report

The wartime reporting in the local press of the impact on the town of knowing that some of Alloa's servicemen were POWs had generally been on the positive side; it was all to do with urging them to keep their spirits up, and holding dances and whist drives to collect money for sending parcels and Christmas messages. The real day-by-day impact on their families however, remains part of Alloa's hidden history of those times; as is the continuing impact in the many years following the war, of dealing with these damaged and mistreated men. You get the impression that the normal response in the town was to believe that little more was needed to help these men back onto their feet than a few parties held in their honour. Late 1945 and 1946 saw a whole series of 'Welcome Home' socials run by various works organisations in Alloa. Patons and Baldwins held 5 such events; after all, they had 380 members in the forces so they needed a few of them.[17] The last of these was reported in the *Journal* on 16th November 1946 which noted that these 'socials' were held in the Patons Sports Pavilion and largely paid for by the Patons and Baldwins Welcome Home and Comforts Funds, which had raised and disbursed £3,500 over the years of the war. At these 'Welcome Homes' they normally catered for about 50-60 returning servicemen at a time and made sure that each got £5.

In December 1946 the *Journal* reported on the Co-operative Society's 'Welcome Home' which was a town hall function with 400 guests. It was noted that out of 435 employees of Alloa Co-operative Society, 135 were in the forces, 114 had returned, 14 were still in military service and 7 had fallen.[18]

COMMEMORATION

BURGH OF ALLOA ROLL OF HONOUR AND WAR MEMORIAL

The names of the 125 people from Alloa who died in the Second World War were added in as a double-page spread at the end of the existing Burgh of Alloa Roll of Honour which had been created after the Great War, in 1920. The figure was made up of 123 men and 2 women. I suspect the idea of seeing these names in the Great War tradition of 'The glorious dead' had somewhat paled by the end of almost six more years of war, and their treatment on the two pages at the back of the Roll of Honour was neat although somewhat cursory compared to the stylish and informative arrangement of those names from the

Great War. However, at least the Roll of Honour got it right this time and its figure agreed with the number on the War Memorial.[19]

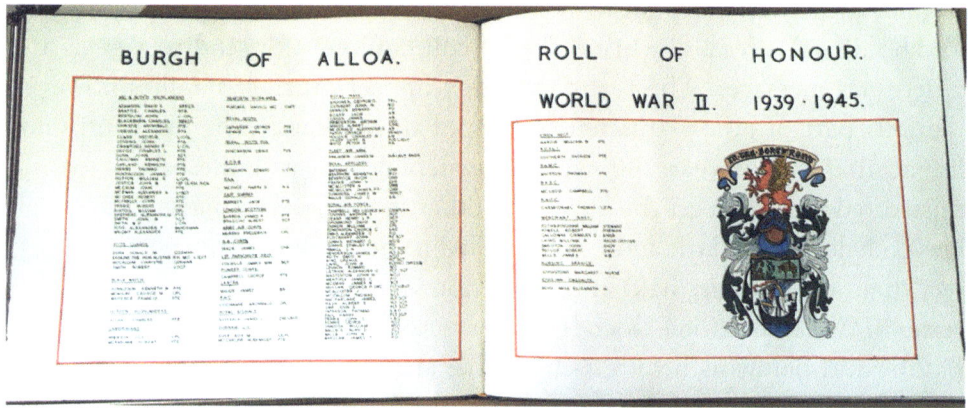

The Burgh of Alloa Roll of Honour, showing the names of all Alloa deaths
in the Second World War

In the Great War, Alloa's losses had been most grievously borne by the 7th Battalion of the Argyll and Sutherland Highlanders: it had 72 out of the 385 names on Alloa's War Memorial. The Second World War shows the impact of the policy of conscription which had started in April 1939.[20] Men of enlistment age did not get to just join their local regiment; they went where they were sent. Therefore, although it may have been convenient for the military authorities to let a fair number of local men join the Argylls [and indeed, 28 out of the 125 Alloa deaths were of men fighting in various battalions of the Argylls], the realities of modern war meant that there was a constant need for a stream of men into the RAF rather than ground forces, since that was the main way, for much of the war, that Britain was taking the war to the enemy. Now, it isn't clear whether proportionally more Alloa men were actually conscripted into the RAF,[21] or whether it was the consequence of a horrifyingly high death rate; but the fact of the matter is that with a total of 34 names in the Roll of Honour, more Alloa men died in the RAF in the Second World War, than in any other branch of the fighting forces.

It has to be mentioned that with adverts like this in the *Circular* in January 1941, no wonder the RAF attracted so many Alloa recruits. The local press, again and again in its reports of the registration of different age groups, made comments such as '1903 Class Registers at Alloa – RAF the most popular preference'.[22] The *Circular* went on to note that for the month of April 1941 there were 214 registrations, of which 81 preferred the RAF, a figure only exceeded by the 84 who stated no preference.

Pilots of the R.A.F. . . . . . .

Alloa Circular 15th January 1941

R. A. F.
RECRUITING VISIT

Volunteers (Age 17¼ to 39) for Flying Duties in the R.A.F.

should call at

THE EMPLOYMENT EXCHANGE, ALLOA

on **Wednesday, 26th January, 1944**

Between 4 - 6 p.m.

W.A.A.F. is Now Open to Recruiting - Age Limits 17½ - 19.

Alloa Journal 22nd January 1944

After making amendments to the Roll of Honour came the task of making suitable amendments to Alloa's War Memorial. This took longer than one might have thought given that only 2 bronze panels were being added to the pillars on the back wall (which were very much in keeping with the existing arrangement), and there were no major revisions needed to the general architecture of the memorial sculpture itself apart from a re-writing of the inscription at the bottom of the front of the plinth.

It is also not clear who was paying for this;[23] the Council minutes do not seem to refer to it and even when it was due to have the extra panels unveiled, the Council minute was very muted in its enthusiasm. It merely noted that; 'Unveiling of New Panels. – It was intimated that it was expected the new panels bearing the names of local members of HM Forces who died as a result of the last war would be in place by Armistice Day and it was agreed that the Provost and Town Clerk should make the necessary arrangements to hold a service of Dedication on the morning of that day'.[24] A notice was put in the local press advising of the order of service for this dedication ceremony. It was to take place on Armistice Day 1951.

LEFT: Alloa War Memorial. The left hand memorial panel

ABOVE: Alloa War Memorial. The new inscription
on the plinth

RIGHT: Alloa War Memorial. The right hand memorial panel

BELOW: *Alloa Journal* 10th November 1951

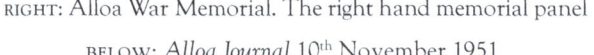

BURGH OF ALLOA WAR MEMORIAL

The dedication of the new panels to the memory of those who sacrificed their lives during the 1939-45 War will take place on SUNDAY, 11th NOVEMBER, 1951, at 10.30 a.m. prompt.

ORDER OF SERVICE

Voluntary - - -	ALLOA INSTRUMENTAL BAND
Praise - - -	2nd PARAPHRASE, verses 1 to 3
Prayer - - -	REV. KEITH M. McROBB, M.A

THE ACT OF DEDICATION

Memorial Panels handed over to Town Council for safe keeping - - - REV. W. D. MacGREGOR, M.A
Acceptance of Custody - - - PROVOST BROWN

UNVEILING OF MEMORIAL PANELS
by
PROVOST BROWN

Dedication and Prayer - REV. PETER P. BRODIE, B.D., LL.B
Praise - - - - HYMN 601

THE LAST POST
LAMENT

11 a.m.—2 minutes silence

REVEILLE

PROVOST BROWN WILL PLACE BURGH WREATH ON
MEMORIAL

THE NATIONAL ANTHEM
LAYING OF WREATHS

Members of the public who desire to attend the Service should congregate at the Memorial in due time keeping clear of the centre past of Bedford Place between the front of the Post Office and the War Memorial, this being reserved for those who will form a parade to the Memorial.

So, in November 1951, a little more than 6 years after the ending of the war, the *Journal* reported that 'At the eleventh hour of the eleventh day of the eleventh month, the folk of Alloa gathered in blustery weather and an uneasy peace to see the panels dedicated in memory of the dead of another Great War'.[25] Alloa Instrumental band supplied the music before the dedication, and there was a squad of Territorials and some regular soldiers to provide a guard of honour. Provost William Brown unveiled the two panels, the first holding 55 names, the second bearing 70. 'Speaking slowly, and obviously deeply conscious of the solemnity of the occasion, the Provost said 'We accept these panels as a sacred trust, and we shall guard them in honour of these faithful lives, in whose honour they have been set up." He then pulled a cord connected to the two Union Jacks covering the side panels, 'and with hardly a check they fell away to reveal the new panels, looking bright and unweathered beside their older companions'. The dedication was by Rev. Keith McRobb and Rev. W.D. Macgregor, while Rev. Peter Brodie gave the prayer. Two minutes silence was observed at 11 o'clock, followed by Reveille.

Alloa Circular 2nd January 1952

ALLOA ACADEMY

Apart from its framed Roll of Honour, the Academy had not got any other memorial to the Former Pupils who had died in the Great War. After the Second World War, the Rector, D.N. Stewart, was determined that this omission would not be repeated. He put in motion the plans to design and fund-raise for a memorial which would do justice to the FPs who had died in both wars. By 11th October 1946 he was able to report on the work done by the Academy's Head of Art; that 'Mr McLeod submitted a sketch for a Memorial window which was exhibited at FP's general meeting. Decided to proceed with it'. This was all reported in the *Journal*; there was still £36 in the FP's Christmas Fund for Servicemen, and this would be transferred into the Memorial Fund and help kick-start the campaign to raise between £150-175 to pay for the FP's memorial.[26] On 25th October 1946 the log book noted that 'Miss Young, Hon. Treasurer of the FPs Association, agreed to act as Treasurer for War Memorial Fund. Rector issued an appeal to

FPs and also arranged for PPs [*present pupils*] to make a weekly contribution'.[27] This memorial stained glass window was unveiled in 1947. A distinguished former pupil, Rev. Charles M. Hepburn, had the honour of dedicating it.[28]

The FPs Association decided that there would also be a Roll of Honour for those FPs killed in the Second World War. This was largely designed and worked by Miss W.M. Young in the Art Dept. Mr R.W. Robertson in the Technical Dept. designed an oak lectern for it to rest on.[29] In addition to the actual

LEFT: Two pages of the Alloa Academy Roll of Honour

Roll of Honour, which would be on display in the school, it was decided to produce a smaller version. This would take the form of a slim grey-covered booklet with the names and photographs of those who were killed. All the pupils in the school at that time were given a copy; plus the families of any FP who had died, plus anyone else in Alloa who wished to have one.[30]

ADDITIONS TO EXISTING MEMORIALS

Patons Mills already had a bronze memorial to the dead of the Great War in the Kilncraigs building, on a pillar to one side of the main stairs going up to the board room. It added another bronze memorial panel for the dead of the Second World War on the pillar to the other side of the stairs.

Alloa's churches did not all seem quite so keen, following the Second World War, to memorialise the dead from their congregations in the same way as most of them had done in the years after 1918, with long lists of names on a memorial tablet. St Mungo's for instance went for a stained glass window on the north side of the church. It does have two Second World War references in it; the dates 1939-1945 near the top and representations of the military crests of the armed forces right at the top; but apart from that there are few other emphatic commemorative military metaphors. Even the wording along the bottom of the panels; 'He will dwell with them and they shall be his people', is only quite a subtle reference to the fact that this window is a memorial.[31] However, the addition of an

explanatory plaque on the wall makes it clear that this window is there to commemorate the 33 members of the congregation who gave their lives in the Second World War.

Three other churches took action, of a more traditional nature: St John's Church added a panel of names below and very much in keeping with their existing Great War memorial, whilst Moncrieff Church and St Andrew's Church each created a new wall plaque.[32]

St John's Church

St Andrew's Church

Moncrieff Church

ENDNOTES

[1] Alloa Burgh Council minute book 27th November 1944, *Alloa Journal* 2nd December 1944 and *Alloa Circular* 24th January 1945

[2] *Alloa Advertiser* 23rd December 1944

[3] *Alloa Advertiser* 29th January 1945

[4] Alloa Burgh Council minute book 26th April 1945

[5] *Alloa Advertiser* 5th May 1945

[6] *Alloa Advertiser* 12th May 1945

[7] *Alloa Journal* 12th May 1945

[8] *Alloa Advertiser* 28th April 1944

[9] *Alloa Journal* 23rd September 1944

[10] *Alloa Journal* 30th September 1944

[11] *Alloa Journal* 7th February 1945

[12] *Alloa Journal* 21st April 1945

[13] *Alloa Journal* 15th September 1945

[14] *Alloa Journal* 6th October 1945

[15] *Alloa Journal* 21st March 1942. My thanks to Robert Ross for drawing my attention to this story, and John Gallacher's son, also called John, for providing some of the evidence

[16] Reported by his son, John Gallacher

[17] *Alloa Circular* 5th September 1945

[18] *Alloa Journal* 21st December 1946

[19] For the Great War deaths, the figure on Alloa War Memorial is 5 different from the figure on the Burgh of Alloa Roll of Honour. For the Second World War the Roll of Honour and the War Memorial positioned names and regiments in a slightly different order but they do agree on the final figure. The Roll of Honour for the Second World War didn't seem to appreciate that FAA and Fleet Air Arm were the same thing so they did not need both to be listed

[20] Military Training Act of 27th April 1939 introduced partial conscription and this was completed by the National Service (Armed Forces) Act of 3rd September 1939

[21] It was certainly the case that the RAF Recruiting Office was the only one of the services that regularly put adverts in the local press trying to attract Alloa's young men who were coming up to enlistable age, to consider the merits of joining the RAF

[22] *Alloa Circular* 16th April 1941

[23] The report in the *Alloa Journal* on 17th November 1951 says that the responsibility for the panels only passed formally into the hands of the Burgh Council at the ceremonial unveiling.

[24] Alloa Burgh Council minute book 23rd October 1951

[25] *Alloa Journal* 17th November 1951. The original war memorial was unveiled **just under** 6 years after the end of the Great War

[26] *Alloa Journal* 19th October 1946

[27] All of Miss Young's financial and donor records for this War Memorial appeal were kept in Alloa Academy until February 2020, and were then passed on to the care of Clackmannanshire Archives and Local History Service

[28] He had been the Dux of Alloa Academy in 1912, rose to be a Captain in the 7th Argylls during the Great War, and then became a Minister in the Church of Scotland until his retirement in 1964. See Alloa Academy Magazine 1966, p13-14

[29] The stained glass window and both of the other memorials are still in Alloa Academy and can be viewed by request. The Miss Young who designed the Book of Remembrance was **not** the same Miss Young who was Treasurer of the War Memorial Fund

[30] Alloa Academy still possesses two copies of this memorial booklet; one of them including an invitation card and the order of service for the day of dedication in October 1947

[31] Information found in *St Mungo's Parish Church The Story So Far,* a history celebrating the bi-centenary of the church's foundation (2019)

[32] This memorial is presently in Ludgate Church, where most of Alloa's Great War church memorials were aggregated, as Alloa's churches declined or joined together in the years following the war.

CHAPTER 10

ALLO SERVICEMEN IN THE WAR

Around about the time of the 100th anniversary celebrations of the Great War, there seemed to be a national outburst of a feeling that we, as a nation, had not done enough to preserve and respect the memory of all those who had fought and died in that war, and that a greater tribute should be paid. One sign of this was that throughout the country there was a proliferation of books detailing the life and career of every soldier on the local war memorial. My contribution to that outburst was *In the Forefront: Alloa at War 1914-1919* which tried to paint a bigger picture of how a whole community went through a war and survived its challenges. It was never my intention to do the research involved in a man-by-man study of the dead servicemen of Alloa during the Great War.

I do recognise however the merits of that form of uplifting 'tribute' for the present generation of students of war studies and I also recognise that, back at the time of the war itself, the members of the community of Alloa were indeed uplifted by the stories of heroism and glory that were associated with 'their' servicemen, even if that was sometimes accompanied by a sense of loss and grief. It was the case that 'the greater the bravery, the greater the local pride'. One of the problems about compiling such a roll-call of heroes however is that it largely depends on trawling through the local press to see what they reported; if the press weren't informed by locally-living relatives or didn't pick up the local connection themselves then the hero got missed. I feel there are bound to be some of the brave sons and daughters of Alloa who have been missed out. The press also sometimes picked up on a fairly tenuous connection in order to create a 'local hero'.

This book, so far, has been an echo of my first book; how did a community face up to the demands placed on it by the pressures of wartime life; but I readily concede both the value and interest in a section on these 'local heroes'. This chapter on servicemen with a connection to Alloa in the Second World War is therefore in two sections; the brave who survived and the brave who sacrificed their lives.

SERVICEMEN WITH A CONNECTION TO ALLOA: BRAVE AND SURVIVED

The Chalmers Family is mentioned partly out of uniqueness; because there was no family like this in Alloa in the Great War! The *Advertiser* in August 1940 contained a notice about this family from Carron Street which had 7 sons serving in the forces...[1] and there was even an eighth son waiting to join up. There is no mention of a Chalmers name on the Burgh of Alloa Roll of Honour, but there was a reference in the *Journal* in 1941 to one of the sons, John, becoming a POW.

The Younger Family were still prominent in the community; after all Younger's was the largest brewery in the town, although the main family lived in Gargunnock in Stirlingshire. The local press were proud to report in November 1940 that Captain Edward George Younger, eldest son of Viscount Younger of Leckie, had been awarded the OBE [military] for service in the field.[2] He also received the Territorial

ALLOA FAMILY'S NOTABLE RECORD

SEVEN BROTHERS SERVING WITH THE COLOURS

A notable record of war service is provided by the family of an Alloa lady, Mrs T. Chalmers, Carron Street, who has seven sons serving with the colours. Four are in the R.A.F., one in the Navy, one in the Army, and one in the Home Guard.

Of the four brothers in the Air Force, Thomas, the eldest, has been in this branch of the services for a period of nine years, and is now acting as a recruiting sergeant. In his civil employment he was a joiner and served his apprenticeship on the Alloa Estate.

Alec and Andrew joined the R.A.F. the same week and are now aircraftsmen. Alec is married and was formerly employed as a vanman with the Alloa Co-operative Society. In peace time, Andrew was a brewer with Messrs George Younger and Sons Ltd.

The other brother in the Air Force, George, was previously employed as a butcher with Mr Peter Sinclair, High Street. His experience has now been advanced a stage further in food front activities—he is at present acting as cook to an R.A.F. squadron.

David, who is a stoker in the Royal Navy, has been away for four years.

John joined the R.A.S.C. in September, 1938. He is a motor driver and was sent to France at the beginning of the war. He was previously employed with Messrs W. Alexanders and Sons, Ltd.

Jim is in the Home Guard. He joined at the time of the earlier recruiting.

One son, William, is awaiting his calling-up papers.

Alloa Circular 14th August 1940

Decoration in 1943. This was in recognition of his 16 years of long service in the Territorial Army. He was now entitled to put the letters TD after his name. The *Journal*'s report on this award contained the information that Captain

Younger 'was in one of the brigades evacuated from France after our former ally capitulated. The brigade escaped via La Havre. He is now a major'.[3] He served in the 7th Argylls, and his obituary in 1997 noted that 'He showed an unusual aptitude for staff work; not many TA officers rose to the ranks of full colonel'.

Brigadier Robert Gifford Moir DSO MC

He was from a well-known local family; his late father was AP Moir, the solicitor at Marshill. Robert had won his medals for gallantry in the Great War, and his elder brother Archie had been killed at Ypres in 1915. Robert was a career soldier and by 1939 had risen to the rank of Brigadier and was Commanding Officer of the Northern Area in Malaya. In 1941-42 he was General Officer Commanding of the Malayan Lines of Communications Area when Japanese forces invaded the Malay Peninsula and captured Singapore on 15th February 1942. In the last hours before the Japanese came he buried his valuables and his wife's jewels in a cash box under the hedge near his HQ in Tanglin, then surrendered. He became a POW in Changi Camp and his wife was interned at Changi Gaol. It was not until 2 months after his capture that the local press was able to report that he was in trouble; under the heading of 'Brigadier Robert Gifford Moir and his wife, missing in Malaya'.[4] He was to spend more than 3 years as a Japanese prisoner of war. In September 1945 the *Journal* reported on his release from Japanese captivity.[5] He was transferred to Formosa and Manchuria and then flown to England. In January 1946 the *Journal* proudly noted that 'Alloa this week had a visit from one of her notable sons' when Brigadier-General Moir came to the town.[6] 'Although he had been incarcerated in very bad conditions, 'Bobby'… was looking very well when he called on old acquaintances this week…' The story of the retrieval of his box of valuables can be found in the *Straits Times* (Singapore) dated 19th January 1947 under the heading of 'Mine-finder spots Brigadier's jewels'. Basically, after the war was over Brigadier Moir got a friend of his in Singapore, Major Goldman, to organise the use of a REME sapper with a mine detector to locate where the cash box had been hidden. This search was successful and 'a rusty box, crumbling with decay was lifted from the hole. In it were Mrs Moir's jewels and Brig. Moir's gold cigarette case, cash, war medals and other valuables'.

Flight Sergeant John Kesson DFM

Alloa Academy Magazine

His Distinguished Flying Medal was the first medal for gallantry awarded to a man from Alloa in the Second World War. The website www.yorkshireaircraft.co.uk has good information about him as an air gunner on a Whitley bomber on a raid over Hamburg in September 1940.

It adds that 'He was born in Alloa, Clackmannanshire in 1920 and he worked as a road surveyor [for Alloa Burgh Council] before joining the RAF in 1939'. He was born on 3rd September 1922 and went to Alloa Academy [Admission No. 3258]. He was the only Alloa serviceman to be mentioned by name in the Minutes of Alloa Burgh Council during the whole of the war; when on 28th July 1941 the 'Council congratulated Sergeant John Kesson on his DFM'. He received this award for service with 77 Squadron, gazetted on 18th July 1941. He eventually received his commission to the rank of Pilot Officer on probation (emergency) on 1st September 1943 (157481) and was later confirmed in this appointment and rose to Flying Officer (war subs) on 1st March 1944. He relinquished his commission on the grounds of being medically unfit for Air Force service on 31st May 1947.

(l to r.) Sgt. J. C. Kesson, D.F.M., Mrs Kesson, Cpl. Margaret Inglis, A.T.S., and Police Sgt. D. Kesson.

The Kesson family at John Kesson's investiture. *Alloa Circular* 12th November 1941

Squadron Leader HHK Gunnis DFC and bar

Alloa Academy Magazine

Alloa's most highly decorated war hero was Herbert Horatio Kitchener Gunnis [born 2nd June 1916]. He was a former pupil of Alloa Academy [Admission No. 2510] where he was a member of the Rugby 1st XV and the Cricket 1st XI. He had left school to go to Glasgow Technical College as a pharmaceutical student before joining up. He was brought up at Cora Linn on Hilton Road. You can't help thinking that there is no-one more deserving of gallantry medals than someone with a name like that.[7] He joined the RAF (Service No. 61508) and became a pilot, serving firstly in North Africa. His first Distinguished Flying Cross was awarded in 1942. He received his award from the King in October 1943. Both the *Journal* and the *Advertiser* had articles[8] which gave a fuller picture of his family circumstances; one brother, also a pilot, had lost his life over Rotterdam earlier in the war,[9] another brother had joined the merchant navy and was lost at sea on his first voyage,[10] three more brothers were in the RAF and a sister was a nurse.[11]

It does seem that he was a genuine air hero; see comments in the following books: Christopher Shores and Clive Williams in *Aces High: A Tribute to the Most Notable Fighter Pilots of the Second World War* write that HK Gunnis 'claimed 5 victories flying Bristol Beaufighters with 252 Squadron in the Mediterranean area in 1942'. At that time it appears that the name by which he was commonly referred was 'Alec'. Andrew Thomas in *Beaufighter Aces of World War 2* has an account on p48 of how Gunnis shot down three enemy bomber aircraft on one day, 11th March 1942. Then, on p49 an account from a fellow flyer, of how he shot down another German aircraft to reach the tally of 5 needed to become an 'Ace'. The *Circular*'s account on how he won his first DFC included the observation from this friend that 'That action in fooling the enemy was typical of Herbert' in reference to the fact that he had run out of ammunition during his attack but had continued to harass and fool the enemy by feint attacks.[12]

Only the *Circular*, in January 1945, picked up on the circumstances of his wedding – maybe because they wanted to use what seemed the aviation-appropriate headline of 'A Hurricane Courtship', even though he generally flew either Beaufighters or Mosquitos.[13] There were indeed unusual circumstances. The bride, Elizabeth, was the sister of the navigator of the plane in which his brother Stanley was killed in September 1941. She was Canadian and had lost her husband in a flying accident in Canada. Over the years, through correspondence with Herbert Gunnis's sister, the two ladies had become friends and this led to Elizabeth being invited to Scotland to see the New Year in to 1945. This was where the 'hurricane' part now came in. Herbert Gunnis came home on leave, he met her for the first time on Hogmanay; they got engaged two days later and married two days after that at the West Church!

The *Advertiser* in December 1944 gave a good account of his part in an attack by his squadron of de Havilland Mosquito 'ship-busters' on a German merchant vessel and its escorting flak-ship in the Kraakhellesund Fjord in Norway.[14] However, when returning from a raid on 25th January 1945, his Mosquito collided in mid-air with another Mosquito of his flight. This happened about 2 miles south of RAF Banff. The other aircraft crashed, killing both of the crew. Squadron Leader Gunnis and his navigator Albert Mudd managed to land safely in their seriously damaged aircraft and both escaped with no serious injury.

The *Journal* in May 1945 had an article under the headline '2 U-Boats Sunk by RAF-Attack led by Alloa pilot[15] and Roy C. Nesbitt in *The Strike Wings: Special Anti-Shipping Squadrons 1942-45* has a detailed account [p238-39] of this action; with Squadron Leader H.K. Gunnis leading his squadron of Mosquitos in April 1945 over the Kattegat, Norway, where his flight sank 2 German U-boats in a sustained cannon-fire and rocket attack. Gunnis said 'I have never seen such an explosion on the sea as the first U-boat made. All the torpedoes must have exploded. An intense volume of smoke went up to about 1000 feet, and then, when it died down – just nothing left'.[16] It was for leading a whole series of successful attacks like this that he was awarded a second DFC in 1945. It was announced in the Supplement to the *London Gazette* on 27th July 1945 (page 3878). Part of the citation, quoted in the *Journal*, read 'Squadron Leader Gunnis has always pressed home his attacks to the utmost, even in the face of intense opposition. He has proved to be an excellent leader'.[17] At that time he was serving in 248 Squadron.

Captain Leslie Millar MC

In March 1943 the *Advertiser* had a piece on the award of the Military Cross to Captain Millar in the Gordon Highlanders. It did not give his full name but noted that he was from Primrose Street.[18] There was nothing on this award in the *Journal*. The *Circular* however, printed a fuller piece describing how Captain Leslie Millar from 39 Primrose St had won his MC during service in North Africa. He was 33 years old and had left Alloa around about the start of the war to become a hotelier in London. He had a wife and son, and the family home was in Paignton.

Captain Hutcheson Burt MC

From the Commando
Veterans Archive

The *Journal*'s article on his award gave some of his background; he had come to Alloa in 1928, worked at Carsebridge distillery and lived in Ward Street. He had joined the army in the Scots Guards and risen to the rank of Warrant Officer 1st Class before being commissioned as a 2nd Lieutenant on 23rd April 1942 (Service No. 231543).

He was trained as a commando and rose to be Captain and the commander of E Troop of No. 4 Commando. He took part in the D-Day landings on 6th June 1944 at La Breche, Ouistreham.[19] He was involved in constant fighting for the next 4 days until being sent for one day's rest on 11th June, then fighting on right through the rest of June and into July. In the second week of July he was injured by shrapnel from a shell at the Chateau in Breville. One of his squad remembered that 'Hutch Burt, our captain got peppered and was injured...'[20] When Field Marshall Montgomery visited nearby Amfreville to officiate at a medal investiture on 16th July, Captain Burt was one of three officers in the regiment to be awarded the Military Cross;[21] but he 'was not present, being still in hospital in England'.[22] The Alloa press did not have information about the award of his MC until September[23] when it reported that he had won it in recognition of 'gallant and distinguished service during operations in Normandy'.

Flying Officer Edward McPhee Graham DFC

The *Journal* in May 1944 noted that he won the Distinguished Flying Cross and that prior to enlisting with the RAF on 1st March 1943, he had been well known in Alloa as a member of Clackmannan County Police Force which he had joined on 2nd April 1938.[24] The Supplement to the *London Gazette*[25] noted that he was flying in 90 Squadron. At the time of the award of his DFC he was probably flying Short Stirlings but their operations were restricted to Special Duties i.e. dropping sea mines, low level supply dropping to the French resistance and shorter bombing raids on invasion objectives. 90 Squadron was active on all these fronts.

Sergeant Thomas Dawson MM

Any award for gallantry to a local man naturally received due praise and recognition. The award of the Military Medal to Sgt Thomas Dawson of 37 Claremont received a full report partly because the medal was bestowed on him personally in a 'field investiture' by Field Marshall Montgomery, and partly because of the heroic nature of the deed. The local press did have the full story of his bravery at a bridgehead over the River Odon, near Caen on 29th June 1944 because they quoted the citation. This stated that, under attack 'by infantry supported by tanks, artillery and mortars', he had pulled soldiers from burning vehicles and attended to the wounded 'with utter disregard for his own personal safety'.[26]

Flying Officer Donald Beaton DFC

From the honour roll of 214 FMS Squadron

The *Advertiser* reported the news in November 1944 of the award of Donald Beaton's Distinguished Flying Cross, for 'the utmost fortitude, courage and devotion to duty on numerous operations against the enemy'. Donald was born on 19th July 1922 in Blantyre, Malawi but moved to Scotland and lived at 4 Moir Street. He was a former pupil of Alloa Academy [Admission No. 3415] and had worked for George Younger's brewery in its labs before enlisting. He was awarded his DFC on 14th November 1944 and was only aged 22. He had been in the RAF since 1942.[27] From the wording on the citation it looks like this was the decoration most officers in the RAF expected to receive if they completed a 'tour' of 30 operations. He served in 214 (Federated Malay States) Squadron which, from 1944 was flying American Boeing B17 Flying Fortresses out of Downham Market. These planes were equipped for radio counter-measures (detection and jamming of enemy radio and radar equipment). He was a member of the 9-man crew of SR388 BU-H.

Pilot Officer James Hamilton DFC

James Hamilton was born in 1920 and attended Grange School. He had joined the RAF before the war and was training at Cranwell from 1936 to 1939. He received his commission only in October 1944.[28] He served in 86 Squadron which was attached to Coastal Command and flew reconnaissance and air-sea rescue missions, anti-shipping strikes, and anti-submarine patrols. The citation for the award of his Distinguished Flying Cross in April 1945 noted that he had completed two tours of duty, and 'By his skill and determination he materially contributed to the successful completion of many sorties'.[29] The *Circular* noted that at the time of his award he lived at 39 Broad Street with his wife and two sons.[30]

Flying Officer Horace Dempster DFC

He was born on 16th December 1920 and he came from Ashley Terrace and went to Sunnyside School before attending Alloa Academy [Admission No. 3136].

He was serving in 149 Squadron (Service No. 179844) when he was awarded his Distinguished Flying Cross on 21st September 1945.[31] 149 Squadron was equipped with heavy bombers, flying Short Stirlings from November 1941 and Avro Lancasters from August 1944. The citation noted that it was 'in recognition of his gallantry and devotion to duty in the execution of air operations against the enemy'.[32]

Alloa Academy Magazine

The report in the *Journal* went on to refer to his sporting abilities; both as a playing member of Clackmannan County CC and as a former vice-captain of Alloa Rugby Club.

Lieutenant John Hall MC

Alloa Academy Magazine

He was born on 28th November 1918 and was a former pupil of Alloa Academy [Admission No. 2844]. In August 1943 he married a girl from Alva and they lived at 28 Clackmannan Road.[33]

He was wounded in March 1944[34] but resumed active service. On 12th April 1945, serving in northern Italy, the 8th Argylls (in 36 Brigade) took part in a three-mile thrust inland, accompanied by Churchill tanks at the Santerno Bridgehead. Lt Hall was in command of a platoon and showed great initiative in moving his men rapidly forward by having them climb onto the advancing tanks. He was able to attack and overcome enemy positions 'on five separate occasions, taking twenty-two prisoners and killing six in all'. On the following day he 'pressed on in the lead with his platoon reconnoitring tank routes and directing their fire on enemy held positions. He displayed great personal bravery and devotion to duty. His coolness and courage in action were a great incentive and inspiration to his men'. The action took place in April, but the news of the award of his Military Cross did not come through until October 1945, when the *Journal* had a full report.[35]

Lance-Sergeant Peter Rutherford Scott MM

He served with the Cameronians (Scottish Rifles) in North-West Europe and was awarded his Military Medal for his services in that sector. The citation read that 'Since 1st November 1944, Corporal Scott has been section commander in a rifle company. On numerous occasions he has shown himself a junior leader of exceptional ability... This N.C.O. has made a name for himself for his coolness and courage under fire and as a result he has frequently been chosen to carry out tasks of a dangerous nature which would otherwise have been given to more senior N.C.O.s, such as commanding patrols, but he has invariably succeeded in his tasks and has gained the confidence of the men under his command'. The *Journal* reported on his bravery on 7th July 1945 but gave no clue as to what part of Alloa he came from.

Flight Lieutenant John Ritchie Stein DFC

He was born on 7th October 1920; he lived in Hill Street and was a former pupil of Alloa Academy [Admission No. 3101]. He enlisted in 1939 (Service No. 176733) and was trained in the Middle East, before receiving his commission in 1944. He was awarded his Distinguished Flying Cross on 17th August 1945.[36] He was a member of 234 Squadron and the citation for his award outlines his heroic conduct: 'This officer is now on his third tour of operations. During his first tour he completed many convoy patrols. Whilst on his second tour he was shot down and taken prisoner in Italy. He succeeded in escaping and reached the British lines in September 1943. He commenced his third tour, since when he has completed 40 long-range escort sorties. He is a capable flight commander and has always shown outstanding devotion to duty'.[37]

Lieutenant Colonel William McKinlay OBE

Alloa Circular
3rd October 1945

He was the eldest son of Provost McKinlay and had trained as an engineer. In April 1942 the *Journal* noted that he had been promoted from Captain to Major in the Royal Army Ordnance Corps.[38] Less than a year later, under a heading of 'Rapid Promotion', it noted that he had been transferred and was now a Lieutenant Colonel in the Canadian RCOC (engineers).[39] He got the OBE for his services as an engineer attached to the Canadian Army. The *Journal* in September 1945 had a full report[40], giving his history as an Alloa Academy FP, his work for Abercrombie and Co, his training as a mechanical engineer at the Royal Technical College Glasgow, then as an engineer for Younger's Brewery. In April 1939 he had joined the Territorial Army 'as a ranker' but 'was promoted to 2nd Lieutenant and went to France… as acting Captain'.[41]

He went to France with the 51st Highland Division in January 1940; where 'he came through the Dunkirk episode, when he was mentioned in dispatches'. He was seconded to the Canadian Army and, following the invasion of Europe, went to the continent in 1944 with the 1st Canadian Army, where 'he took part with the Dominion Forces in the liberation campaign in western Europe…' The *Circular* ended its own report with the comment that he 'expects to be relieved in the near future of his service duties and he will then take up appointment as Chief Mechanical Engineer with Messrs George Younger and Son – a position presently held by his father'.[42] His OBE investiture was in December 1945.[43]

Able Seaman Samuel Hunter DSM

He came from Greenfield Street and was awarded his Distinguished Service Medal in 1945 'for courage and leadership'. He was a member of a gun crew on HM Submarine *Torbay* which took part in a Mediterranean action in the course of which six heavily escorted enemy merchantmen were destroyed, and the bombardment of Amorgos loading-station carried out.[44]

Alloa Circular
3rd November 1945

SERVICEMEN WITH A CONNECTION TO ALLOA; THEIR SACRIFICE RECOGNISED

Sergeant James Colville MM

He was born on 18th February 1921 and lived at 157 Ashley Terrace. He went to South School, then Alloa Academy [Admission No. 3134]. He only spent two years at the Academy but left to get employment at Sellars implement makers.

He joined 1st Parachute Brigade in 1941 and, after completion of the selection course at Hardwick Hall, was posted to the 1st Parachute Battalion then in the process of forming up, and assigned to S Company, 7th Platoon.

Alloa Academy Magazine

He then undertook the 1st advanced training course at RAF Ringway in Cheshire, from 4-15th November 1941. This course involved a night descent from a balloon and aircraft descents with arms containers. He was awarded the Military Medal for his gallant actions in North Africa. He was killed in action on 8th March 1943 aged 22. His award of the MM was gazetted on 23rd September 1943 on p4220 of the Supplement to the *London Gazette*.

It was a posthumous award and his father received the MM at Buckingham Palace on behalf of his son.[45] In March 1944 James Colville's parents received a letter from the commanding officer of their son's unit saying that a memorial had been erected 'on the site of the unit's hardest battles' in memory of all their comrades who had been killed. A photo of the memorial was enclosed with the letter.[46] James Colville was buried at CWGC Medjez-El-Bab Cemetery in Tunisia.[47]

Captain David Gilbert Purgavie MC

Alloa Academy Magazine

He was born on 20th June 1918 and lived at 20 Fenton Street. He was a FP of Alloa Academy [Admission No. 3248] but was only at the school for his V[th] form classes, having come from Dollar Academy.

The *Circular* in November 1943 printed a glowing account of his history and upbringing;[48] charmed by the idea that he had joined the territorials as a private at the outbreak of the war, had then been commissioned, then 'Promoted to Captain on the field'. He served in North Africa and in one letter home in January 1943 he told his parents how one of the bren gun carriers under his command had been decorated with slogans such as 'The Wee Alloa Bus' and 'Good Old Alloa' by its homesick driver. This information found its way into the *Journal*.[49] He won his Military Cross in Sicily in 1943 when he was a lieutenant in the 5th Battalion, Seaforth Highlanders; it was gazetted on 18th November 1943. He was killed on Saturday 19th August 1944 in Normandy; the *Journal* had a note about his death.[50] The *Circular* later noted in October 1945 that Mr and Mrs Purgavie 'went to Holyrood Palace last week' and received the posthumous award of the MC from the hands of the king... for gallantry during the North African Campaign.[51] The *Journal* had a fuller report of the citation, which was very imprecise on details of where the heroic action actually took place. He had led his platoon and his bren-gun carriers to knock out an anti-tank gun, and they then guarded a vital road against constant enemy night attacks... 'The courage and leadership displayed was of the highest order...'[52] He was buried at CWGC Banneville-la-Campagne Cemetery, France; grave ref. VIII.D.8

Flight Lieutenant (Navigator) George Patrick Mullan DFC

Alloa Academy Roll of Honour

He was born on 11th March 1916 and lived in Garvally House, 13 Grange Road when he attended school at Alloa Academy [Admission No. 2000]. He became a Tillicoultry resident, but his name is on Alloa's War Memorial.

He died on 1st January 1945. The *Journal* for 6th January had a note on his death but no recognition that he had been awarded a medal. His award of the Distinguished Flying Cross was gazetted on 16th February 1945 on p932 of the Supplement to the *London Gazette*. The *Journal* noted that it was awarded for 'having completed numerous operations against the enemy in the course of which he invariably displayed the utmost fortitude, courage and devotion to duty'.[53] It was a posthumous award in that it was gazetted 6 weeks after he was killed, although the *Journal* makes the counter-claim that 'his death took place after the award of the DFC had been made'. Maybe he was told about it before it actually appeared in the *Gazette*. He served in 128 Squadron. He had served in the ranks but was commissioned in 1942.[54] He was married and left a widow, Catherine. He was buried at Tillicoultry Cemetery L(West) Grave 16. There is also a Garden of Remembrance stone with his name inscribed on it in that cemetery.

Squadron Leader Rev. George Adam Gordon Campbell

He was the son of Rev G.G. Campbell, the minister of Chalmers Church. He joined the ministry and was licensed as a probationer minister in the Church of Scotland on 9th April 1940.[55] He joined the services as an RAF Chaplain in 25 (South African Air Force)Squadron, Royal Air Force; RAFVR Service No.106468. He served as chaplain in Iceland, Tealing (near Dundee), North Africa and Italy. The *Journal* contained a full story of his background and glowing academic career. The article was aware that he had lost his life in an air accident on Thursday 28th September 1944 in Italy[56] but didn't know he was drowned in an air crash.[57] He was buried at CWGC Bari Cemetery, Italy; grave ref. VII.E.5

Lieutenant the Hon. Alistair Robert Erskine MC

Alistair Erskine was <u>not</u> an Alloa man. He was born at Ickworth, Bury St Edmunds, and his parents' address at the time of his military service and death was still in Bury St Edmunds. His father, Lord Erskine, had not lived in Alloa since the early 1920s [he was Governor of Madras Presidency from 1934-1940 and lived there, and was MP for Brighton in 1940-41]. Alistair's connection to Alloa was due to family association not place of residence; it was because his grandfather was the Earl of Mar. The local press certainly regarded him as a 'son of Alloa' and his name is on Alloa's War Memorial.

Reproduced by kind permission of National Trust for Scotland. In the collection of The Earl of Mar & Kellie at NTS Alloa Tower

Alistair Erskine was born on 21st March 1923, the second son of Lord Erskine. He was educated at Eton and joined the Scots Guards (Service No. 247095). In December 1944 he won the Military Cross for his service in Italy, following the landings at Salerno. His MC was gazetted on 21st December 1944. The *Advertiser* had a full story of his heroic actions and quoted from the citation.[58] He was leading an ambush patrol which itself ran into a German patrol; there was a firefight and Lt. Erskine lead his men with great bravery and coolness and was a constant inspiration to his men.

Barely three months after reporting his heroism the *Advertiser* had to report his loss. He was killed on 19th April 1945. Nine days later the *Advertiser* broke the news of his death in action in Germany;[59] he was killed in the last month of the war in Europe.[60] The *Advertiser* reported the sad loss but added no further details. A fuller description of his final action can be found on the website 'British Aristocracy Losses in World War 2'. It reported that '…The G Company platoon has been less fortunate; a burst of Spandau fire from a projecting window, when they were in a position of comparative safety between a tank and a wall, hit Lieutenant ERSKINE and every member of his Platoon Headquarters, Lieutenant ERSKINE died while being taken to the rear in an ambulance later in the day. He had earned the reputation of being 'the best soldier in the Battalion', and 'soldiering came naturally to him … he could concern himself therefore with the embellishments while we were struggling with the fundamentals'. He was buried at CWGC Becklingen Cemetery, Niedersachsen, Germany; grave ref 4.D.13. The cemetery overlooks Luneburg Heath.

Sunnyside Cemetery in Alloa is the last resting place of 20 servicemen from the Second World War who died in Britain and were able to be given a grave in these shores. Some died in accidents, some were wounded abroad but died of their wounds in Britain; not all of them came from Alloa, but they all have a CWGC headstone.

Victor Aish	Pvt	1946	Royal East Kents	Sussex
David Anderson	Sgt	1945	Argylls	Sauchie
Kenneth Bearpark	WO1	1944	RA	Alloa
Thomas Bernard	Driver	1945	RE	Sauchie
George Campbell	Pvt	1941	Pioneer Corps	Alloa
Henry Deans	Sgt	1946	RAFVR	Alloa
James Hamilton	Pvt	1947	Argylls	Alloa
David Keith	AC1	1943	RAFVR	Edinburgh
Alexander Letham	Flt Sgt	1941	RAFVR	Alloa
Hector Lockie	Gunner	1940	RA	Alloa
Alexander McAllister	Gunner	1946	RA	Alloa

Henry McPhee	Naval airman	1944	RN	Alloa
James Mack	Gunner	1941	RA	Alloa
Robert Mackison	Pvt	1944	RAPC	Glasgow
Joseph Padden	Stoker	1945	RN	Lancashire
David Sharp	Sub Lieut	1945	RNVR	Alloa
W Snaddon	AC2	1940	RAFVR	Alloa
Donald Walls	Bombardier	1941	RA	Alloa
James Wardlaw	Pilot Officer	1940	RAF	Alloa
Thomas Whitton	Pvt	1946	RAMC	Alloa

Seven of these man had died after the war in Europe was over, 11 are listed in Alloa's Roll of Honour

ENDNOTES

1 *Alloa Advertiser* 17th August 1940

2 *Alloa Advertiser* 2nd November 1940

3 *Alloa Journal* 19th June 1943

4 *Alloa Advertiser* 18th April 1942 and *Alloa Circular* 22nd April 1942

5 *Alloa Advertiser* and *Alloa Journal* 29th September 1945

6 *Alloa Journal* 19th January 1946

7 He was born three days before the death of Horatio Herbert, Lord Kitchener, which occurred when *HMS Hampshire* was lost at sea off the Orkney Islands

8 *Alloa Journal* and *Alloa Advertiser* 2nd October 1943

9 *Alloa Journal* 20th December 1941 noted that Stanley Gunnis who had been reported missing in September 1941, was now confirmed as dead. He was buried in the Hook of Holland. The Bristol Blenheim Society noted that he was part of a crew of three on aircraft no V6436 when they were hit by flak and the aircraft crashed. All three were killed

10 This death is not listed in the CWGC records. That may well be because merchant navy personnel were only listed if their deaths could be **proven** to be attributable to enemy action.

11 *Alloa Advertiser* 6th June 1942

12 *Alloa Circular* 3rd June 1942

13 *Alloa Circular* 10th January 1945

14 *Alloa Advertiser* 23rd December 1944

15 *Alloa Journal* 19th May 1945

16 For more information on this action, see a website called www.wrecksite.eu which gives details of the loss of U-804 and U-1065 in the Kattegat on 9th April 1945. There were no survivors from either U-boat

17 *Alloa Journal* 11th August 1945 and *Alloa Circular* 1st August 1945

18 *Alloa Advertiser* 13th March 1943

19 This information and some of that which follows can be found on the Facebook public page of No. 4 Commando

20 This information can be found in *World War 2; People's War*, the BBC archive which included the memories of Ernest Brooks, contributed 9th September 2005

[21] MC gazetted in *London Gazette* Supplement (p4045)

[22] Facebook public page of No. 4 Commando

[23] *Alloa Journal* 9th September 1944 and *Alloa Advertiser* 16th September 1944

[24] *Alloa Journal* 27th May 1944

[25] Supplement to *London Gazette* dated 23rd May 1944 (p2349)

[26] *Alloa Advertiser* 21st October 1944 and 28th October 1944, and *Alloa Journal* 4th November 1944

[27] *Alloa Advertiser* 14th November 1944

[28] Second Supplement to *London Gazette* dated 17th November 1944 (p5327) states that he was appointed to rank of Pilot Officer as from 17th August 1944

[29] *Alloa Advertiser* 14th April 1945

[30] *Alloa Circular* 18th April 1945

[31] DFC gazetted in *London Gazette* Supplement dated 21st September 1945 (p4703)

[32] *Alloa Journal* 29th September 1945

[33] *Alloa Circular* 24th August 1943

[34] *Alloa Circular* 8th March 1944

[35] *Alloa Journal* 27th October 1945

[36] Supplement to *London Gazette* dated 17th August 1945 (p4187)

[37] *Alloa Circular* 22nd August 1945

[38] *Alloa Journal* 25th April 1942

[39] *Alloa Journal* 6th February 1943

[40] *Alloa Journal* 29th September 1945

[41] *Alloa Circular* 3rd October 1945

[42] *Alloa Circular* 3rd October 1945

[43] *Alloa Journal* 22nd December 1945

[44] *Alloa Journal* 3rd November 1945. Wikipedia lists HM Submarine *Torbay*'s exploits before being reassigned to the Far East in May 1945. These include sinking a German floating dock [which presumably is the Amorgos loading station], and a selection of merchant ships

[45] *Alloa Advertiser* 28th February 1944

[46] *Alloa Journal* 11th March 1944

[47] This information can be found on the website 'Airborne Assault ParaData'

[48] *Alloa Circular* 17th November 1943. This report was printed the day before his MC award was gazetted

[49] *Alloa Journal* 30th January 1943. On the subject of Alloa-related military graffiti; John McClelland has also posted on-line a short movie clip from a BBC documentary in the 1950s, of British Sherman tanks in Normandy [near Falaise], one of which has ALLOA stencilled on the side. The Imperial War Museum also has a photo of a Sherman tank in Burma, serving with the 255th Indian Tank Brigade which is clearly marked with Alloa 288795 on the side [Catalogue JFU 109]

[50] *Alloa Journal* 26th August 1944

[51] *Alloa Circular* 10th October 1945

[52] *Alloa Journal* 6th October 1945

[53] *Alloa Journal* 24th February 1945 and *Alloa Circular* 21st February 1945

[54] *Alloa Advertiser* 24th February 1945

[55] *Alloa Journal* 13th April 1940

[56] *Alloa Journal* 7th October 1944

[57] This information can be found on a website called 'They Gave Their Today'

[58] *Alloa Advertiser* 6th January 1945

[59] *Alloa Advertiser* and *Alloa Journal* 14th April 1945

[60] *Alloa Advertiser* 28th April 1945

CONCLUSION

When I wrote the book on Alloa in the First World War, I very much felt it was a book that was able to speak just about that time, basically saying 'This was what faced the people of Alloa as they went through the strains of a war and this is how they reacted to it'. After all, it wasn't as if anyone at that time was seriously able to compare it to anything else they had experienced before. Back in 1914-1918 there was no feeling in Alloa that the townsfolk were looking back at the Boer War or even Crimean War for pointers as to what they could expect this time round.[1] I do not believe you can make that same claim about the people of Alloa in the way they reacted to the Second World War. This war started less than 21 years after the Great War had ended, well over half the population of Alloa had got a clear memory of what that first war was like; they naturally compared this second war to the one they had gone through earlier; in reality it only made sense when a comparison was made. In the years of the Second World War the evidence suggests there was a constant sense that the Alloa townsfolk were basically saying; 'We've been through this before, this is what we can expect, this is how we know we can deal with it'. Again and again, in looking at the evidence from those times, a sense of déjà vu emerges in people's responses; partly because so many of the same leading local and civic figures from the time of the Great War were still around; to them this was 'Alloa at War: The Sequel'. Maybe that helps to explain why there was so much of an attitude of 'business as usual' about social, economic, religious and educational life for the Alloa townsfolk; they knew how bad it could get but they weren't going to let it get to them, so in many ways they ignored it and just soldiered on. Then the reference to 'these critical times' in the main title of this book, is not a long way from the phrase 'this present crisis' which was so regularly used in the local press, found in Kirk Session minutes and the minutes of the bowling club. It does have a sort of temporary ring to it;

as though the Alloa folk recognised that it wouldn't last that long and things would soon get better.

This was absolutely summed up by some comments in the editorial of the *Alloa Academy Magazine* in 1940. The opening words of this article, by the anonymous Jembee,[2] showed they well remembered that people had been through a war already... 'Twice in a lifetime has the Peace been blown sky high...' The article ended with 'Those who remember the deadly years that led to Versailles now know full well that, having survived the worst that Germany could do last time, Britain is profiting from experience'. How was that for the optimistic view with five more hard years of war still to come? It was the case though, that the war was a grind; this was particularly so in 1940-41 when there was the prospect of losing it and things looked very grim. There was an enormous amount of government control and restriction on every aspect of Alloa people's lives on the home front; the growing list of rationing restrictions on just about everything they wanted, shortages of fuel, limited travel due to no petrol, blackout, compulsory billeting, 'essential workers' powers controlling who worked and where they could do it; with quite stiff punishments for disobedience of any of these rules. The Alloa people stuck at it; the tedious interference in their everyday lives was stoically tolerated, and the government's constant message to them about their importance to the war effort was believed and acted upon.

By April 1945, the *Circular*'s editorial showed it was well-aware, after the years of hardship, that we were on the brink of victory and commented that 'it will be a signal for a new way of life for the majority of people in this country'.[3] Not everyone shared that view; the *Alloa Academy Magazine* for 1945 contained another long article by Jembee on 'What will victory bring?' which was much more pessimistic in its tone with its comments like 'So Utopia is not just yet? No, not by a long chalk...'[4] Maybe this writer was remembering the mistakes made at the end of the Great War and wondering if they would be repeated. It has to be said that I don't think they were, and this is a point worth considering. All wars leave their impact in the years which follow, but compared to the Great War, which left its social legacy in the shape of Lloyd George's vision of 'Homes fit for heroes', the social legacy of the Second World War was much deeper and more widespread and longer lasting. Unlike in 1919, there wasn't an attempt to turn back the clock to the pre-war 'good old days'.

The *Circular*'s editorial boldly stated this in January 1945; 'We do not want things to return to the state of 1939, or the years immediately preceding, with their international strife and domestic apathy'.[5] Amongst other things, the Beveridge Report of 1942 had provided a beacon of hope – 'This is what we are fighting for'– and the first post-war election showed how the British people really wanted root and branch reform of their entire social system; and only trusted the Labour Party to do it.[6] So, the consequence of the Second World War for the British people, with its much smaller casualty and death rates, was not decades of grief but a determination to recast the nature of British society, especially in terms of the structure of industrial ownership, social security, a national health service and housing. Not all of it worked or lasted but the attempt was made. That is why that same January 1945 editorial in the *Circular* continued; 'Our post-war tasks will demand of us the same singleness of mind and the same determination and faith that we have put in our wartime jobs. Otherwise we shall have won the war only to lose the peace, and let slip by the glorious opportunities of building a better world…' This book's sub-title is *Alloa at War 1939-1945* but the end-date of this study really should be taken many years further on, to properly see how the consequences of what we thought the war had been fought for, panned out for the people of Alloa.

ACKNOWLEDGEMENTS

Susan Yule at the Clackmannanshire Archives and Local History Service for her helpful support at all times
Stirling Archives; for access to the Kirk Session records of several Alloa churches
For proof reading and general good advice; Celia Hunt, George Hutchison and John McClelland

Archivists/Guardians of records:
George Marshall at Alloa Golf Club
John Glencross at Alloa Athletic Football Club
David Lobley at St John's Church
Elizabeth Ramsay at St Mungo's Church
Donna Maguire at Scottish Catholic Archive

University of Glasgow: Scottish Brewing Archive
The Mitchell Library, Glasgow
Ian Riches at National Trust for Scotland

Clackmannanshire Archives and Local History Service for the use of extracts and photographs from the *Alloa Advertiser*, *Alloa Journal* and *Alloa Circular*; the microfilms of these newspapers are in their care.

For photographs:
Several members of the *Auld Clackmannanshire* Facebook public group and the *Old Alloa photos* group who either possessed or tracked down some of the photos of Alloa during the Second World War that appear in this book. Clackmannanshire Archives and Local History Service also provided some of the original photos used, especially in Chapter 2.

Once again, despite all the help I received from those listed above, this is my book not theirs and any mistakes are mine alone.

ENDNOTES
_____

[1] In respect of the Great War echoing the Boer War, I suppose you could argue that the local press in 1914 did think that there would be some use for the Boy Scouts as messengers, but that was about all!

[2] I'm sure the identity of this writer could be discovered: they must be a former pupil, the made-up name suggests a set of initials, a trawl through the admissions register could probably provide the rest; I just haven't done it!

[3] *Alloa Circular* 25th April 1945

[4] Alloa Academy Magazine 1945 p21

[5] *Alloa Circular* 17th January 1945

[6] As a convenient shorthand it is called the 'first post-war election', but in fact the war was not yet over because Japan did not surrender until a fortnight after the 1945 General Election

ALSO BY THE SAME AUTHOR

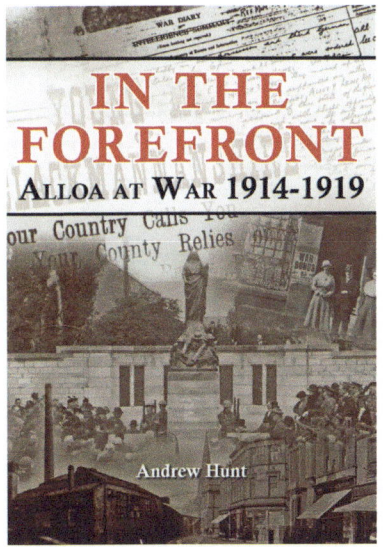

Andrew Hunt's first book was about the impact that the Great War had on the town of Alloa. It gives an insight into the role of Scotland's people in the war, and the part individuals played on the local, regional, national and international stage of the battlefields of France, Flanders and across Empires.

Available from all booksellers and online retailers.

ISBN: 978-1-999890-05-6
Price: £17.99

BV - #0031 - 240225 - C15 - 244/170/13 - PB - 9781999890025 - Gloss Lamination